Leeds Studies in English

New Series XLIX

© *Leeds Studies in English* 2020
School of English
University of Leeds
Leeds, England

ISSN 0075-8566
ISBN 978-1-84549-771-2

Publishing Office

Abramis Academic
ASK House
Northgate Avenue
Bury St. Edmunds
Suffolk
IP32 6BB

Tel: +44 (0)1284 700321
Fax: +44 (0)1284 717889
Email: info@abramis.co.uk
Web: www.abramis.co.uk

Leeds Studies in English

New Series XLIX

2018

Edited by

Alaric Hall

Leeds Studies in English

<www.leeds.ac.uk/lse>
School of English
University of Leeds
2018

Leeds Studies in English

<www.leeds.ac.uk/lse>

Leeds Studies in English is an international, refereed journal based in the School of English, University of Leeds. *Leeds Studies in English* publishes articles on Old and Middle English literature, Old Icelandic language and literature, and the historical study of the English language. After a two-year embargo, past copies are made available, free access; they can be accessed via <https://www.leeds.ac.uk/lse>.

Notes for Contributors

Contributors are requested to follow the *MHRA Style Guide: A Handbook for Authors and Editors*, 3rd edn (London: Modern Humanities Research Association, 2013), available at <www.mhra.org.uk/publications/MHRA-Style-Guide>.

Where possible, contributors are encouraged to include the digital object identifiers or, where a complete free access text is available, stable URLs of materials cited (see *Style Guide* §11.2.10.1).

The language of publication is English and translations should normally be supplied for quotations in languages other than English. Each contributor will receive a free copy of the journal, and a PDF of their article for distribution. Please email all contributions to <lse@leeds.ac.uk>.

Reviews

Copies of books for review should be sent to the Editor, *Leeds Studies in English*, School of English, University of Leeds, Leeds LS2 9JT, United Kingdom.

Contents

Ála flekks saga: An Introduction, Text and Translation   1
        Jonathan Y. H. Hui   *University of Cambridge*
        Caitlin Ellis
        James McIntosh
        Katherine Marie Olley
        William Norman
        Kimberly Anderson

Ála flekks saga: A Snow White Variant from Late Medieval Iceland   45
        Jonathan Y. H. Hui   *University of Cambridge*
        Caitlin Ellis
        James McIntosh
        Katherine Marie Olley

Wise Aggressors and Steadfast Victims: The Shift in Christian   65
Feminine Ideals from Old to Middle English Religious Poetry
        Judith Kaup   *Universität zu Köln*

Chaucer's Osewold the Reeve and St Oswald the Bishop (from the   87
South English Legendary and Other Sources)
        Thomas R. Liszka   *Penn State Altoona*

Worthy, Wycht, and Wys: Romance, Chivalry, and Chivalric   101
Language in John Barbour's *Bruce*
        James W. Titterton   *University of Leeds*

Middle Yiddish and Chaucer's English Considered as Fusion   121
Languages
        Jennifer G. Wollock   *Texas A&M University*

Reviews:

P. S. Langeslag, *Seasons in the Literatures of the Medieval North*.   135
Cambridge: Brewer, 2015
        [Alaric Hall]

David R. Carlson, *John Gower: Poetry and Propaganda in*   137
Fourteenth-Century England. Cambridge: Brewer, 2012
        [Trevor Russell Smith]

Editorial note

2018 was the fifty-first anniversary of the new series of *Leeds Studies in English* and the year of its forty-ninth issue — neither quite a round number, yet each tantalisingly close to being one. 1967 was a busy year for medievalists at the University of Leeds: Arthur Cawley and Robin Alston published the first issue of *Leeds Studies in English* (whose precursor, *Leeds Studies in English and Kindred Languages*, had lapsed in 1952); John Le Patourel, along with Cawley and others, established what at the time was the Leeds Graduate Centre for Medieval Studies; and Peter Sawyer founded the International Medieval Bibliography.

The mid-1990s saw another burst of activity: in 1994, Leeds hosted the first International Medieval Congress; in 1995, Alan Murray began editing the *Bulletin of International Medieval Research* under the aegis of the International Medieval Bibliography; and in 1996 the Centre for Medieval Studies made its first direct appointment, Mary Swan, leading to the establishment of its Ph.D. programme.

In 2003 all of these endeavours barring *Leeds Studies in English* came together as the Institute for Medieval Studies. It is now time for *Leeds Studies in English*, which has always shared the temporal focus, internationality, and commitment to interdisciplinary scholarship of the Institute, to join the fold, and enter its third incarnation. The present volume is therefore the last of *Leeds Studies in English* under that name: the journal will merge with the *Bulletin of International Medieval Research* to become *Leeds Medieval Studies*.

The first of the annual issues of *Leeds Medieval Studies* will be published in 2021. The journal will sustain and develop the commitment of *Leeds Studies in English* to the study of the literature, culture, and languages of medieval north-west Europe — including our proud tradition, unusual in academic journals, of publishing editions and translations. But, in keeping with the *Bulletin*, its scope will reflect the wide and ever-developing intellectual commitments of the Institute to interdisciplinary medieval studies at large.

Both *Leeds Studies in English* and the *Bulletin* have always been published by scholars, for scholars. From 2009 we digitised the *Leeds Studies in English* back-catalogue and made it freely available online, making subsequent publications available free-access after a two-year embargo. (In addition to their home at <https://digital.library.leeds.ac.uk/view/lse/>, all *Leeds Studies in English* volumes can now also be found at <https://archive.org>.) Ten years ago, this was a fairly progressive move for a long-established print journal. But the open-access movement has since advanced and it is time for us, too, to change.

Leeds Medieval Studies will be a fully free-access publication (neither requiring authors to pay to publish, nor requiring readers to pay for immediate online access). We will also be digitising and opening up the Leeds Texts and Monographs archive, alongside many of the University of Leeds's other medieval studies publications.

The notes for contributors and contact details published in this volume will remain valid for the foreseeable future for *Leeds Medieval Studies*.

Alaric Hall, Leeds, May 2020

Ála flekks saga: An Introduction, Text and Translation

Jonathan Y. H. Hui, Caitlin Ellis, James McIntosh, Katherine Marie Olley, William Norman
and Kimberly Anderson[1]

1. Background

The Old Norse *riddarasögur* ('sagas of knights') were one of the most popular genres of saga literature in Iceland down the centuries, as demonstrated by the extant manuscript evidence.[2] The corpus encompasses a diverse array of texts which can be positioned along a scale spanning from reworkings of texts from continental Europe to original compositions which more closely resemble the native saga tradition. On the one hand, the early Norwegian translations of texts from the Continent seem to have been translated in the court of King Hákon Hákonarson, who ruled Norway from 1217 to 1263. These include the romances *Tristrams saga ok Ísöndar* (translated from Thomas of Britain's *Tristan*), *Elis saga ok Rósamundu* (*Elie de Saint-Gilles*), *Parcevals saga* (Chrétien de Troyes' *Le Conte du Graal*), *Ívens saga* (Chrétien's *Le Chevalier au Lion*) and *Erex saga* (Chrétien's *Erec et Enide*), as well as *Möttuls saga* (*Le mantel mautaillé*) and the *Strengleikar* (Marie de France's *lais*). Old Norse translations of many other diverse texts, such as *Breta sögur* (Geoffrey of Monmouth's *Historia Regum Britanniae*) and *Pamphilus saga ok Galatheu* (the elegiac comedy *Pamphilus de amore*), are now also classified by scholars as *riddarasögur*.

On the other hand, the indigenous *riddarasögur* were composed in Iceland and are not thought to be direct translations of Continental works, though they are still influenced by them to varying degrees. These sagas 'take place in an exotic (non-Scandinavian), vaguely chivalric milieu, and are characterised by an extensive use of foreign motifs and a strong supernatural or fabulous element'.[3] They also tend to follow set narrative patterns, to such an extent that they have often been criticised as 'formulaic'.[4] The disdain with which these sagas

[1] The project was run as a collaborative effort among graduate students at the Department of Anglo-Saxon, Norse and Celtic at the University of Cambridge. The authors would also like to thank Lucie Hobson and Jonathan Wright for their contributions during the early stages of the translation, Brynja Þorgeirsdóttir for her invaluable comments and suggestions on successive drafts of the translation, and the anonymous peer-reviewers, whose recommendations were especially useful in helping us improve the focus of the introduction.
[2] Marianne E. Kalinke, 'Norse Romance (*Riddarasögur*)', in *Old Norse-Icelandic Literature: A Critical Guide*, ed. by Carol J. Clover and John Lindow (Ithaca, NY: Cornell University Press, 1985), pp. 316–64 (p. 316).
[3] Matthew J. Driscoll, 'Late Prose Fiction (*lygisögur*)', in *A Companion to Old Norse-Icelandic Literature and Culture*, ed. by Rory McTurk (Malden, MA: Blackwell, 2005), pp. 190–204 (p. 190).
[4] Driscoll, 'Late Prose Fiction', p. 198.

were dismissed as derivative and unaesthetic by late-nineteenth- and early-twentieth-century scholars is well-documented.[5]

Ála flekks saga ('the saga of Áli flekkr') lies far to the indigenous end of the *riddarasaga* spectrum. It is thought to have been composed around the early fifteenth century,[6] placing it among the youngest medieval Icelandic romances — though this is something of an arbitrary statement given that the tradition of saga composition continued to flourish for centuries after the Reformation.[7] The saga is an entertaining tale in its own right, and the first-time reader wishing to discover this for themselves may prefer to read the translation before continuing with this spoiler-laden introduction. The story was certainly popular in Iceland down the centuries, as evinced by its thirty-seven extant manuscript witnesses as well as its adaptation into three sets of *rímur* (rhymed metrical ballads indigenous to Iceland). Despite this, the saga fell victim to the aforementioned scholarly disdain for — and consequent disinterest in — the genre. Few early scholars paid any attention to it at all. One who did, Finnur Jónsson, called it 'ret ubetydelig' ('rather insignificant'), though he did concede that 'den er så at sige mere rationel i sit indhold end de flestre andre' ('it is, so to speak, more rational in its content than most of the others [late romances]').[8] It is a sign of just how neglected and underappreciated the saga has been that this latter remark remains one of the only — and therefore highest — compliments it has ever received.

Part of the 'rationality' that Finnur Jónsson identified in *Ála flekks saga* undoubtedly derives from the careful construction of its cohesive narrative around a set of curses. The saga is, in the words of Alaric Hall, Steven D. P. Richardson and Haukur Þorgeirsson, 'the pre-eminent Old Icelandic example of an *álög* tale—a story whose plot [...] centres on breaking a stepmother's curse (*álög*)'.[9] This motif is commonly found in medieval Irish and Welsh and modern Gaelic tales. It was therefore probably of Celtic origin, although by the fifteenth century it had become firmly crystallised as a stock element of late medieval Icelandic romances.[10] The use of the motif in *Ála flekks saga* has been relatively understudied compared to some of its contemporary Icelandic analogues. Of particular curiosity to the folklorist will be the fact that this motif plays a central role in the saga's use and adaptation

---

[5]   See, for instance, the summaries of scholarship by Kalinke, 'Norse Romance', p. 316, and Driscoll, 'Late Prose Fiction', pp. 196–97. Perhaps the most famous criticism of these prose romances was by W. P. Ker, who remarked that 'they are among the dreariest things ever made by human fancy' (*Epic and Romance: Essays on Medieval Literature* (London: Macmillan, 1908), p. 282).

[6]   Finnur Jónsson, *Den oldnorske og oldislandske litteraturs historie*, 3 vols (Copenhagen: Gad, 1920–24), iii, 110; Stefán Einarsson, *A History of Icelandic Literature* (New York: Johns Hopkins Press, 1957), pp. 163–64.

[7]   On this, see Matthew J. Driscoll, *The Unwashed Children of Eve: The Production, Dissemination and Reception of Popular Literature in Post-Reformation Iceland* (London: Hisarlik Press, 1997). It should also be stressed that medieval *fornaldarsögur* and *riddarasögur* continued to be widely copied and adapted in the post-medieval period, and a number of recent doctoral projects and monographs have addressed the post-medieval production, transmission and reception of some of these sagas: see Tereza Lansing, 'Post-Medieval Production: Dissemination and Reception of *Hrólfs saga kraka*' (unpublished Ph.D. thesis, University of Copenhagen, 2011); Silvia Hufnagel, '*Sörla saga sterka*. Studies in the Transmission of a *fornaldarsaga*' (unpublished Ph.D. thesis, University of Copenhagen, 2012); Jeffrey S. Love, *The Reception of Hervarar saga ok Heiðreks from the Middle Ages to the Seventeenth Century* (Munich: Utz, 2013); Philip Lavender, 'Whatever Happened to *Illuga saga Gríðarfóstra*? Origin, Transmission and Reception of a *fornaldarsaga*' (unpublished Ph.D. thesis, University of Copenhagen, 2014); and Sheryl McDonald Werronen, *Popular Romance in Iceland: The Women, Worldviews, and Manuscript Witnesses of Nítíða saga* (Amsterdam: Amsterdam University Press, 2016).

[8]   Finnur Jónsson, *Den oldnorske og oldislandske litteraturs historie*, iii, 110.

[9]   Alaric Hall, Steven D. P. Richardson and Haukur Þorgeirsson, '*Sigrgarðs saga frækna*: A Normalised Text, Translation, and Introduction', *Scandinavian-Canadian Studies*, 21 (2013), 80–155 (p. 88).

[10] Margaret Schlauch, *Romance in Iceland* (New York: Princeton University Press, 1934), pp. 125–34.

of the narrative structure of the Snow White tale-type, something that has never before been noted in scholarship; a substantial discussion on both the saga's use of the *álög* motif and the Snow White connection can be found in a separate article later in this issue.[11] Furthermore, a number of episodes and motifs heavy in folkloric overtones, including a wolf-transformation episode and a dream which causes grave wounds to the hero's physical body, can tell us much about the saga's place not simply among the literature of medieval Iceland, but among contemporary European romance as well.

This translation represents part of a recent wave of English translations of indigenous *riddarasögur*.[12] Since the turn of the millennium, English translations have been produced of *Mírmanns saga* (2002),[13] *Kirialax saga* (2009),[14] *Nítíða saga* (2010),[15] *Sigurðar saga fóts* (2010),[16] *Sigrgarðs saga frækna* (2013),[17] *Þjalar-Jóns saga* (2016),[18] and *Vilmundar saga viðutan* (forthcoming).[19] *Ála flekks saga* has in fact been translated into English on one previous occasion, in a popular translation by W. Bryant Bachman and Guðmundur Erlingsson, as part of their *Six Old Icelandic Sagas*.[20] This volume is now out of print and difficult to get hold of. It is the intention of the present authors to provide a new and scholarly translation, freely accessible to academics, students and enthusiasts alike, in order to help the saga gain a wider audience and some long-overdue attention.

2. Genre

Ála flekks saga displays more direct influence from the native saga tradition than from the Continental tradition, and has usually been considered one of the clearest examples of an indigenous romance, formerly termed *lygisögur* ('lying sagas') by some scholars.[21] Stefán Einarsson remarks that '[t]he influence of chivalrous romance on these sagas is slight for

[11] See Jonathan Y. H. Hui, Caitlin Ellis, James McIntosh and Katherine Marie Olley, '*Ála flekks saga*: A Snow White Variant from Medieval Iceland', *Leeds Studies in English*, 49 (2018), 45–64.

[12] For more on recent trends in *riddarasaga* translation, see Alaric Hall, 'Translating the Medieval Icelandic Romance-Sagas', *The Retrospective Methods Network*, 8 (2014), 65–67.

[13] *Icelandic Histories and Romances*, trans. by Ralph O'Connor, 2nd edn (Stroud: Tempus, 2006), pp. 235–96.

[14] Alenka Divjak, *Studies in the Traditions of Kirialax saga* (Ljubljana: Institut Nove revije, zavod za humanistiko, 2009), pp. 298–352.

[15] Sheryl McDonald, '*Nítíða saga*: A Normalised Icelandic Text and Translation', *Leeds Studies in English*, 40 (2010), 119–45. A revised version of this translation can be found in Sheryl McDonald Werronen, *Popular Romance in Iceland*, pp. 235–48.

[16] Alaric Hall and others, '*Sigurðar saga fóts* (The Saga of Sigurðr Foot): A Translation', *Mirator*, 11 (2010), 56–91.

[17] Hall, Richardson and Haukur Þorgeirsson, '*Sigrgarðs saga frækna*', 80–155.

[18] Philip T. Lavender, '*Þjalar-Jóns saga*: A Translation and Introduction', *Leeds Studies in English*, 46 (2016), 73–113.

[19] '*Vilmundar saga viðutan*': The Saga of Vilmundur the Outsider, ed. and trans. by Jonathan Y. H. Hui (London: Viking Society of Northern Research, forthcoming).

[20] *Six Old Icelandic Sagas*, trans. by W. Bryant Bachman and Guðmundur Erlingsson (Lanham: University Press of America, 1993), pp. 41–61. The saga has also been translated into German by Gert Kreutzer, in *Isländische Märchensagas*, ed. by Jürg Glauser and Gert Kreutzer (Munich: Diederichs, 1998), pp. 20–40, into French by Ásdís Rósa Magnúsdóttir and Hélène Tétrel, in *Histoires des Bretagnes: 3. La petite saga de Tristan et autres sagas islandaises inspirées de la matière de Bretagne*, ed. by Ásdís Rósa Magnúsdóttir and Hélène Tétrel (Brest: Centre de Recherche Bretonne et Celtique, 2012), pp. 123–41, and into Czech by Markéta Podolská, in *Lživé ságy starého Severu*, ed. by Jiří Starý (Prague: Herrmann & synové, 2015), pp. 73–91.

[21] The term *lygisögur* has one medieval attestation, which has become well-known because of its relevance to questions of genre in the *fornaldarsögur*: in the thirteenth-century *Þorgils saga ok Hafliða*, we are told that King Sverrir complimented the telling of **Hrómundar saga Gripssonar* at a wedding in Reykjahólar in 1119. No

their chief characteristics are native motifs and native style';[22] and it was on account of the saga's simple syntax and infrequent use of loanwords that Åke Lagerholm, who produced the first edition of the saga, wrote that '[a]us diesem gesichtspunkte stellt sich die saga als eine der isländischesten lygisǫgur dar, die wir besitzen' ['from this viewpoint, the saga presents itself as one of the most Icelandic *lygisögur* that we possess'].[23] The translated *riddarasögur*, of course, share 'their courtly setting, their interest in kingship, and their concerns with the ethics of chivalry and courtly love',[24] and, under this influence, a large number of indigenous *riddarasögur* contain overt textures of chivalry, with traces also found in some *fornaldarsögur* ('sagas of an ancient time', or mythic-heroic sagas). However, so far removed from this courtliness is *Ála flekks saga* that it belies the narrowest sense of the term *riddarasaga*: it contains no knights, no jousting tournaments, nor any overt chivalric texture at all. Probably the closest thing to an overt chivalric feature in the saga is Áli greeting his father *kurteisliga*, 'courteously', in chapter 11.

It has long been recognised that the boundary between the genres of *fornaldarsögur* and *riddarasögur* is an arbitrary one, and *Ála flekks saga* contains many similarities with some of the *fornaldarsögur*. The designation of the *fornaldarsaga* corpus is itself arbitrary, and its extended history has been laid out in a recent article by Philip Lavender.[25] The term '*fornaldarsögur norðrlanda*' was coined by Carl Christian Rafn in his 1829–30 edition of the corpus, which he defined as Icelandic sagas detailing events that happened 'á Norðrlöndum' ('in Northern Lands', meaning Scandinavia), before the settlement of Iceland.[26] Lavender notes that these two chronological and geographical criteria were the same criteria used by Peter Erasmus Müller in volume two of his *Sagabibliothek*, published in 1818, whose choice of texts would also influence Rafn's own. Müller was open-handed with his choice of sagas, including sagas dealing with seemingly ancient heroic traditions as well as younger sagas which seemed to him to have drawn on other old traditions.[27] Lavender remarks that 'the juxtaposition of seemingly ancient subject matter with later works that use the features of such sagas for coloring led to a heterogeneity in the collection, which can be seen to have had as a consequence several later attempts to subdivide the *fornaldarsögur* genre'.[28] These 'later attempts' all subdivide the corpus on roughly similar lines. Helga Reuschel (and Kurt Schier after her) divided them into *Heldensagas* ('Heroic sagas'), *Wikingersagas* ('Viking sagas') and *Abenteuersagas* ('Adventure sagas'),[29] while Hermann Pálsson divided them into 'hero legends'

---

medieval versions of **Hrómundar saga* survive, but Hrómundr's narrative tradition survived in medieval *rímur* from which the postmedieval *Hrómundar saga* derives. For a history of the usage of the term *lygisögur* and the texts it encompasses, see Driscoll, 'Late Prose Fiction', pp. 190–204.

[22] Stefán Einarsson, *A History of Icelandic Literature*, pp. 163–64.

[23] *Drei lygisǫgur: Egils saga einhenda ok Ásmundar berserkjabana; Ála flekks saga; Flóres saga konungs ok sona hans*, ed. by Åke Lagerholm (Halle (Saale): Niemeyer, 1927), p. lvi. There are still a number of Irish-influenced elements in the saga, for instance the dream discussed in Section 3.ii., but here Lagerholm was referring to the lack of an overt chivalric texture.

[24] Margaret Clunies Ross, *The Cambridge Introduction to the Old Norse-Icelandic Saga* (Cambridge: Cambridge University Press, 2010), p. 81.

[25] Philip Lavender, 'The Secret Prehistory of the *Fornaldarsögur*', *Journal of English and Germanic Philology*, 114 (2015), 526–51.

[26] *Fornaldar sögur Nordrlanda*, ed. by Carl Christian Rafn, 3 vols (Copenhagen: Popp, 1829–30), I, p. v.

[27] Peter Erasmus Müller, *Sagabibliothek med anmaerkninger og indledende afhandlinger*, 3 vols (Copenhagen: Schulz, 1817–20), I, p. xvi; Lavender, 'Secret Prehistory', p. 532.

[28] Lavender, 'Secret Prehistory', p. 532.

[29] Helga Reuschel, *Untersuchungen über Stoff und Stil der Fornaldarsaga* (Bühl-Baden: Konkordia, 1933), and Kurt Schier, *Sagalitteratur* (Stuttgart: Metzler, 1970), pp. 86–91.

and 'adventure tales'/'Viking romances'.[30] Stephen Mitchell qualified this heterogeneity by suggesting the applicability of a scale of engagement with 'traditional materials'.[31] Whichever subdivision we apply, there are clear differences between the two poles of the *fornaldarsaga* spectrum in terms of key generic aspects. Key differences noted by Elizabeth Ashman Rowe include the following: the heroic legends span several generations, are set in 'the pagan world of Scandinavian legend', are driven by heroic values and are always tragic in mood; while the adventure tales cover a single generation, are not limited to Scandinavian settings, often contain commoner heroes and are invariably comic.[32]

It is with the adventure-tale *fornaldarsögur* that *Ála flekks saga* shares many stylistic and generic similarities. Indeed, the saga is one of around six indigenous *riddarasögur* which have been designated 'borderline *fornaldarsögur*', because they each have strong literary connections to a number of *fornaldarsögur*. Besides *Ála flekks saga*, this group consists of: the fragmentary *Hrings saga ok Tryggva*, *Sigurðar saga fóts*, *Sigrgarðs saga frækna*, *Vilmundar saga viðutan* and *Þjalar-Jóns saga*.[33] Regarding these texts, Matthew Driscoll notes that 'the scene of the action lies outside Scandinavia proper, but in a Viking, rather than a chivalric, milieu'.[34] The reason that the 'borderline *fornaldarsögur*' are not classified with the adventure-tale *fornaldarsögur* is simply that this latter group either involve Scandinavian heroes or feature a Scandinavian setting (with the exception of *Hjálmþés saga ok Ölvis*, which does not explicitly name a Scandinavian location, and whose heroes are from a place called 'Mannheimar'). The 'borderline *fornaldarsögur*' have neither. Therefore, a dominant factor in why they have usually been (and continue to be) classified as *riddarasögur* is that they were excluded from the *fornaldarsaga* corpus on geographic grounds. This separation has become further entrenched with each publication of an edition of either the *fornaldarsaga* or *riddarasaga* corpus.

Although it features neither a Scandinavian character nor a Scandinavian setting, *Ála flekks saga* is in the highly unusual position of having a non-Scandinavian hero who is genealogically linked to a *fornaldarsaga* hero, that is, a legendary Scandinavian hero. Áli flekkr is said both in *Hálfdanar saga Brönufóstra* and in most manuscripts of *Ála flekks saga* to be the grandson of Hálfdan Brönufóstri, since Ríkarðr, the father of Áli flekkr, is the son of Hálfdan Brönufóstri and his wife Princess Marsibil, through whom Hálfdan inherits the English throne. Áli is thus not only the son of the king of England but the grandson of the king of both Denmark and England.

Áli's heroic career mirrors that of his illustrious grandfather in many ways. Most notably, both Áli and Hálfdan are aided on their adventures by supernatural female helpers. Áli is liberated from the clutches of the troll-woman Nótt by Hlaðgerðr, her half-human daughter, in much the same way that Brana, the daughter of the giant Járnhauss and a kidnapped Norman princess, aids Hálfdan by killing her father.[35] Both Hlaðgerðr and Brana explicitly choose

---

[30] Hermann Pálsson, 'Fornaldarsögur Norðurlanda', in *Dictionary of the Middle Ages*, 13 vols, ed. by Joseph L. Strayer (New York: Scribner, 1985), VI, 137–43 (p. 138).

[31] Stephen A. Mitchell, *Heroic Sagas and Ballads* (Ithaca, NY: Cornell University Press, 1991), pp. 15–18.

[32] Rowe's observations are tabulated in her contribution in Judy Quinn and others, 'Interrogating Genre in the *Fornaldarsögur*: Round-Table Discussion', *Viking and Medieval Scandinavia*, 2 (2006), 275–96 (pp. 284–86).

[33] Driscoll, 'Late Prose Fiction', p. 191.

[34] Driscoll, 'Late Prose Fiction', p. 191.

[35] *Hálfdanar saga Brönufóstra*, ch. 6, in *Fornaldar sögur Norðurlanda*, ed. by Guðni Jónsson, 4 vols (Akureyri: Íslendingasagnaútgáfan, 1954–59), IV, 303–4. All references to *fornaldarsögur* will be to this edition, which will subsequently be abbreviated as *FAS*.

to identify with their human parent and thereby with the human heroes they encounter.[36] While there is never any liaison between Áli and Hlaðgerðr as there is between Brana and Hálfdan, Áli does support Hlaðgerðr's eventual marriage to King Eireikr and acts as her bride-giver. Much as Hlaðgerðr's mixed parentage was an inversion of Brana's, Áli's role as bride-giver likewise inverts Brana's role in arranging Hálfdan's marriage to Marsibil.[37] Chapter 9 of *Hálfdanar saga Brönufóstra* even mentions a female figure called Hlaðgerðr, who is said to rule over Hlaðeyjar (the fictitious Hlaðir Islands),[38] though there is no explicit connection made between this Hlaðgerðr and her namesake in *Ála flekks saga*. As a final note, Marianne Kalinke has raised the possibility that Marsibil and Þornbjǫrg could also be considered to parallel one another (somewhat in the manner of Brana and Hlaðgerðr), since they both represent what she calls 'nonfunctional' maiden kings.[39] Marsibil is never explicitly referred to as a maiden king (*meykonungr*) in *Hálfdanar saga Brönufóstra*, nor does she independently rule a kingdom as Þornbjǫrg does, but it is apparent that both *Hálfdanar saga* and *Ála flekks saga* selectively draw on aspects of the maiden-king motif, further strengthening the narrative connections between them.

Similar genealogical connections to that between Hálfdan and Áli are also found in two other 'borderline *fornaldarsögur*'. Firstly, the Russian hero Vilmundr of *Vilmundar saga* is the grandson of the East-Gautish Bósi of *Bósa saga ok Herrauðs*. Secondly, the Hunnish king Ásmundr Húnakappi in *Sigurðar saga fóts* is said to be the grandfather of the half-brothers of *Ásmundar saga kappabana*, the half-Danish-half-Swedish protagonist Ásmundr and the half-Swedish antagonist Hildibrandr Húnakappi.[40] In the cases of Hálfdan Brönufóstri-Áli flekkr and Bósi-Vilmundr, the ending of the grandfather's saga also corroborates the genealogical connection.[41]

It is helpful to draw a further comparison between Áli and Vilmundr of *Vilmundar saga*. Vilmundr is the son of Sviði (a minor character named in several *fornaldarsögur*), who is the son of one of the East-Gautish heroes of *Bósa saga*, Bósi, and this makes Vilmundr the descendant of a legendary Swede. During the seventeenth century and eighteenth centuries, the medieval Icelandic *fornaldarsögur* were of particular interest to Swedish and Danish scholars, who were keen to 'suggest continuities between their respective modern societies and the heroic spirit of the ancient Goths'.[42] Accordingly, this nationalistic impulse saw the publication of editions of many *fornaldarsögur* involving those respective countries; indeed,

---

[36] *Hálfdanar saga Brönufóstra*, ch. 6, in *FAS*, IV, 302.

[37] *Hálfdanar saga Brönufóstra*, ch. 7, in *FAS*, IV, 305.

[38] *Hálfdanar saga Brönufóstra*, ch. 7, in *FAS*, IV, 306.

[39] Marianne E. Kalinke, *Bridal-Quest Romance in Medieval Iceland* (Ithaca, NY: Cornell University Press, 1990), p. 102 n. 46.

[40] Hall and others, 'Sigurðar saga fóts', p. 91. Notably, *Sigurðar saga fóts* states that Ásmundr Húnakappi's son was the father of both Ásmundr and Hildibrandr Húnakappi, meaning that the half-brothers' common parent was the father. However, in *Ásmundar saga kappabana*, their common parent is their mother, Hildr, and neither of their fathers is called Hrólfr (Ásmundr's is called 'Áki', and Hildibrandr's 'Helgi'). There is no such intertextual discrepancy in the Hálfdan-Áli and Bósi-Vilmundr connections, where the linking genealogical figure is given the same name in both pairs of sagas, Ríkarðr in *Hálfdanar saga* and *Ála flekks saga*, and Sviði in *Bósa saga* and *Vilmundar saga*.

[41] For *Hálfdanar saga Brönufóstra*'s mention of Áli flekkr, see *Hálfdanar saga Brönufóstra*, ch. 17, in *FAS*, IV, 318. For *Bósa saga*'s mention of Vilmundr, see *Bósa saga*, ch. 16, in *FAS*, III, 322. For *Vilmundar saga*'s mention of Bósi, see *Vilmundar saga viðutan*, ch. 8, in *Late Medieval Icelandic Romances*, ed. by Agnete Loth, 5 vols (Copenhagen: Munksgaard, 1962–64), IV, 152.

[42] Andrew Wawn, 'The Post-Medieval Reception of Old Norse and Old Icelandic Literature', in *A Companion to Old Norse-Icelandic Literature and Culture*, ed. by McTurk, pp. 320–37 (p. 324).

the first ever Icelandic sagas to appear in a printed edition were the Gautland-based *Gautreks saga* and *Hrólfs saga Gautrekssonar*, published by Olaus Verelius in 1664.[43] One such edition was of *Sturlaugs saga starfsama*, by Guðmundur Ólafsson in 1694. In his introduction to the saga, Guðmundur stated his belief that *Sturlaugs saga* was part of a group of true stories, and he listed eight sagas as named examples.[44] Seven of these involve prominent Scandinavian heroes and/or locations and are today classified as *fornaldarsögur*, and the other is *Vilmundar saga*. Philip Lavender points out that *Vilmundar saga* follows *Hálfdanar saga Eysteinssonar* in Guðmundur's list, and that *Hálfdanar saga* features Vilmundr's father Sviði. Lavender suggests that '[a] genealogical principle (rather than a geographical one [...]) seems to determine inclusion on Guðmundur's list', noting that Vilmundr 'could [...] be seen as a type of Swedish hero by blood'.[45]

Yet while there is some evidence for Swedish nationalistic interest in *Vilmundar saga*, there seems to be no evidence that *Ála flekks saga* was seen in a similar light by the Danes, despite Áli being the grandson of a legendary Dane, Hálfdan Brönufóstri, and the fact that their sagas share some noticeable similarities. This means that, unlike *Vilmundar saga*, there is no evidence that *Ála flekks saga* was viewed in scholarly discourse as having a particularly close relationship with Scandinavia-based romances. This is in spite of the fact that it travelled frequently with *fornaldarsögur* in Icelandic manuscripts that were being produced through to the nineteenth century, and the fact that the saga it travels with most frequently in extant manuscripts is *Hálfdanar saga Brönufóstra*.[46] However, there is one prominent and relatively recent instance in which scholars have grouped *Ála flekks saga* with some *fornaldarsögur* in publication: in Bachman and Guðmundur Erlingsson's *Six Old Icelandic Sagas*. There, it appears alongside translations of five *fornaldarsögur*, namely *Hrómundar saga Gripssonar*, *Yngvars saga víðförla*, *Illuga saga Gríðarfóstra*, *Sörla þáttr* and *Ásmundar saga kappabana*. This marked the first time that *Ála flekks saga* had ever been edited or translated alongside *fornaldarsögur*. Groundbreaking as this decision was, the translators did not give a reason for the specific inclusion of *Ála flekks saga* alongside five *fornaldarsögur*, although they did note that the *álög* central to the saga's structure is common in the *fornaldarsögur* and *riddarasögur*.[47] They do not mention the Hálfdan Brönufóstri connection in their introduction, so it seems likeliest that they included it purely because they recognised the strong stylistic similarities with some of the *fornaldarsögur*.

In *Ála flekks saga*, therefore, we have an indigenous Icelandic romance without much of a chivalric texture, whose hero is descended from a legendary Scandinavian hero, and which has significant connections to *fornaldarsögur* and *riddarasögur* alike. Therefore, in

---

[43] Matthew J. Driscoll, 'What's Truth Got to Do with it? Views on the Historicity of the Sagas', in *Skemmtiligastar lygisögur: Studies in Honour of Galina Glazyrina*, ed. by Tatjana N. Jackson and Elena A. Melnikova (Moscow: Dimitriy Pozharskiy University, 2012), pp. 15–27 (pp. 17–18).

[44] Philip Lavender, '*Illuga saga Gríðarfóstra* in Sweden: Textual Transmission, History and Genre-Formation in the Seventeenth and Eighteenth Centuries', *Arkiv för Nordisk filologi*, 129 (2014), 197–232 (pp. 204–5).

[45] Lavender, '*Illuga saga Gríðarfóstra* in Sweden', pp. 227–28.

[46] Of the eight manuscripts which contain both *Ála flekks saga* and *Hálfdanar saga Brönufóstra*, the two sagas appear consecutively in five of them. These are AM 589 e 4to (1450–1500), AM 571 4to (1500–1550), AM 297 b 4to (1650–1700), Lbs 272 fol. (1700) and Lbs 840 4to (1737). The full contents of these manuscripts can be found on *Stories for All Time: The Icelandic 'fornaldarsögur'*, compiled by Matthew Driscoll, with Silvia Hufnagel and others (Copenhagen: Nordisk Forskningsinstitut, 2016): http://fasnl.ku.dk. AM 589 e 4to and AM 571 4to are the only surviving medieval witnesses to *Ála flekks saga*, and two out of three of the only surviving medieval witnesses to *Hálfdanar saga Brönufóstra* (the other being AM 152 1 fol., which dates to 1500–1525).

[47] *Six Old Icelandic Sagas*, p. xxi.

spite of its usual classification as a *riddarasaga* — an arbitrary classification essentially based on geographical setting rather than generic markers — *Ála flekks saga* must be studied as part of a fluid generic spectrum that invites a more natural association with the sagas in the *fornaldarsaga* corpus. Just as *Vilmundar saga* has been argued to be 'a Russia-based spin-off of the Scandinavia-based romances',[48] it is not only useful, but also generically accurate, to consider *Ála flekks saga* to be another 'spin-off of the Scandinavia-based romances'.

3. Notable Motifs

Ála flekks saga contains a number of interesting features which deserve a brief introduction in their own right. Previous scholarly interest in the saga has focussed principally on two notable episodes: Áli's werewolf transformation in chapters 8–10 and his supernatural dream in chapter 12. This section will provide an introductory overview of these episodes and their literary context. Additionally, although it has received little scholarly attention, readers may also be curious to learn more about the birthmark from which Áli's takes his cognomen and the saga takes its title, and this notable feature will be discussed at the end of this section.

3.i. The Werewolf Episode

Ála flekks saga is one of fourteen indigenous Icelandic works that feature a werewolf episode, all of which are more fully discussed in Aðalheiður Guðmundsdóttir's survey of the werewolf in medieval Icelandic literature.[49] Aðalheiður follows Einar Ólafur Sveinsson's division of the motif into two variants, the first an indigenous variant characterised by the innate ability to shift into wolf-form and associated with 'war and warlike behaviour' and the second a Continental variant, ultimately deriving from Celtic tradition, in which the transformation results from an external spell or curse.[50] It is the cross-fertilisation between these two variants, she suggests, which resulted in the werewolf episode in *Ála flekks saga*, which shows influence from both indigenous and Celtic traditions.

The clearest parallels, however, are found in *Völsunga saga* and *Hrólfs saga kraka*. Like Áli, Sigmundr and Sinfjötli both take on wolf form, in chapter 8 of *Völsunga saga*. Though their initial donning of wolf pelts is voluntary, unlike Áli's forced transformation, the father and son find themselves trapped and unable to remove the skins until ten days have passed. In both sagas, the wolf skins are clearly cursed, overwhelming the wearer with murderous aggression which seeks to kill indiscriminately, both men and beasts, rather than hunt for prey. As Sigmundr turns on his son Sinfjötli, whom he has begotten incestuously by his sister, nearly killing him, so Áli's aggression is directed at his family, first ravaging the livestock of his future wife and then that of his father. When Áli finally sheds the wolf-skin, his foster-mother, Hildr, directs her husband, Gunni, to burn it, just as Sigmundr and Sinfjötli take theirs 'ok brenna í eldi ok báðu engum at meini verða' ('and burn them in fire and pray no

---

[48] '*Vilmundar saga viðutan*', ed. and trans. by Hui, forthcoming.

[49] For a full discussion of these works and their handling of werewolves see Aðalheiður Guðmundsdóttir, 'The Werewolf in Medieval Icelandic Literature', *The Journal of English and Germanic Philology*, 106 (2007), 277–303.

[50] Aðalheiður Guðmundsdóttir, 'The Werewolf', p. 279; Einar Ól. Sveinsson, 'Keltnesk áhrif á íslenzkar ýkjusögur', *Skírnir*, 106 (1932), 100–23 (pp. 118–19). See also Einar Ól. Sveinsson, 'Celtic Elements in Icelandic Tradition', *Béaloideas*, 25 (1957), 3–24.

further harm should occur').[51] *Sigrgarðs saga frœkna* provides a further example of animal skins being burnt, when the princesses, Hildr and Signý, are released from their cursed forms, as a pig and as a foal respectively, suggesting that fire was a common solution to the obvious magical potency of such skins.

The *Ála flekks saga* episode also bears notable similarities to the transformation of Björn in *Hrólfs saga kraka*. Transformed by his step-mother, Hvít, into a bear, Björn ravages the livestock in his father's kingdom. Only his sweetheart, Bera, still knows him since 'í þessum birni þykkist hún kenna augu Bjarnar konungssonar' ('in the bear she thought she recognised the eyes of the king's son, Björn'), just as Áli's foster mother Hildr recognises the wolf's eyes as those of Áli flekkr.[52] By contrast, Björn's father, Hringr, leads a hunting party to kill his son, mirroring the actions of Áli's father Ríkarðr, but with deadlier results since Björn is granted no last-minute quarter and is instead killed by his father's men.

3.ii. Áli's Dream

The motif of physical wounds sustained in a dream is exceptionally rare in medieval Icelandic literature. Apart from *Ála flekks saga*, versions of the motif appear in three other sagas: the thirteenth-century *Fóstbrœðra saga* and the fourteenth-century *Bárðar saga Snæfellsnáss*, both *Íslendingasögur*; and the fourteenth-century *riddarasaga Sigurðar saga þögla*. A fuller discussion of the motif in these three sagas can be found in John Roberts' dissertation on dreams in the medieval Icelandic romances,[53] but none of these three instances will be discussed here, since they are too dissimilar to Áli's dream to assume a connection. For instance, Áli's dream is entirely recounted in the first-person, while the other three sagas recount their dreams in the third-person. Another key difference is the specificity of the wound sustained; Áli's wounds are described very generally and presumably located all around his body, while in the other three sagas, the wounds are localised to the eyes in two cases, and the head in one.[54]

However, Áli's dream does have an uncannily close parallel in another medieval text. Einar Ól. Sveinsson noted the strong similarities between Áli's dream and that of Cú Chulainn in the Old Irish *Serglige Con Culainn* ('The Wasting Sickness of Cú Chulainn').[55] In this tale, the legendary hero Cú Chulainn is persuaded to catch beautiful lake-birds for the Ulsterwomen, and he attempts to catch two particularly special birds for his own wife. He throws a stone, but misses, and then throws a spear which pierces one of the birds. He then falls asleep, and two women appear to him in a dream, whipping him in turn until he is near death. He lies under these wounds for close to a year, before being visited by Lí Ban, one of the women from his dream and one of the two birds he had attacked, who asks him to go to Fand, the other dream-woman, and fight a battle in the otherworld on her behalf, in exchange for fully healing him.

---

[51] *Völsunga saga*, ch. 8, in *FAS*, I, 124.

[52] *Hrólfs saga kraka*, ch. 26, in *FAS*, I, 48.

[53] John J. Roberts, 'Dreams and Visions in Medieval Icelandic Romance' (unpublished Ph.D. thesis, University of Leeds, 2007), pp. 163–75. Roberts discusses *Ála flekks saga* immediately afterwards, at pp. 175–83.

[54] The instances of eye-pain in the dreams of the two *Íslendingasögur* are discussed in Kirsi Kanerva, '"Eigi er sá heill, er í augun verkir": Eye Pain in Thirteenth- and Fourteenth-Century *Íslendingasögur*', *Arv: Nordic Yearbook of Folklore*, 69 (2013), 7–35.

[55] Einar Ól. Sveinsson, 'Celtic Elements in Icelandic Tradition', pp. 16–17. For an edition of this text, see Myles Dillon, 'The Trinity College Text of *Serglige Con Culainn*', *Scottish Gaelic Studies*, 6 (1949), 139–75. For a

The similarities are obvious: in both cases the hero is visited in a dream by a woman or women whom he had previously met in person; in both cases the hero is being punished in retaliation for an offence against the woman; in both cases wounds are inflicted by whips; in both cases these wounds render the hero bedridden for an extended period of time; and in both cases it is stipulated that the wounds are only to be fully healed by someone living in a faraway paranormal otherworld. There are also some differences, such as the fact that Áli is given an expiration date while Cú Chulainn is not, but the specificity of some of the similarities, such as the whip-wielding women, strongly implies a connection between the two.[56] This in itself is not evidence that *Serglige Con Culainn* was known in late medieval Iceland, as the rest of the narrative differs drastically from that of *Ála flekks saga*. However, at the very least, it is probable that the key aspects of Áli's dream were based on a source with some connection to the much older tradition of Cú Chulainn's dream, even if it is difficult to say how direct this connection is, whether this source was oral or literary, or how close the source was to the versions of *Serglige Con Culainn* that survive.[57]

3.iii. Áli's Fleck

The fleck on Áli's right cheek is integral to his identity, but it is nothing more than a blind motif. There does not seem to be an immediate source for it,[58] but in medieval romance, the birthmark is frequently a marker of royalty and usually has a single narrative function, namely to prove a hero or heroine's royal identity.[59] However, in *Ála flekks saga*, this birthmark is only

---

translation, see Myles Dillon, 'The Wasting Sickness of Cú Chulainn', *Scottish Gaelic Studies*, 7 (1953), 47–88.

[56] Beyond the dream, there is one other similarity between the two texts: in the Icelandic saga, Glóðarauga's curse that turns Áli into a wolf is followed by the provision that he will never be released 'unless a woman should ask for quarter for you when you are captured'; in the Irish tale, Cú Chulainn's charioteer Láeg is told that he will not depart from Fand's land alive unless protected by a woman.

[57] Alaric Hall has noted that several aspects of *Serglige Con Culainn* (and to a lesser extent other Irish and Welsh texts) find parallels in the description of the death of Vanlandi in *Ynglinga saga* (Alaric Hall, *Elves in Anglo-Saxon England: Matters of Belief, Health, Gender and Identity*, Anglo-Saxon Studies, 8 (Woodbridge: Boydell and Brewer, 2007), pp. 137–9, 144), suggesting therefore that the form of Snorri's narrative has 'deeper roots' (p. 139). He draws further parallels between *Serglige Con Culainn* and an account of a witchcraft trial on Orkney in 1616 (2007, 152–3; for further details see Alaric Hall, 'Hoe Keltisch zijn elfen eigenlijk?', trans. by Dennis Groenewegen, *Kelten*, 37 (2008), 2–5). Orkney has been suggested as a possible staging post in the travel of Irish or Gaelic folklore and literary ideas to Iceland; see for example Michael Chesnutt, 'An Unsolved Problem in Old Norse-Icelandic Literary History', *Mediaeval Scandinavia*, 1 (1968), 122–37 (p. 129); Bo Almqvist, *Viking Ale: Studies on Folklore Contacts Between the Northern and the Western Worlds* (Aberystwyth: Boethius Press, 1991), pp. 1–29, esp. 24–5. For a more minimalist view of Orkney as a conduit see Gísli Sigurðsson, *Gaelic Influence in Iceland: Historical and Literary Contacts: A Survey of Research*, 2nd edn (Reykjavik: University of Iceland Press, 2010), pp. 42, 47.

[58] Two others characters have the cognomen *flekkr* in the corpus of Old Norse saga literature. In *Óláfs saga helga* there is a farmer called Þorgeirr flekkr. Additionally, there is a Barðr flekkr in *Hákonar saga Hákonarsonar*. The origin of the nickname is not explained in the case of either Þorgeirr or Barðr, nor do their 'flecks' serve any narrative purpose.

[59] Under Stith Thompson's motif-index classification, this is motif number H71, 'mark of royalty' (Stith Thompson, *Motif-Index of Folk-Literature: A Classification of Narrative Elements in Folktales, Ballads, Myths, Fables, Mediaeval Romances, Exempla, Fabliaux, Jest-Books and Local Legends*, rev. and enl. edn, 6 vols (Bloomington: Indiana University Press, 1955–58), III, 379–80), and the best-known Norse example of this can be found in the birthmark of Sigurðr ormr-í-auga in *Ragnars saga loðbrókar*. A wider survey of the literary and linguistic associations of the birthmark can be found in Karl Jaberg, 'The Birthmark in Language and Literature', *Romance Philology*, 10 (1956), 307–42, with the 'mark of royalty' motif only briefly discussed at p. 311. The birthmark has been a well-established motif since classical antiquity. In his *Poetics*, Aristotle refers to two legends involving inherited birthmarks: 'the spear which the earth-born race bear on their bodies' (the birthmark of the descendants

mentioned as part of the brief physical description of Áli given immediately after his birth, and it serves no narrative function in the saga other than to provide him with his cognomen while he is being fostered by Gunni and Hildr. It does not even feature at the moment his real mother recognises him — for there he is recognised not by his fleck, but by his eyes.

One prominent example of this form of the birthmark motif, and one with a tantalising set of similarities to *Ála flekks saga*, is the thirteenth-century Middle High German romance *Wolfdietrich*.[60] The eponymous hero is born with the following birthmark: 'im zwischen schultern ein rôtez kriuzelin' (stanza 140, 'between his shoulders a red cross'); and in the very next line, the poet reveals its function: 'dâ bâ si dâ erkante ir liebez kindelîn' (st. 141, 'by which she [his mother, Princess Hildeburg of Salonika] recognised her dear baby later').[61] Wolfdietrich is exposed as a baby, but is found by his unknowing grandfather, King Walgunt of Salonika, and recognised not long afterwards by Hildeburg (st. 189).[62] Following this, the truth of Wolfdietrich's parentage is revealed to all. In Wolfdietrich's case, this is only the backstory to his adventures as an adult, as opposed to constituting the full drama. Wolfdietrich in fact shares notable biographical similarities to Áli. Both are born into royalty, but are exposed as children and are later brought back into their true family by being recognised by their mother. In both cases, the exposure, recognition and return are only the backstory to their adventures proper. Both have a birthmark of some implied significance, though only in *Wolfdietrich* is it used as proof of identity. Wolfdietrich briefly lives among the wolves while Áli is temporarily transformed into one. Another curious similarity, albeit a minor one, is that both are at one point associated with the same number of companions: Áli is said in chapter 3 to have sixteen *leiksveinar* ('playmates'), who are never named and whose only action in the saga is to inform the king and queen of Áli's disappearance; while Duke Berchtung gives Wolfdietrich his sixteen sons as vassals, along with himself and five hundred knights — though six of his sons and all of the other knights are killed shortly afterwards. Berchtung and his remaining ten sons do feature again at the very end of the romance and are therefore, unlike Áli's playmates, of some structural importance. Tantalising though it is, this evidence remains too thin for us to posit a definite relationship between *Wolfdietrich* and *Ála flekks saga*, but the similarities remain noteworthy nevertheless.

of the *spartoi* spawned from the dragon teeth sowed by Cadmus); and 'the "stars" introduced by Carcinus in his *Thyestes*' (the birthmark of the Pelopids, the descendants of the ivory-shouldered Pelops) (*Aristotle: Poetics. Longinus: On the Sublime. Demetrius: On Style*, ed. and trans. by Stephen Halliwell, W. Hamilton Fyfe, Donald Russell, W. Rhys Roberts and Doreen Innes (Cambridge, MA: Harvard University Press, 1995), pp. 82–83). Another notable ancient example can be found in Heliodorus of Emesa's third- or fourth-century novel *Aethiopica*, in which the final and conclusive proof of the true identity of Chariclea, lost daughter of the king and queen of Ethiopia, is the birthmark above her left elbow. Prominent birthmarks are also to be found in Shakespeare (in *Cymbeline*, for instance, there is the mole on Imogen's left breast and Guiderius' birthmark of a 'sanguine star') and Cervantes (for instance the moon-shaped mark under Preciosa's left breast in *La Gitanilla*, and the mole behind Isabela's ear in *La española inglesa*); and this timeless fascination with the dramatic and symbolic potential of congenital bodily marks continues to be seen in modern literature, with a prominent example being Toni Morrison's *Sula* (1973).

60 *Wolfdietrich* survives in three thirteenth-century versions, two of which are fragmentary, and in another version dating to around 1300; see J. W. Thomas, *'Ortnit' and 'Wolfdietrich': Two Medieval Romances*, Studies in German Literature, Linguistics, and Culture, 23 (Columbia, South Carolina: Camden House, 1986), p. xvii. For more on the manuscripts containing the romance, see *Deutsches Heldenbuch*, ed. by Oskar Jänicke, Ernst Martin, Arthur Amelung and Julius Zupitza, 5 vols (Berlin: Weidmannsche Buchhandlung, 1866–1873), III, pp. v–viii.

61 *Ortnit und die Wolfdietriche nach Müllenhoffs Vorarbeiten*, ed. by Arthur Amelung and Oskar Jänicke, 2 vols (Berlin: Weidmannsche Buchhandlung, 1871–73), I, 188.

62 *Ortnit und die Wolfdietriche*, ed. by Amelung and Jänicke, I, 196.

The motif of the royal birthmark does not always provide proof of both royalty and identity. In some cases, the birthmark is simply a proof of royalty, rather than identity, to those who do not actually know the hero. Examples from medieval European romance include the thirteenth-century Old French romance *Richars li Biaus*, in which the hero is said to have the mark of two crosses on his right shoulder (ll. 668–69),[63] as well as in the late thirteenth-century Middle English romance *Havelok*, in which Havelok is said to have a 'kine-merk' ('king-mark') on his 'right shuldre' ('right shoulder') (ll. 604, 2140–47).[64] In other cases, we also have instances in which a royal birthmark appears without fulfilling an identification role at all. One example is found in the Middle English *Emaré*, which dates to the late fourteenth century but which claims to have been based on an Old French poem (ll. 1030–2).[65] In it, Segramour is said to have a 'dowbyll kyngus marke' ('double king's mark'; l. 504),[66] but it does not fulfil the usual identification function because he is never separated from his mother, Emaré. It is nevertheless clearly supposed to be the same motif with all the connotations of royalty, and it is possible that the dual crosses might be interpreted to represent Segramour's descent from both the Welsh and Roman royal houses.[67] In a Norse context, a royal birthmark without narrative function is found in *Jarlmanns saga ok Hermanns*, an indigenous *riddarasaga* probably composed in the fourteenth century — in this saga, Ríkilát, daughter of the emperor of Miklagarðr (Constantinople), has the mark of a golden cross on the back of her right hand.[68]

The fact that the motif of the royal birthmark could appear as a blind motif is illuminating. Like Segramour's in *Emaré*, Ríkilát's birthmark is never used for any sort of identification or royal verification, but the fact that it is shaped like a cross strongly suggests that it was drawing on this wider European motif, and, accordingly, Inger Boberg catalogues it as a sign of royalty in her *Motif-Index of Early Icelandic Literature*.[69] That this is deployed as a blind motif in *Jarlmanns saga* is important here because it raises the possibility that the same process underlies Áli flekkr's birthmark, which is similarly functionless but lacks the cross-shape and is therefore not as obviously connected to the wider European motif (although it is on his right cheek, which may be related to other right-sided manifestations of the motif). However, Áli's exposure as an infant and his return to his real, royal family are consistent with other instances in which the motif is deployed, and it is therefore plausible that Áli's fleck was based on this common European motif.

[63] *Richars li Biaus: Roman du XIIIe siècle*, ed. by Anthony J. Holden (Paris: Champion, 1983), p. 45.

[64] *Havelok the Dane*, in *Middle English Verse Romances*, ed. by Donald B. Sands (Exeter: University of Exeter Press, 1986), pp. 74, 108. On the relationship between *Richars li Biaus* and *Havelok*, see Maldwyn Mills, 'Havelok's Return', *Medium Ævum*, 45 (1976), 20–35. The earlier Old French and Anglo-Norman versions of the Haveloc/Havelok legend do not contain the birthmark (for editions of these, see *The Anglo-Norman Lay of 'Haveloc'*, ed. and trans. by Glyn S. Burgess and Leslie C. Brook (Cambridge: Brewer, 2015)).

[65] *Emaré*, in *The Middle English Breton Lays*, ed. by Anne Laskaya and Eve Salisbury (Kalamazoo: Medieval Institute Publications, 1995), p. 167.

[66] *Emaré*, in *The Middle English Breton Lays*, ed. by Laskaya and Salisbury, p. 182.

[67] *The Middle English Metrical Romances*, ed. by Walter H. French and Charles Brockway Hale, 2 vols (New York: Russell and Russell, 1964), I, 439.

[68] *Jarlmanns saga ok Hermanns*, ch. 2, in *Late Medieval Icelandic Romances*, III, 7–8. In the younger version of the saga, the mark is on the back of Ríkilát's left hand; see *Jarlmanns saga ok Hermanns i yngre handskrifters redaktion*, ed. by Hugo Rydberg (Copenhagen: Møller, 1917), p. 4.

[69] See motif H71.5 in Inger M. Boberg, *Motif-Index of Early Icelandic Literature* (Copenhagen: Munksgaard, 1966), p. 148.

4. Manuscripts, Editions and Notes on the Translation

Ála flekks saga is preserved in some form in a total of thirty-seven known extant manuscripts, the earliest of which was produced in the fifteenth century, and the latest in the late nineteenth century.[70] The total of thirty-seven manuscript witnesses may be relatively low within the exceptionally popular corpus of surviving medieval indigenous *riddarasögur*, in which Matthew Driscoll observes that 'over half are preserved in 40 manuscripts or more, and two, *Mágus saga* and *Jarlmanns saga ok Hermanns*, in nearly twice that many',[71] but it is still a high number in the context of the entire corpus of saga literature, and it indicates that the saga was relatively popular through the centuries. The popularity of the Áli flekkr tradition is also evident from the fact that the saga spawned three sets of *rímur*: one composed in the seventeenth century, possibly by a certain Gísli Jónsson; one by Ingimundur Jónsson of Sveinungsvík in the eighteenth century; and one by Lýður Jónsson of Skipaskagi, composed in 1854.[72] Study of the *rímur* does not come into the scope of this article, but it remains an important and as-yet unexplored avenue of the Áli flekkr tradition (and this is also true of most other narrative traditions which were adapted into *rímur*).

Of the thirty-seven manuscripts containing *Ála flekks saga*, the oldest is AM 589 e 4to (hereafter 589e), which dates to the second half of the fifteenth century and contains, in order, *Þorsteins þáttr bæjarmagns*, *Egils saga einhenda ok Ásmundar berserkjabana*, *Hálfdanar saga Brönufóstra*, *Ála flekks saga* and *Hákonar þáttr Hárekssonar*.[73] It is one of six manuscripts that once formed a single volume, but which are now separate and have the individual shelfmarks AM 589 a 4to, AM 589 b 4to, AM 589 c 4to, AM 589 d 4to, AM 589 e 4to and AM 589 f 4to;[74] all six are now housed at the Árni Magnússon Institute in Reykjavik. Although the 589e text of *Ála flekks saga* (and indeed *Hálfdanar saga Brönufóstra*) is now fragmentary, it was very fortunately copied in entirety before it lost its opening.[75] That copy now survives as AM 181 k fol. (hereafter 181k) and was produced around 1650.[76]

Apart from 589e, *Ála flekks saga* survives in another very late medieval manuscript, AM 571 4to (hereafter 571), which dates to the first half of the sixteenth century and contains, in order, two fragments of *Ála flekks saga*, two of *Hálfdanar saga Brönufóstra*, one of *Þorsteins þáttr bæjarmagns* and three of *Grettis saga*.[77] Although the text of *Ála flekks saga* in 571 is fragmentary, it is closely related to the (completely intact) text of the saga in the seventeenth-century manuscript AM 182 fol. (hereafter 182), and it may even have been its direct source.[78] The 571-182 text of *Ála flekks saga* bears some minor differences to that of 589e-181k, mostly in the form of omissions of short phrases, and they therefore represent two different, though very close, stemmatic branches of the saga's transmission.[79]

[70] Marianne E. Kalinke and P. M. Mitchell, *Bibliography of Old Norse-Icelandic Romances* (Ithaca, NY: Cornell University Press, 1985), pp. 19–20.

[71] Driscoll, 'Late Prose Fiction', p. 194.

[72] Finnur Sigmundsson, *Rímnatal*, 2 vols (Reykjavik: Rímnafélagið, 1966), I, 13–15.

[73] AM 589 e 4to, viewed at *Stories for All Time* (http://fasnl.ku.dk) [accessed 19 May 2017].

[74] *Fornaldarsagas and Late Medieval Romances: Manuscripts No. 586 and 589 a–f, 4to in the Arnamagnæan Collection*, ed. by Agnete Loth (Copenhagen: Rosenkilde and Bagger, 1977), pp. 7, 9.

[75] *Drei lygisǫgur*, p. lxix, cf. *Fornaldarsagas and Late Medieval Romances*, p. 15.

[76] Kristian Kålund, *Katalog over den Arnamagnæanske håndskriftsamling*, 2 vols (Copenhagen: Gyldendalske boghandel, 1889–94), I, 153.

[77] AM 571 4to, viewed at *Stories for All Time* (http://fasnl.ku.dk) [accessed 19 May 2017].

[78] *Drei lygisǫgur*, p. lxix.

[79] *Drei lygisǫgur*, p. lxix. In footnote 1 on the same page, Lagerholm lists examples of differences between the two

Only one critical edition of the saga has been produced, by Åke Lagerholm in 1927, and the text he used was 589e-181k. The same text was reproduced, in Modern Icelandic orthography, in volume five of Bjarni Vilhjálmsson's six-volume *Riddarasögur*.[80] The translation here is of Lagerholm's edition, though it is in substance the exact same text as the translation by W. Bryant Bachman and Guðmundur Erlingsson, who used Bjarni's edition.

We have opted to present Lagerholm's text — with his original normalisation to Old Norse — as a facing text for our translation. We recognise that it is nowadays — with good reason — usual to present the text of a late medieval Icelandic romance normalised to the pre-thirteenth-century conventions of 'standard Old Norse'. We have chosen to retain Lagerholm's text with its anachronistic features here because it is the orthography most familiar to the student of Old Norse.[81] *Ála flekks saga* is a simple text in both narrative and language, and it was felt that retaining this more familiar orthography would make the saga singularly accessible, particularly for those less experienced with the Old Norse language. Nonetheless, four changes have been made to the text. Firstly, in order to avoid confusion over inflections and vowel lengths, we have removed from personal and place names the superfluous accents which Lagerholm had added. Therefore, we have normalised, for instance, Lagerholm's 'Pólícáná' to 'Pólícana', 'Tartaríá' to 'Tartaría', 'Indíá' to 'Indía', 'Mandán' to 'Mandan' and 'Andán' to 'Andan'. Secondly, we have changed Lagerholm's Roman numerals into their equivalent Norse words, for instance 'II þrælar' into 'tveir þrælar'. Thirdly, in two instances of morphological levelling where a first-person plural pronoun is accompanied by the third-person plural verb (in both cases 'eru vit'), we have amended the verb to the first-person plural conjugation more familiar to students ('erum vit'). Fourthly, we have normalised the definite article to 'inn/in/it'; the base manuscripts use the younger forms 'hinn/hin/hit', while Lagerholm mostly normalises them to the older forms 'enn/en/et'. We hope that our decision to retain Lagerholm's orthography, with these changes, will give students and enthusiasts every opportunity to engage with the language in the saga, with the help of the translation.

In terms of the orthography of our translation, we have followed scholarly convention by keeping personal, animal and object names in their nominative form. For the sake of consistency, we have retained the orthography of these names as they appear in Lagerholm's text, rather than using the more modern forms that tend to appear in scholarship. For instance, our translation uses 'Ríkarðr' instead of 'Ríkarð', 'Richard' or the equivalent of the name in modern Icelandic orthography, 'Ríkarður'; and where names contain an 'ǫ', such as 'Þornbjǫrg', this letter has not been converted to the more modern 'ö' ('Þornbjörg'). However, place-names have all been rendered in their English forms, with the exception of 'Pólícana', which probably cannot be identified with a real place. A list of names of characters, animals and objects, followed by one of places, can be found at the end of this introduction. Regarding our translation style, we have sought to follow the text as closely as possible. On the whole, therefore, we have tried to maintain the verb tenses of the original text, although on rare occasions where the text contained tense changes that would have been too awkward in translation, such as in a single sentence with more than two verbs, we have rendered

---

branches of the saga.

[80] *Ála flekks saga*, in *Riddarasögur*, ed. by Bjarni Vilhjálmsson, 6 vols (Reykjavik: Íslendingasagnaútgáfan, 1951), v, 123–60.

[81] For instance, in *An Introduction to Old Norse*, ed. by E. V. Gordon, rev. by A. R. Taylor, 2nd edn (Oxford: Clarendon Press, 1957) or *A New Introduction to Old Norse. Part I: Grammar*, ed. by Michael Barnes, 3rd edn (London: Viking Society for Northern Research, 2008).

present verbs as present participles. However, we have been selective in our translation of the conjunctions 'en' ('but') and 'ok' ('and') and the adverb 'þá' ('then'), sometimes omitting them from the translation in order to preserve the flow of the story. We have also divided up long sentences in some instances, for the same reason.

5. Lists of names

Characters, animals and objects (in order of first mention)

- **Ríkarðr** — king of England.

- **Sólbjǫrt** — Ríkarðr's wife. Hers is a rare name, meaning 'Sun-bright', but it also appears in *Úlfhams saga*.

- **Áli flekkr** — the saga hero, and son of Ríkarðr and Sólbjǫrt. Assumes the name **Stutt-theðinn** ('Short-cloak') at first while in Tartary, and **Gunnvarðr** while in Jǫtunoxi's kingdom.

- **Gunni** and **Hildr** — a poor couple who find and adopt Áli.

- **Blátǫnn** — sister of Nótt, Glóðarauga, Jǫtunoxi, Leggr and Liðr. Her name means 'Black-Tooth', or, alternatively, 'Blue-Tooth'.

- **Hlaðgerðr** — daughter of Nótt and a human man.

- **Nótt** — sister of Blátǫnn, Glóðarauga, Jǫtunoxi, Leggr and Liðr, and mother of Hlaðgerðr. Her name means 'Night'.

- **Þornbjǫrg** — maiden-king of Tartary. Assumes the name **Gunnvǫr** while in Jǫtunoxi's kingdom.

- **Bjǫrn** — a kinsman of Þornbjǫrg and a protector of the borders of Tartary.

- **Álfr** and **Hugi** — two earls who rule over India.

- **Ingifer** — father of Álfr and Hugi. As a common noun attested as early as the fourteenth century, his name refers to the ginger plant, and it may have been assigned to an Indian noble on account of its exoticism. Alternatively, it may derive from Yngvi-Freyr, one of the names of the Norse deity Freyr.

- **Gergín** — a champion of Álfr and Hugi. His name may be derived from *Gergen*, an old genitive form of the German name 'Georg', or it may be a variant of the Danish and Norwegian *Jørgen*.

- **Glóðarauga** — brother of Blátǫnn, Nótt, Jǫtunoxi, Leggr and Liðr. His name means 'Ember-eye', although in modern Icelandic it refers to a 'black eye'.

- **Rauðr** — a counsellor of Ríkarðr. His name means 'Red'.

- **Jǫtunoxi** — brother of Blátǫnn, Nótt, Glóðarauga, Leggr and Liðr. His name means '*jǫtunn*-ox' (*jǫtunn* being a type of giant), and as a common noun, refers to the hairy rove beetle (*Creophilus maxillosus*), which, according to Icelandic folklore, has some healing properties.[82] In rare medical contexts, it refers to a festering wound (or a cancer). Both meanings are curiously appropriate for the character, given Áli's physical state during their initial interaction.

- **Leggr** and **Liðr** — brothers of Blátǫnn, Nótt, Glóðarauga and Jǫtunoxi. These two brothers' names mean 'Limb' and 'Joint' respectively.

- **Mandan** and **Andan** — sons of an earl called Polloníus, and the only human servants of Jǫtunoxi. Their names may be Irish in origin.

- **Gunnbjǫrn** — supposedly an earl in Russia, whom Þornbjǫrg claims to be the father of Áli and herself while they are under the assumed names Gunnvarðr and Gunnvǫr.

- **Polloníus** — father of Mandan and Andan. The name may derive from Latin *polonius* (meaning 'Polish', but used here without any apparent connection to its etymological meaning). This seems to be the earliest extant attestation of this personal name; the saga antedates, by approximately two centuries, the Polonius of Shakespeare's *Hamlet*, whose source for the name has never convincingly been identified.[83] It may alternatively be a rendering of *Apollonius*, a name well known in medieval Europe through the popular legend of Apollonius of Tyre. 'Apollonio' (the Latin dative form of 'Apollonius') is indeed found in the 182 witness of the saga, but the fragmentary 571 witness lacks the corresponding passage.

- **Bremill** — a sword taken from Jǫtunoxi's hall by Áli. Its name is probably based on *brimill*, which refers to a male of a species of large seal.

- **Kolr** — a giant in Mirkwood. His name means 'Coal'.

- **Bárðr** — a farmer in Scythia.

- **Eireikr** — king of Scythia and an unspecified kinsman of Áli.

- **Krákr** — a black horse given by Eirekr to Áli. Its name means 'Crow'.

- **Vilhjálmr, Ríkarðr** and **Óláfr** — sons of Áli and Þornbjǫrg.

Place-names (in order of first mention)

- **England** — England.

- **Tartaría** — Tartary. A land in central Asia, which features in several *fornaldarsögur* and indigenous *riddarasögur*, including *Egils saga einhenda ok Ásmundar berserkjabana*, *Rémundar saga keisarasonar*, *Sigrgarðs saga frækna* and *Sigurðar saga þögla*.

---

[82] Jónas Jónasson, *Íslenzkir þjóðhættir*, ed. by Einar Ól. Sveinsson, 4th edn (Reykjavik: Bókaútgáfan Opna, 2010), pp. 325–30.

[83] J. Madison Davis and A. Daniel Frankforter, *The Shakespeare Name Dictionary* (New York: Garland, 1995), pp. 391–92.

- **Pólícana** — Unattested elsewhere in Old Norse literature as a place-name. It is clearly Latinate, given that it is declined according to the Latin first declension accusative ending *-am* in chapter 7. 'Policana' does feature as the name of Marcolf's wife in the widespread Solomon and Marcolf tradition, including in the accusative 'Policanam' form, a form which also appears in *Ála flekks saga*.[84] There exists an Icelandic variant of this tradition from the fourteenth century, *Melkólfs saga ok Salomons konungs*, but only the beginning of the text survives, and Melkólfr, whose youth is emphasised, is not mentioned to have a wife.[85] It may also be of potential interest that in some postmedieval manuscripts of the fourteenth-century *riddarasaga Saulus saga ok Nikanors*, the sister of Duke Nikanor is called 'Pólisíana',[86] but we cannot read much into this similarity given that in medieval manuscripts, she is called 'Potenciana'.[87] An alternative explanation for this place-name is that it may be a rendering of '-politanus', found in such Latin adjectives as 'Constantinopolitanus' ('from Constantinople').

- **Indía(land)** — India.

- **Affríca** — Africa.

- **Ásía** — Asia.

- **Rússía** — Russia.

- **Svíþjóð in mikla** — Also referred to in this saga as '**Svena**' or abbreviated to **Svíþjóð**, this place is usually identified as Scythia. The literal meaning of this name is 'Sweden the Great'. According to the opening of *Ynglinga saga*, 'Svíþjóð in mikla' (there also called 'Svíþjóð in kalda', 'Sweden the Cold') is a vast north-eastern land which extends down to the Black Sea. However, some geographical treatises use the term to refer to the Kievan Rus'.[88]

- **Myrkviðr** — Mirkwood, a mythological forest which is named in several eddic poems, as well as in *Hervarar saga ok Heiðreks*.

- **Valland** — Gaul, although perhaps denoting France more generally in this saga since *Frakkland* is not mentioned.

- **Saxland** — Saxony.

[84] *The Dialogue of Solomon and Marcolf*, ed. by Nancy M. Bradbury and Scott Bradbury (Kalamazoo: Medieval Institute Publications, 2012), p. 28.

[85] For an edition, see John Tucker, 'Melkólfs saga ok Salomons konungs', *Opuscula*, 10 (1996), 208–11.

[86] *Fjórar riddarasögur*, ed. by H. Erlendsson and Einar Þórðarson (Reykjavik: E. Þórðarson, 1852), p. 35.

[87] *Sálus saga ok Nikanors*, in *Late Medieval Icelandic Romances*, II, 8.

[88] Tatjana N. Jackson, 'The North of Eastern Europe in Early Nordic Texts: The Study of Place-Names', *Arkiv för nordisk filologi*, 108 (1993), 38–45 (p. 43).

Ála flekks saga

Chapter 1

Ríkarðr hefir konungr heitit;[89] hann réð fyrir Englandi. Hann var allra konunga vitrastr, svá at hann vissi fyrir óorðna hluti. Hann átti sér dróttningu, þá er Sólbjǫrt hét. Hon var hverri konu vænni ok vitrari. Þau konungr ok dróttning áttu ekki bǫrn, ok þótti þeim þat mikit mein.

Kotbœr einn var skammt frá hǫllinni. Þar átti atsetu karl, sá er Gunni hét. Hann átti sér kerlingu, þá er Hildr hét. Þau váru bæði mjǫk órík. Karl átti skóg, þann er honum þótti beztr af sínum eigum; þangat fór hann hvern dag at veiða dýr ok fugla sér til matar.

Einn tíma segir konungr, at hann vill láta búa skip ór landi, ok svá var gǫrt, ok váru búin sextán skip. Síðan velr konungr með sér ina frœknustu menn er í váru ríkinu, ok gerir þat bert fyrir alþýðu, at hann ætlar at halda í leiðangr ok ætlar at vera í burtu í þrjá vetr. Dróttning mælti þá til konungs:

'Ek fer eigi kona einsaman, ok er ek með barni.'

Konungr mælti þá: 'Ef þú fœðir sveinbarn, þá skal þat út bera, ok hverr er eigi vill þat gera, skal lífit láta.'

Dróttning frétti, því svá skyldi breyta. Konungr mælti þá:

'Ek sé, ef þat heldi lífi, at hann muni eiga æfi bæði harða ok langa. En ef þu átt mey', segir hann, 'þá skal hana upp fœða.'

Dróttning var óglǫð við þessi orð konungs. Skilja þau nú þetta tal.

Chapter 2

Þegar sem konungr var nú allbúinn, þá gekk hann til skipa, ok kvaddi áðr dróttningu ok aðra menn; sigldi síðan í burt af Englandi, ok fær frægð mikla hvar sem hann kom. En dróttning var eptir mjǫk hljóð, ok kemr sú stund, er hon skal léttari verða. Hon fœðir sveinbarn. Sá sveinn var bæði mikill ok vænn; hann hafði flekk á hœgri kinn. Dróttning skipar tveimr þrælum at bera út sveininn. Þeir gera svá, taka barnit ok bera til skógar Gunna, ok bjuggu um undir einu tré, ok fóru heim síðan, ok sǫgðu dróttningu, at þeir hefðu týnt sveininum.[90] Hon trúði því.

Einhvern dag gekk Gunni til skógar síns, ok ætlar at veiða dýr. Hann heyrði þá óp mikit, ok skundaði þangat, ok sér barn eitt, ok sýniz sveininn fagr; tekr upp ok berr heim til kerlingar sinnar, ok sýnir henni ok segir, hvar hann hefði fundit, ok biðr hana leggjaz á golf. Hon gerir svá, ok lætr sem hon fœði svein þenna. Þau karl ok kerling unnu mikit sveininum, ok óx hann þar upp. En hvert þat nafn, sem þau gáfu honum at kveldi, mundu þau aldri at morni.

Chapter 3

Nú skal þar til máls taka, er konungr kemr heim ór leiðangri, ok fann dróttningu. Hon sagði honum, hversu hon hefði breytt. Konungr spurði, hvar þeir væri, sem sveininn hefðu út borit. En þeir gengu fyrir konung ok sǫgðuz hafa deytt sveininn; en konungr kvez eigi trúa því.

---

[89]   This is the point at which most manuscripts call Ríkarðr 'sonr Hálfdanar Brönufóstra' ('son of Hálfdan, Brana's foster-son').

[90]   The verb *týna* can mean 'to lose' or 'to kill' in Old Norse (though not in modern Icelandic, where it only means the former). In this case, the slaves are probably claiming to have killed the boy, given the corresponding scene at the beginning of chapter 3, in which they tell the king that they have killed the boy (the meaning of *deyða* being unequivocal), but the king, unlike the queen, does not believe them.

The Saga of Áli flekkr

Chapter 1

There was a king called Ríkarðr; he ruled over England. He was the wisest of all kings, such that he knew beforehand of things that had not yet happened. He was married to a queen called Sólbjǫrt. She was more beautiful and wise than any woman. The king and queen had no children, and that was a great sorrow to them.

There was a cottage a short way from the hall. An old man called Gunni had his residence there. He was married to an old woman called Hildr. They were both very poor. The old man owned a forest, which he considered the best of his possessions; he went there every day to hunt game and birds for food.

One time, the king says that he wants to have ships prepared for a voyage abroad, and so it was done, and sixteen ships were prepared. Then the king selects the most valiant men in the kingdom to accompany him, and makes it known to all his people that he intends to make a naval expedition and to be away for three winters. Then the queen spoke to the king:

'I do not walk alone: I am with child.'

The king spoke: 'If you give birth to a boy, he must be exposed, and anyone who will not do that shall lose his life.'

The queen asked why this should be done. The king spoke:

'I foresee that if he remains alive, he will lead a life both hard and long. But if you have a girl', he says, 'then she must be brought up.'

The queen was unhappy with the king's words. Now they drop the subject.

Chapter 2

When the king was fully prepared, he went to the ships. He first bade farewell to the queen and other people, and then sailed away from England, and gained much fame wherever he went. But the queen became very quiet after this, and the time comes for her to deliver. She gives birth to a boy. This boy was both large and handsome. He had a fleck on his right cheek. The queen orders two slaves to expose the boy. They do so; they take the child, carry it to Gunni's forest and laid him under a tree. Then they went home and told the queen that they had killed the boy. She believed that.

One day, Gunni went to his forest intending to hunt game. He heard a great cry and hastened towards it, and sees a child, and the boy seems fair to him. He picks him up and carries him home to his wife, shows him to her and tells her where he had found him, and asks her to lie down on the floor. She does so, and acts as if she is giving birth to the boy. The old man and woman loved the boy greatly, and he grew up there. But whatever the name they gave him in the evening, they never remembered it in the morning.

Chapter 3

Now the tale will be taken up when the king arrives home from his expedition and met the queen. She told him what she had done. The king asked where those who had exposed the boy might be. They went before the king and said that they had killed the boy, but the king said that he did not believe this.

Einhvern morgun stóð karl upp snemma, ok gekk at rúmi því, er sonr hans lá í, ok þá mælti hann:

'Sefr þú, Áli flekkr?' En hann sagði sik vaka.

Þetta nafn bar hann síðan. Þá var hann átta vetra. Bæði var hann mikill vexti ok vænn áliti.

Konungr lætr nú búa veizlu ok til bjóða ǫllum beztum mǫnnum, er í váru hans ríki; ok at ǫllum þeim þar komnum verðr mikill príss ok gleði í hǫllinni ok hǫfuðborginni. Gunni ok kerling fóru til veizlunnar; þau sátu útarliga í hǫllinni. Áli var með þeim, ok gekk innarr fyrir konungsborðit. Dróttning sat á einum stóli, ok er hon sér Ála, þá roðnaði hon mjǫk ok horfði á hann. Þetta gat konungr skjótt at líta, ok mælti till hennar:

'Hví horfir þú svá á þenna mann, eða þykkiz þú hafa sét hann fyrr?'

Dróttning svarar: 'Ek þekki hann til fulls ekki, en þó hefi ek sét hann fyrri.'

Konungr mælti þá: 'Hvar er Gunni ok kerling hans? Komi þau hér!'

Þeim var sagt, at þau kœmi til konungs. Ok þeir gera svá, ganga fyrir konung ok kveðja hann. Konungr tók svá til máls:

'Grunr er mér á, hvárt þau Gunni ok Hildr eiga þenna mann inn unga, er hér stendr, ok vil ek, at þit segið satt frá, hversu þat er til komit.'

Gunni tekr þá mál: 'Þessi sveinn er víst ekki okkarr sonr. Ek fann hann á skógi mínum, ok hǫfum vit hann síðan upp fœddan.'

Konungr fann þá af sinni vizku, at þessi sveinn var hans sonr. Var þá bert gǫrt fyrir alþýðu, at Áli var konungs sonr. Tók konungr hann þá með miklum heiðri, en gaf Gunna karli góðar gjafir. Fór karl þá ok kella hans til síns heimilis. Var svá slitin veizlan, ok var Áli heima með fǫður sínum. Hann hafðu sextán leiksveina, ok gengu þeir með honum út ok inn.

Chapter 4

Blátǫnn hét ambátt ein, er var í konungsgarðinum. Hon var at ǫllu illa fallin. Eitt kveld var þat, er Áli konungssonr var úti staddr einn saman, þá kom þar Blátǫnn. Hon grenjaði hátt ok mælti svá:

'Þú, Áli!' segir hon, 'hefir mik aldri kvatt með góðum orðum, ok skal ek nú launa þér þat: þú skalt þegar í stað verða at fara á skóg, ok eigi fyrr létta, en þú kemr til Nóttar, systur minnar; henni sendi ek þik til bónda.'

Áli mælti þá: 'Þat mæli ek um, at þú farir framm til eldahúss, ok verðir at einni hellu, ok kyndi þrælar eld á þér. En ef ek komumz frá Nótt trǫllkonu, þá skaltu klofna í sundr, ok láta svá lífit.'

Þá mælti Blátǫnn: 'Þat vil ek, at þetta haldiz hvárki.'

Áli kvað þetta verða statt at standa. Þegar fór Áli á skóg, en Blátǫnn í eldahús, ok varð hon at hellu, ok gerðu þrælar á henni elda; stóð hennar æfi þann veg.

Sveinar sakna hans nú, ok leita at honum allsstaðar nær borginni, ok finna þeir hann eigi. Þeir segja konungi ok dróttningu hvarf konungssonar. Konungr mælti: 'Nú er þat framm komit, er ek vissa fyrri, at þessi sveinn mundi fyrir miklum óskǫpum verða. Veit ek, at hann er horfinn í trǫlla hendr, ok mun ek ekki leita hans.'

Við þetta allt saman grét dróttningin mjǫk sárliga.

One morning, the old man woke up early and went to the bed in which his son lay, and then he spoke: 'Are you sleeping, Áli flekkr?' But he said that he was awake.

He bore that name thereafter. He was then eight winters old. He was both large in stature and fair of face.

The king now has a feast prepared and invites all the best men in his kingdom; and when all of them had arrived, there was much pomp and merriment in the hall and the capital city. Gunni and his wife went to the feast; they sat on the fringes of the hall. Áli was with them, and went farther in up to the king's table. The queen sat on a chair, and when she sees Áli, she reddened greatly and stared at him. The king immediately noticed that, and spoke to her:

'Why do you stare so at that person, or do you think you have seen him before?' The queen replies: 'I do not fully recognise him, but even so I have seen him before.'

The king spoke: 'Where are Gunni and his wife? Have them come here.'

They were told that they should come to the king. And they do so, going before the king and greeting him. The king began to speak thus:

'I am doubtful whether Gunni and Hildr are the parents of that young man who stands here, and I want you two to speak the truth about how this came to pass.'

Gunni begins to speak: 'This boy is indeed not our son. I found him in my forest, and we two have brought him up since then.'

The king realised through his wisdom that this boy was his son. Then it was made known to all the people that Áli was the king's son. The king received him with great honour, and gave the old man Gunni good gifts. Then the old man and his wife went to their homestead. The feast was concluded thus, and Áli stayed at home with his father. He had sixteen playmates, and they accompanied him inside and outside.

Chapter 4

There was a bondwoman called Blátǫnn in the king's court. She was wholly malevolent. It happened one evening, when the king's son Áli was outside alone, that Blátǫnn arrived there. She howled loudly and spoke thus:

'You, Áli', she says, 'have never greeted me with kind words, and I will now repay you for that: you shall immediately have to go away into the forest, and not stop until you come to Nótt, my sister. I send you to her as a husband.'

Áli spoke: 'I pronounce that you will go forth to the kitchen and become a stone slab, and slaves will kindle fires on you. But if I should escape from Nótt the troll-woman, you shall be cloven asunder, and thus lose your life.'

Blátǫnn spoke: 'I wish that neither of these would hold true.'

Áli said that it would have to come to pass. Áli went at once into the forest, and Blátǫnn into the kitchen, and she became a stone slab, and slaves lit fires on her. Her life was spent in this way.

The boys now miss Áli and search for him everywhere near the city, but they do not find him. They tell the king and the queen of the disappearance of the king's son. The king spoke: 'It has now come about as I foresaw, that this boy would suffer a very evil fate. I know that he is lost into the hands of trolls, and I will not look for him.'

Because of all this, the queen wept very bitterly.

Chapter 5

Nú skal segja frá Ála, at hann liggr úti á mǫrkum átján dœgr, ok um síðir kemr hann í dal einn. Áli var þá illa klæddr. Hann sér þá hús eitt mikit; þangat gengr hann, ok sér þar eina fríða konu. Hon heilsar honum með nafni, en hann undrar þetta geysimjǫk, ok mælti svá:

'Hvert er nafn þitt, kona?' segir hann, 'er þú heilsar mér svá kunnugliga, en ek þykkjumz eigi hafa sét þik.'

Hon mælti þá: 'Gǫrla kenni ek þik, Áli!' segir hon, 'ok svá veit ek, hvert þú ert sendr. Fyrir dal þessum ræðr móðir mín, er Nótt heitir, ok til hennar ertu sendr. Faðir minn var mennskr maðr, ok til hans bregðr mér meirr at betr er, ok heiti ek Hlaðgerðr. En er þú ferr í burt héðan, muntu hitta helli stóran; honum stýrir móðir mín. En er þú kemr, muntu engan mann sjá, þvíat eigi er Nótt heima, ok aldri kemr hon, fyrr en langt er af nótt. En er hon kemr heim, mun hon fyrst neyta fœzlu. Hon mun bjóða þér at eta með sér, en þat skaltu eigi gera. Hon mun segja, at þú skalt eigi mat fá. Því næst mun hon til sængr fara, ok biðja þik at liggja hjá sér, en þú skalt þat eigi vilja; en þat mun henni illa líka, ef þú liggr í ǫðrum stað; en þó mun hon sofna brátt. Þú munt ok brátt sofna, ok eigi muntu vakna fyrr en byrgðar eru hellisdyrr. Burt mun þá Nótt horfin.

Þá skal ek senda þér skikkjurakka[91] minn með þá hluti, er þér þarfaz, ok með því einu muntu lauss verða, at hann leysi þik út. En ef hann ferr með flesk af svíni, þá tak þat; er þú kemr upp á þat fjall, er fyrir ofan er helli Nóttar, legg þat niðr í gǫtuna, ok mun hon þá ekki eptir þér fara; enda fartu nú í burt, þvíat móðir mín veit, at þú ert hér.'

Áli kvað svá vera skyldu, ok fór hann í burt ór dyngjunni í þann hluta dalsins, er myrkt var í. Hann kemr at einstigi; þar váru í klǫppuð spor. Áli hafði øxi eina sér í hendi, er Hlaðgerðr hafði gefit honum; hann krœkti øxarhyrnunni upp í sporit, ok las sik spor af spori, þar til er hann kom upp á bjargit. Hann sér þar helli stóran; þóttiz hann þá vita, at Nótt trǫllkona mundi fyrir þeim ráða eiga. Snýr hann þá at hellinum, ok skjótliga gengr hann inn; þar var bæði fúlt ok kalt. Hann settiz niðr við hellisdyrr, ok beið þar allt til dagsetrs, ok kom flagðit eigi heim. En þá er vera mundi þriðjungr af nótt, heyrði konungssonr dunur ok dynki stóra; sá hann þá, at flagðit skauz í hellinn. Hon var í skorpnum skinnstakki; hann tók eigi á lendar á bakit, en á tær fyrir. Enga skepnu þóttiz Áli ferligri sét hafa.

Nótt tók svá til orða: 'Vel verði Blátǫnn, systur minni, er hon sendi þik, Áli, mér til handa ok bónda! En þú gerðir þat illa, er þú lagðir á hana.'

Áli svaraði engu. Nótt bjó sér fœdu, hrossakjǫt ok manna, ok bauð Ála með sér til matar; en Áli neitaði því.[92] Hon kvað hann eigi fyrr skyldu hafa, en hann yrði feginn.

---

[91] The term *skikkjurakki* only appears in this saga, *Hálfdanar saga Eysteinssonar*, and *Orkneyinga saga*. Although the Cleasby-Vigfússon and Zoega dictionaries of Old Norse translate it as 'lapdog', none of these attestations portrays the dog as the small, domesticated and pampered dog to which the modern English term refers. The noun *skikkja* means 'cloak' or 'mantle', so the literal translation is 'cloak-dog'. It is unclear what this refers to. One possibility is that it refers to a dog who follows by its master's cloak, or perhaps more metaphorically, a dog who watches its master's back closely. This fits the attestations of the word, since the dogs of *Ála flekks saga* and *Hálfdanar saga* are loyal and physically capable (and in *Hálfdanar saga Eysteinssonar*, protective). Another possibility is that it refers to a type of dog with a saddle coloured differently to the rest of its body, such as modern-day German shepherds or Siberian huskies; the modern Icelandic term *skikkja* in fact is used in this context. We are grateful to Brynja Þorgeirsdóttir for these suggestions.

[92] The verb *neita*, 'to refuse', may be a pun on its homophone *neyta*, 'to consume', which is used when Hlaðgerðr introduces Nótt and also later in this chapter.

J. Y. H. Hui, C. Ellis, J. McIntosh, K. M. Olley, W. Norman and K. Anderson

Chapter 5

The next thing to say about Áli is that he spends eighteen days in the forest, and comes at last to a valley. By then Áli was poorly clothed. Then he sees a large house. He walks to it and sees a beautiful woman there. She greets him by name, and he wonders greatly at that and spoke thus:

'What is your name, lady', he says, 'who greets me so familiarly, though I don't think I've seen you before?'

She spoke: 'I know you well, Áli', she says, 'and I also know where you've been sent. My mother, who is called Nótt, rules over this valley, and you have been sent to her. My father was human, and I resemble him more, which is fortunate, and I am called Hlaðgerðr. When you go away from here, you will find a large cave. My mother rules it. But when you arrive, you will see no one, because Nótt is not at home, and she never returns until it is late into the night. And when she comes home, she will first of all eat food. She will invite you to eat with her, but you must not do that. She will say that you will not get any food. Next, she will go to the bed and invite you to lie with her, but you must resist the desire to do that. She will take it badly if you lie somewhere else, but she will nevertheless fall asleep quickly. You will also fall asleep quickly, and you will not wake before the cave-door is shut. Nótt will have disappeared by then.

'Then I shall send you my dog with the things that you need, and you can only become free by him letting you out. And if he brings some pork, then take it. When you come up onto the mountain above Nótt's cave, lay it down on the path, and she will not follow you. Go away now, because my mother knows that you are here.'

Áli said that it would be so, and he went out of the bower and into the part of the valley which lay in darkness. He comes to a narrow path; footholds were chiselled there. Áli had an axe in his hand, which Hlaðgerðr had given to him; he hooked the heel of the axe-blade into the foothold and pulled himself up from foothold to foothold until he came up onto the ledge. He sees a great cave there, and he realised that Nótt the troll-woman must rule it. Then he turns to the cave and walks in briskly. It was both foul-smelling and cold inside. He sits down by the cave-door, and waited there all the way until nightfall, and the ogress did not come home. But when a third of the night had passed, the king's son heard thunderous noises and a great clamour, and then he saw the ogress burst into the cave. She was in a shrivelled skin-cloak; it did not reach her buttocks down the back, but fell to her toes in the front. Áli thought that he had never seen a more monstrous creature.

Nótt began to speak: 'Blátǫnn, my sister, did well, when she sent you into my power to be my husband, Áli! But you acted badly when you laid a curse on her.'

Áli did not reply. Nótt prepared food for herself, horse-flesh and man-flesh, and invited Áli to eat with her, but Áli refused this. She said that he must not have had it before, but that he would come to like it. And when she had eaten what she wanted, she put away the food

En er hon hafði etit sem hon vildi, geymdi hon fœðuna, en bjó sér sæng með þeim hætti, at hon lagði einn beð undir hǫfuð sér; hann var gǫrr af geitskinnum. Bauð hon Ála at liggja hjá sér, en þat vildi hann eigi. Henni líkaði þat ekki vel, en þó sofnaði hon brátt, því hon var móð. Konungssonr sofnaði ok skjótt, ok eigi vaknaði hann fyrr en hann sá, at alljóst var í hellinum, ok Nótt var ǫll í burtu,[93] en hellisdyrr byrgðar. Áli stendr þá upp ok gengr til hellisdyra. Hann sér, at bora var á hellisberginu; hann sá þar úti, at skikkjurakki Hlaðgerðar var kominn, ok hafði gǫrt rauf á berginu með trýninu. Áli ferr þá ór klæðum sínum, ok getr smogit út þessa boru, ok sér, at hundrinn bar á baki sér flesk af svíni; klæði hafði hundrinn meðferðar, ok svá góða fœðu, at konungssonr mátti vel neyta. Tekr hann þessa hluti alla af hundinum; neytir hann þá fœðu sem hann lysti; klæðin váru Ála mátulig. En sem hann hafði etit ok drukkit sem hann lysti, býz hann til ferðar; gengr upp á fjallit, ok er hann kemr upp þangat, skerr hann fleskit niðr í gǫtuna, þat er Hlaðgerðr hafði gefit honum. Eptir þat gengr Áli á merkr ok skóga marga daga. Eigi kann hann nú veg til fǫður síns, ok aldri veit hann, hvar hann ferr.

Chapter 6

Á einum degi kom Áli ofan í eitt ríki mjǫk stórt. Hann sér þá smá bœi ok stóra, ok eina borg mjǫk stóra sá hann þar. Þangat gengr Áli, ok er hann kom at hallardyrum, beiðiz hann af dyravǫrðum inn at ganga, eptirspyrjandi, hverr fyrir þessarri borg réði. Þeir segja, at fyrir henni réði einn meykonungr, ok ætti hon þar forræði, er Þornbjǫrg hét— 'ok hefir hon nýtekit við fǫðurleifð sinni.'

Síðan lofa þeir honum inn at ganga. Áli gengr nú inn fyrir meykonunginn, ok kveðr hana virðuliga. Meykonungr tók honum vel, ok spurði hann at nafni; en hann sagðiz Stuttheðinn heita— 'ok eru bráð brautingja erendi, ok vilda ek vera hér hjá yðr í vetr.'

Meykonungrinn játar því, ok skipar honum hjá gestum á inn óœðra bekk. Þessi meykonungr var bæði væn ok vitr. Stuttheðinn kom sér í mikla kærleika við meykonunginn, ok mat hon hann mikils vónum bráðara. Allir unnu honum hugástum; en hann var fálátr. Meykonungr spurði sína menn, hvat manna þeir ætluðu hann vera. En þeir sǫgðuz þat eigi vita, ok fréttu hana, hvat hon ætlaði. Hon sagði þá: 'Þat ætla ek', sagði hon, 'at hann sé konungsættar, ok hafi orðit fyrir álǫgum'; ok fell þar niðr þetta mál.

Bjǫrn hét maðr ok var frændi meykonungs ok mikils metinn af meykonungi. Hann varði landit fyrir víkingum ok ránsmǫnnum, er gengu á ríkit. Land þetta, er meykonungr réð fyrir, hét Tartaría. Sat Bjǫrn í ýzta hluta landsins, í borg þeirri, er Pólícana heitir. Var Bjǫrn af því sjaldan með meykonunginum.

Chapter 7

Jarlar tveir réðu fyrir Indía. Þeir hétu Álfr ok Hugi, ok váru Ingifers synir. Þeir váru miklir hǫfðingjar, ok fréttu þeir til þessa meykonungs, ok safna sér liði, ok fóru til Tartaríam þess erendis, at Álfr ætlaði at biðja meykonungsins; en ef hon tœki því fjarri, ætluðu þeir at eyða ríkit með eldi ok vápnum. Fara þeir nú með þrjátigi skipa til Tartaría, ok koma við Pólícanam.

---

[93] This seems to be a pun on *nótt* as a common noun, meaning 'night', such that the phrase could also mean 'night had completely gone away'.

and prepared the bed for herself by laying a pillow under her head; it was made of goat-skin. She invited Áli to lie with her, but he did not want to. She did not take that well, but she quickly fell asleep, because she was exhausted. The king's son also fell asleep swiftly, and he did not wake until it was entirely bright in the cave and Nótt had completely gone away, but the cave-door was closed. Áli stands up and goes to the cave-door. He sees that there was a small hole in the cave-wall. Through it, he saw that Hlaðgerðr's dog had arrived outside, and it had made an opening in the wall with its muzzle. Áli takes off his clothes and manages to slip out through this hole, and he sees that the dog carried some pork on its back. The dog had brought clothes and such good food that the king's son could happily consume it. He takes all these things from the dog, and he eats as much food as he wished. The clothes were suitable for Áli. And when he had eaten and drunk as he wished, he prepares himself for the journey. He walks up onto the mountain, and when he arrives there, he cuts up the meat which Hlaðgerðr had given him and places it down on the path. After that, Áli walks in forests and woods for many days. He does not now know the way to his father, and he has no idea where he is going.

Chapter 6

One day, Áli came down into a very large kingdom. He sees towns both small and large, as well as one very large city. Áli walks to it, and when he came to the hall-door, he asks the door-wardens to let him in, asking who ruled over this city. They say that a maiden-king called Þornbjǫrg ruled over it and had authority there — 'and she has recently come into her patrimony.'

Then they allow him to enter. Áli walks in before the maiden-king and greets her respectfully. The maiden-king received him well and asked his name, and he said that he was called Stuttheðinn — 'the wanderer's business is urgent, and I want to stay here with you this winter.'

The maiden-king grants this and seats him with the guests on the bench for those lower in rank. This maiden-king was both beautiful and wise. Stuttheðinn developed a strong friendship with the maiden-king, and she esteemed him greatly sooner than was expected. Everyone loved him with all their hearts, but he was reserved. The maiden-king asked her men what kind of man they thought him to be. But they said that they did not know, and asked her what she thought. She said: 'I think that he might be of royal birth, and that he has come under a curse', and they dropped the subject there.

There was a man called Bjǫrn who was a kinsman of the maiden-king and was greatly esteemed by her. He protected the land from pirates and robbers who encroached upon the kingdom. This land over which the maiden-king ruled was called Tartary. Bjǫrn resided in the outermost part of the land in the city which was called Pólícana. Because of this, Bjǫrn was seldom with the maiden-king.

Chapter 7

Two earls ruled over India. They were called Álfr and Hugi, and they were the sons of Ingifer. They were mighty chieftains, and having heard of this maiden-king, they gather their host and went to Tartary for this mission: that Álfr intended to ask for the hand of the maiden-king — but if she were to take that badly, they intended to lay waste to the kingdom with fire and weapons. Now they go to Tartary with thirty ships and arrive at Pólícana.

Bjǫrn fór þegar til bardaga við þá, er hann vissi, hvers erendis þeir fóru, ok kvað þá eigi skyldi sjá meykonunginn, ok var þat harðr bardagi. Jarlarnir gengu hart framm. Sá maðr var með þeim, er Gergín hét. Hann mœtti Birni í bardagum, ok hafði kesju eina í hendi, ok lagði til Bjarnar; þat kom í lærit. Bjǫrn hjó kesjuna af skaptinu, ok komz með þat á flótta, ok tveir menn með honum. Bjǫrn kom á fund meykonungs; hann segir henni ferðir jarlanna ok þat, at Álfr vildi biðja hennar. Þornbjǫrg ansar þá á þessa lund: 'Hvernin er Álfr jarl at sjá?'

'Ljótr maðr ok illmannligr', segir Bjǫrn. Meykonungr fréttir þá, hverr vera vildi hǫfuðsmaðr á móti jarlinum fyrir liðinu— 'þvíat eigi vil ek', segir hon, 'eiga jarl; en Bjǫrn er sárr, ok má hann því eigi vera forstjóri yðvarr.'

Enginn af mǫnnum Þornbjargar vildi forstjóri vera. Meykonungr hét þá at ganga með þeim manni, er forstjórinn vildi vera fyrir liðinu. Stuttheðinn segiz þat vildi til vinna, ok geriz hǫfðingi fyrir liðinu; váru þat nærri tvau hundruð manna. Jarlar váru þá komnir á slétta vǫllu, er þar váru nær borginni þeirri, er meykonungr sat í, ok hǫfðu fjǫgur hundruð manna. Stuttheðinn ríðr út af borginni með sína menn. Jarlarnir hǫfðu fylkt liði sínu.

Stuttheðinn ríðr nú hart framm ok allir hans menn á hendr óvinum sínum. Stuttheðinn sér, hvar Gergín berz allhraustliga; vendir hann þá í móti honum, ok hǫggr til hans með mæki þeim, er meykonungr hafði gefit honum, ok kom þat hǫgg á hœgri ǫxlina, ok tók af hǫndina ok þar með síðuna ok fótinn annan fyrir ofan knéit, en annan fyrir neðan, ok fell Gergín dauðr til jarðar. Hugi jarl sér nú fall hans, ok verðr ákafliga reiðr, ok snýr þegar móti Stuttheðni, ok leggr til hans með spjóti. Hann hjó þat af skaptinu, ok kastar eptir þat mækinum, en hleypr undir jarl, ok keyrir hann niðr. Þá koma þar nǫkkrir fylgðarmenn Stuttheðins, ok hǫfðu þá handtekit Álf jarl. Einn af þeim hjó Huga banahǫgg. Stuttheðinn gaf Álfi jarli grið með því móti, at Álfr jarl sœri eiða, at herja aldri á ríki Þornbjargar. Hann helt þegar í burt með lið þat, sem eptir var, heim til Indíalands, ok sez um kyrt. Nú skal segja frá Stuttheðni; hann kemr heim til meykonungs, ok segir frá ferðum sínum, en hon lét vel yfir þeim.

Chapter 8

Nú gerir Áli bert fyrir alþýðu, at hann er sonr Ríkarðar konungs af Englandi. Heimtir hann nú framm þau fǫgr heit, er meykonungr hafði heitit at ganga með honum; mælti meykonungr ekki í móti. Var þá búiz við brullaupi; gekk Áli at eiga Þornbjǫrgu dróttningu, ok var veizla en bezta; ok um kveldit váru þau Áli ok dróttning leidd í eina sæng í eina skemmu vel innan búna; var þat it vænsta herbergi.

Glóðarauga hét þræll einn er var í borginni; hann var bróðir Nóttar trǫllkonu. Hann kom í skemmu, er meykonungi ok Ála var í fylgt. Áli var þá afklæddr ǫllum klæðum nema línklæðum. Þá mælti þræll með ógurligri raust:

'Gott hyggr þú nú til, Áli!' segir hann, 'at sofa hjá meykonungi; en nú skal ek launa þér þat, er þú lagðir á Blátǫnn, systur mína, ok því legg ek þat á þik, at þú verðir at vargi ok farir á skóg ok drepir bæði menn ok fé, ok á þat fé grimmastr, er meykonungr á, ok at því mest leggjaz.'

When Bjǫrn discovered what mission they were on, he immediately engaged in battle with them and said that they would not see the maiden-king, and it was a hard battle. The earls made a bold advance. A man called Gergín was with them. He met Bjǫrn in battle, and he had a halberd in his hand and struck at Bjǫrn; it stabbed him in the thigh. Bjǫrn hewed the halberd from the shaft, and with that he escaped, along with two men.

Bjǫrn came to meet the maiden-king. He tells her of the earls' journey and that Álfr wished to ask for her hand. Þornbjǫrg answers in this way: 'How is Earl Álfr to look upon?'

'He is an ugly and wicked man', says Bjǫrn. Then the maiden-king asks who would like to be her champion at the head of her host against the earls — 'because I do not wish', she says, 'to marry the earl, but Bjǫrn is wounded, and for this reason he is not able to be your leader.'

None of Þornbjǫrg's men wanted to be the leader. Then the maiden-king promised to marry the man who wished to be the leader at the head of her host. Stutteðinn said that he wanted to do that, and he made himself leader at the head of the host, which was nearly two hundred men. The earls had arrived on the flat plains which were near the city in which the maiden-king resided, and they had four hundred men. Stutteðinn rides out of the city with his men. The earls had drawn up their host.

Stutteðinn now rides forth boldly with all his men against his enemies. He sees where Gergín fights most valiantly. He makes his way towards him and hews at him with the short-sword which the maiden-king had given him, and the blow fell upon his right shoulder and took off the arm, and with it the side, and one leg above the knee and the other below it, and Gergín fell dead to the ground. Earl Hugi sees his death and becomes exceedingly angry, and he immediately turns to face Stutteðinn and thrusts at him with his spear. He hewed the spear from the shaft and, throwing down the short-sword, throws himself under the earl and drags him down. Then some followers of Stutteðinn arrive there, having captured Earl Álfr. One of them struck Hugi a fatal blow. Stutteðinn gave Earl Álfr quarter on this condition: that Earl Álfr should swear an oath never to attack Þornbjǫrg's kingdom. He immediately went home to India with what remained of the army, and settles down peacefully. It is now to be told about Stutteðinn that he comes home to the maiden-king and recounts his journey, and she expressed her approval of it.

Chapter 8

Now Áli makes it known to all the people that he is the son of Ríkarðr, king of England. He claims the fair promises which were made when the maiden-king promised to marry him. The maiden-king did not disapprove of that. Then the wedding feast was prepared. Áli went to marry Queen Þornbjǫrg, and there was a magnificent feast, and during the evening, Áli and the queen were led into a bed in a bower which was well-furnished. It was the most beautiful room.

There was a slave called Glóðarauga in the city; he was the brother of Nótt the troll-woman. He came to the bower to which the maiden-king and Áli had been led. Áli was then completely undressed apart from his linen undergarments. The slave spoke with a terrible voice:

'You're looking forward to sleeping with the maiden-king, Áli!' he says, 'but now I shall repay you for the curse which you laid on Blátǫnn, my sister, and so I lay this on you: that you will turn into a wolf and go into the forest and kill both men and livestock and attack most fiercely the livestock which the maiden-king owns — may you pursue them most of all.'

Áli tekr þá svá til máls: 'Með því', segir hann, 'at þú, Glóðarauga! hefir með fullum fjándskap á mik lagt, þá mæli ek þat um, at þú sitir á þeirri sǫmu kistu sem nú ok œpir upp yfir þik sem mest getr þú, alla þá stund, sem ek er í þessum nauðum, svá at aldri hafir þú ró. En ef ek kemz ór þessi þraut, þá skulu tveir þrælar leiða þik til skógar ok hengja á gálga.'

Glóðarauga grenjaði þegar ógurliga ok mælti: 'Þat legg ek þó inn til við þik, Áli! at þá er þú hefir eytt ǫllu fé í ríki Þornbjargar dróttningar, skyndir þú í ríki fǫður þíns ok eirir þar hvárki fé né mǫnnum, ok ekki skal þér til undanlausnar annat um þína æfi, nema at nǫkkur kona verði til at biðja griða fyrir þik, þá er þú verðr handtekinn, ok verðir þú af því lauss; en þat mun aldri verða.'

Svá varð þegar í stað; hljóp Áli á skóg ok verðr at einum vargi, ok svá grimmum, at hann drepr bæði menn ok hesta ok fé; en Glóðarauga œpir bæði nótt ok dag, svá at hann linnir aldri, ok fengu menn dróttningar af þessu inar mestu ónáðir.

Chapter 9

Þat er af Ála at segja, at hann eyðir ǫllu fé Þornbjargar dróttningar; en eptir þat fór hann á burt á merkr ok skóga, ok um síðir kemr hann framm í ríki fǫður síns, ok reif þar bæði menn ok fé til dauðs, ok svá geriz hann þar skœðr, at hann bítr einn veg fé til bana, þótt þat sé læst í grindum. Þetta er sagt konungi. Ríkarðr konungr lætr nú saman kalla þá beztu menn, er í váru ríkinu, ok sagði þeim þat vandkvæði, er þar hafði gǫrz, at vargr sá var þar kominn í ríkit, svá skœðr, at ekki lét ógǫrt, ok dræpi bæði menn ok fé, ok frétti þá ráða. En þeir skutu allir til hans.

'Þat er þá mitt ráð', segir konungr, 'at vér leggjum þrjár merkr silfrs til hǫfuðs varginum, ok gerum hann svá útlægan; þat fé skal sé eignaz, er varginum verðr at bana.'

Ǫllum líkaði þetta vel, ok var við þat slitit þinginu, ok fór hverr til sinna heimkynna. En vargrinn rífr niðr hjǫrð konungs slíkt eðr meirr en fyrr, ok af því býr hann út sína hirð, ok ætlaði at veiða varginn, ok þeir geta slegit hring um hann. Konungr eggjar nú sína menn at ganga at varginum; en í því bili þá hleypr vargrinn upp yfir mannhringinn þar sem konungrinn var sjálfr fyrir, ok síðan fengu þeir ekki vald á honum, ok fóru þeir heim við svá búit.

Chapter 10

Eitt kveld kemr vargrinn í garðshorn til Gunna ok Hildar. Þar lét vargrinn allt í friði, ok settiz í garð þann, er var fyrir bœ karls. Kerling sér þetta, ok mælti við karl sinn:

'Engi augu hefi ek líkari sét, en í vargi þessum ok var í Ála flekk!'

'Ekki sýniz mér svá', segir hann.

Kerling gekk þá framm ok í búr sitt, ok kom út aptr ok hefir með sér trog ok þar í pǫrur ok margt hark, ok setr niðr fyrir varginn. Hann var þá allsvangr, ok tekr til at eta ór troginu, ok lýkr því ǫllu, ok hleypr í burt síðan ok á skóg. En kerling tók trog sitt ok ferr inn síðan, ok er henni tíðrœtt um varginn.

Áli starts to speak in this way: 'Because you, Glóðarauga', he says, 'have laid this on me with complete enmity, I pronounce that you will sit on the same chest as now and shriek as loudly as you can, so that you have no rest, for the whole time that I am in this ordeal. And if I should escape from this hardship, then two slaves will bring you to the forest and hang you on the gallows.'

At once, Glóðarauga howled terribly and spoke: 'Nevertheless I lay another curse on you, Áli: that when you have destroyed all the livestock in Queen Þornbjǫrg's kingdom, you will hasten to your father's kingdom and spare neither livestock nor men, and nothing will release you for the rest of your life apart from a woman asking for quarter for you when you are captured, and then you will be released — but that will never happen.'

Thus it immediately came to pass: Áli ran into the forest and becomes a wolf, and such a ferocious wolf that he kills both men and horses and livestock; and Glóðarauga shrieks both night and day, so that he never ceases, and the queen's men suffered great disturbances from this.

Chapter 9

It is to be told about Áli that he destroys all the livestock of Queen Þornbjǫrg, and after that he went away into the forests and woods, arriving at last in his father's kingdom, where he tears both men and livestock to death, becoming so vicious that he fatally bites livestock in the same way, even if they are locked in pens. This was reported to the king. King Ríkarðr now calls together all the best men in the kingdom and told them of those troublesome events which had happened there: that such a vicious wolf had entered the kingdom and left no stone unturned, killing both men and livestock. He asked for advice, but they all deferred to him.

'It is my decision, then', says the king, 'that we offer three marks of silver as a bounty on the wolf's head, and thus make it an outlaw. The one who kills the wolf shall have that reward.'

This was to everyone's liking, and with that, the meeting was dissolved and each went to his own household. But the wolf tears down the king's herd just as much or more than before. Because of this, the king prepares his followers to go out, intending to hunt the wolf, and they manage to form a circle around it. The king now encourages his men to close in on the wolf, but at that moment, the wolf leaps up over the circle of men out to where the king himself was situated, and after that they could not lay a hand on it. They went home, leaving the matter there.

Chapter 10

One evening the wolf comes to the farmhouse, to Gunni and Hildr. There, the wolf disturbs nothing and settles down in the yard which was in front of the old man's farmstead. The old woman saw that, and said to her husband:

'I have never seen more familiar eyes than this wolf's — they're just like Áli flekkr's.'

'It doesn't seem that way to me', he says.

Then the old woman went into her pantry and came back out with a trough, in which were scraps and a lot of waste, and she places it down in front of the wolf. By then it was famished; it begins to eat out of the trough, finishes it all and then runs away again into the forest. But the old woman took the trough and goes inside, chattering about the wolf.

Þat er nú af varginum at segja, at hann hljóp á skóg, ok reif fé til dauða, ok á þessi nótt drepr hann þrjá hjarðarsveina konungs. Ok um morguninn lætr konungrinn út fara hirðr sína, ok ætlar at veiða varginn, ok er nú hringrinn ferfaldr. Allir menn af inum næstu heruðum váru þangat komnir með konungi; þar váru þau bæði Gunni ok Hildr. Hirðmenn konungs sœkja nú hart at varginum. Hann ætlar þá at støkkva út yfir hringinn; í því kom sjálfr konungrinn ok gat handtekit varginn, ok frétti þá konungr sína menn, hvern dauðdaga þeir vildu at vargrinn hefði; en þeir báðu hann ráða. Í því bili kom framm Hildr kerling fyrir konung, svá mælandi:

'Vilda ek, herra!' segir hon, 'at þér gæfið varginum grið; en ek vil ábyrgjaz, at hann geri engum manni mein.'

Þeir er hjá stóðu báðu konunginn eigi svá gera. Konungr tekr svá til máls: 'Veita mundi Áli þér, Hildr! þessa bœn, ef hann væri hér, ok fyrir hann, Hildr! vil ek veita þér þat, er þú biðr.'

Hon þakkar þá konungi þessa gjǫf, ok ferr heim með varginn, ok svá Gunni karl. En konungr ok hans menn fara til hallar, ok var þá komit at kveldi dags. Alla þessa nótt vakir Hildr í hvílugólfi sínu yfir varginum ok er kemr at miðri nótt, þá kemr svefnhǫfgi at Hildi; ok er hon vaknar, sér hon mann liggja í hvílugólfinu. Þekkir hon þar Ála flekk. En vargshamr sá, sem hann hafði í verit, lá þar niðri fyrir hjá honum. Hildr stendr þá upp skyndiliga ok vekr Gunna ok biðr hann upp standa, ok segir honum, hvat um er, ok segir, at hann fari til ok brenni sem skjótast þenna vargsham; ok hann gerir svá. En Hildr tekr sér vín, ok sez undir herðar honum ok dreypir því á hann, ok tekr hann þá at næraz skjótliga, ok er hann mátti mæla spyrr hann, hverr honum hefði komit ór ánauðum. En Hildr sagði til sín. Áli varð feginn, er hann sá fóstru sína, ok var þar fagnafundr. Þá gekk Gunni at Ála, ok fagnar þar hvárr ǫðrum. Sofa þau nú þat er eptir var nætr ǫll í góðum friði.

Chapter 11

At morni dags fara þau Gunni ok Hildr til konungshallar, ok Áli með þeim. Ok er þau koma þar, segja þau konungi alla hluti, hversu þau hǫfðu breytt. Áli gengr þá fyrir konunginn feðr sinn, ok kvaddi hann kurteisliga. Konungr varð nú harðla glaðr, ok tekr vel syni sínum. Allr borgarlýðr varð þessu feginn, at Áli var heim kominn, ok einna mest dróttningin, móðir hans. Áli tekr þá menn sér til fylgðar, er fyrr hafði hann sér til sveina, ok hvárki skilja þeir nú við hann nótt né dag. Er hann nú heima með feðr sínum um hríð, ok var lofaðr af hverjum manni.

Nú er at segja af Glóðarauga, at þann sama dag sem Áli var ór þeirri ánauð kominn, er hann hafði á hann lagt, leiða tveir þrælar Þornbjargar dróttningar hann til skógar ok reisa þar gálga ok hengja hann síðan, ok lýkr þar hans æfi. Áli er nú heima með feðr sínum, ok er harðla vinsæll af ǫllum lýð, ok er nú kyrt um hans hag.

Chapter 12

Eina nótt liggr Áli í sæng sinni sofandi, en sveinar hans lágu umkring hann. Áli lætr þá illa í svefni, ok eru svefnfarir hans bæði harðar ok langar; en um síðir vaknar hann, ok var þá ákafliga móðr, ok þat sá fylgðarmenn Ála, at hann hafði á sínum líkama mǫrg sár ok stór. Þeir fréttu hann, hverju þetta sætti.

It is now to be told about the wolf that it ran to the forest and tore livestock to death, and that night it kills three of the king's shepherd-boys. And in the morning, the king has his retinue go out and intends to hunt the wolf, and now the circle is four men deep. All the men from the nearest districts had come there with the king. Both Gunni and Hildr were there. The king's followers now charge fiercely towards the wolf. Just as it intends to leap out over the ring, the king himself entered the ring and managed to capture the wolf. The king then asked his men what manner of death they wished the wolf to have, but they asked him to decide. At that moment, the old woman Hildr came before the king, speaking thus:

'I wish, my lord', she says, 'that you grant the wolf quarter; and I want to vouch for it, that it will cause harm to no one else.'

The bystanders asked the king not to do so. The king thus begins to speak: 'Áli would grant you this request, Hildr, if he were here, and for him, Hildr, I will grant you what you ask for.'

Then she thanks the king for this gift and goes home with the wolf, as does the old man Gunni. But the king and his men go to the hall, and by then, evening had come. All that night, Hildr lies awake in bed, watching the wolf, but when the middle of the night comes, drowsiness comes over Hildr, and when she wakes, she sees a man lying in the bed. She recognises Áli flekkr there. But the wolf-skin, which he had had on, lay there down at his feet. Hildr then gets up hastily and wakes Gunni and asks him to get up, and she tells him what is going on, and says that he should go and burn the wolf-skin as quickly as possible, and he does so. And Hildr takes some wine, seats herself under Áli's shoulders and drips it on him. He then begins to recover quickly, and when he is able to speak, he asks who had helped him escape from affliction. And Hildr told him who she was. Áli became joyful when he recognised his foster-mother, and there was a joyous meeting there. Then Gunni went to Áli, and each greets the other. Now they all sleep peacefully for the rest of the night.

Chapter 11

In the morning, Gunni and Hildr go to the king's hall, along with Áli. And when they arrive there, they tell the king everything they had done. Then Áli goes before the king, his father, and greeted him courteously. The king became very glad, and receives his son well. All the townspeople became joyful that Áli had come home, and most of all the queen, his mother. Then Áli takes as followers the men who had previously accompanied him as boys, and they part from him neither night nor day. He now stays at home with his father for a while, and was praised by everyone.

Now it is to be told about Glóðarauga that on the same day that Áli had escaped from the affliction which he had laid on him, two slaves of Queen Þornbjǫrg bring him to the forest, raise a gallows there and then hang him, and there his life ends. Áli stays at home with his father and is very popular among all the people, and he lives in peace.

Chapter 12

One night, Áli lies sleeping in his bed, and his companions lie in a circle around him. Áli was ill at ease in his sleep, and his dreams are both long and difficult. When he wakes at last, he was exhausted, and Áli's followers saw that he had many great wounds on his body. They asked him how that came about.

Hann tekr svá til máls: 'Nótt trǫllkona kom til mín', sagði hann, 'ok barði mik með járnsvipu bæði hart ok tíðum, ok kvaz eigi fyrr hafa mátt hefna mér, er ek hljóp í burt frá henni ór hellinum, ok þat annat, er ek lagða á Glóðarauga bróður hennar, ok lagði hon þat á mik, at þessi sár skyldi aldri gróa fyrr en brœðr hennar grœddi mik; ok í þeim sárum skylda ek liggja tíu vetr, ok ef ek yrða þá eigi grœddr, þá skylda ek andaz ór þeim sárum. Er ek nú svá stirðr ok lerkaðr, at ek má héðan hvergi ganga.'

Sveinar Ála verða mjǫk óglaðir við þetta, ok segja þó konungi til svá búins. Ríkarðr konungr gengr nú til þess húss, sem Áli svaf í, ok er hann kemr þar, kvaddi hann feðr sinn, ok segir honum til, hversu at hafði borit um vanmátt sinn. Konungr ok allr borgarlýðr harma þetta mjǫk. Liggr Áli nú í sárum um þessa tólf mánaði. Fær konungr til þá beztu lækna, sem í váru ǫllu Englandi, ok gátu þeir ekki at gǫrt. Fúnar nú hold Ála, ok gengr af honum mikill óþefr.

Einn dag kom konungr til Ála, en Áli segir þá svá til hans:

'Kæri faðir!' segir hann, 'einn er sá hlutr, er ek hefi yðr leynt.'

'Hverr er sá?' sagði konungr.

'Ek er giptr', segir Áli, 'ok fekk ek Þornbjargar dróttningar af Tattaría, ok vilda ek nú, minn góði faðir! at þér senduð eptir henni.'

En hann játar því, ok skilja at sinni, ok gekk konungr í burt.

Rauðr hét ráðgjafi konungs. Hann sendi hann þessa erendis at sœkja Þornbjǫrgu dróttningu ok segja henni af hag Ála, ok at hon kœmi á hans fund.

Chapter 13

Rauðr býr nú skip sitt, ok fær menn til; ok at því búni heldr hann til Tattaría, ok er eigi sagt af hans ferð fyrr en hann kemr í ríki dróttningar, ok kemr skjótt á hennar fund ok gengr fyrir hana ok kveðr hana. Hon tekr því vel. Hann segir henni þá sitt erendi ok þat, at Áli væri litt haldinn. Dróttning varð við þetta mjǫk óglǫð, ok lætr búa skip ór landi fimm at tǫlu, ok velr með sér ina vǫskustu menn. Dróttning heldr þeim skipum í burt af Tattaría til Englands, ok kemr þar at áliðnu sumri. Ok er hon kemr, fagnar konungr henni vel ok allr landslýðr, ok var þar fyrir búin en bezta veizla. Ok inn fyrsta dag veizlunnar gengr dróttning Þornbjǫrg í þat hús, er Áli lá í; ok þegar þau funduz mintiz hann við hana. Hon spurði þá eptir, hversu at hefði boriz um vanmátt hans. Áli segir henni allt, hversu farit hafði með þeim Nótt trǫllkonu. Dróttning harmaði þetta mjǫk, ok skilja nú sitt tal, ok gengr hon nú í burt ok þiggr ina beztu veizlu, ok er hon með konungi þenna vetr allan vel haldin ok allir hennar menn.

Chapter 14

At várinu komanda búa menn dróttningar skip sín at boði hennar. Konungr lætr ok búa þrjú skip, þvíat Áli lýsir yfir því, at hann ætlar í burt með Þornbjǫrgu dróttningu. Ok at þeim skipum búnum taka þau Áli ok dróttning orlof af konungi, ok halda í burt af Englandi, ok váru þau Áli ok dróttning á einu skipi. Svá er sagt, at þau sigldu allt þetta sumar um alla norðrhálfuna, leitandi eptir þeim læknum, sem hon vissi at beztir váru,

He begins to speak thus: 'Nótt the troll-woman came to me', he said, 'and struck me both hard and often with an iron whip, and said that she had not been able earlier to take revenge on me for running away from her out of the cave, and also for laying a curse on her brother Glóðarauga. And she laid this curse on me: that these wounds would never heal unless her brothers healed me; and that I would lie with these wounds for ten winters, and if I have not been healed by then, I would die from those wounds. I am now so stiff and bruised that I am unable to walk anywhere from here.'

Áli's companions become very unhappy at this, and they tell the king how matters stand. King Ríkarðr goes to the house in which Áli was sleeping, and when he arrives, he greeted his father and tells him how his illness had come about. The king and all the townspeople lament this greatly. Áli lies wounded for the next twelve months. The king gets the best physicians in all England, but they could do nothing. Then Áli's flesh starts to fester, and a great stench rises from him.

One day, the king came to Áli, and Áli speaks to him thus:

'Dear father', he says, 'there is one thing which I have hidden from you.'

'What is that?' said the king.

'I am married', says Áli. 'I wedded Queen Þornbjǫrg of Tartary, and now I want you to send for her, good father.'

The king agrees to this and parts from him, and goes away.

There was a counsellor to the king called Rauðr. He sends him on this mission: to seek Þornbjǫrg and tell her of Áli's condition, and that she should come to meet him.

Chapter 13

Now Rauðr prepares his ship, and gathers men, and when this is done, he sails to Tartary, and nothing is said of his journey until he arrives in the kingdom of the queen. He goes quickly to meet her, and he walks before her and greets her. She receives him well. Then he tells her of his mission, and that Áli was in a bad way. The queen became very unhappy at that, and she has ships prepared to depart the land, five in number, and chooses the most valiant men to join her. The queen sails these ships away from Tartary to England, and arrives there in late summer. And when she arrives, the king, along with all the countrymen, greets her well, and a magnificent feast was prepared. And on the first day of the feast, Queen Þornbjǫrg goes into the house in which Áli lay, and as soon as they met, he kissed her. Then she asked how his illness had come about. Áli tells her everything regarding how things had gone between himself and Nótt the troll-woman. The queen lamented that greatly, and they end their conversation. She now goes away and accepts the magnificent feast, and she stays in comfort with the king during the winter, with all her men.

Chapter 14

The following spring, the queen's men prepare their ships at her bidding. The king also has three ships prepared, because Áli declares that he intends to go away with Queen Þornbjǫrg. And when the ships were prepared, Áli and the queen take their leave of the king and sail away from England, and Áli and the queen were on the same ship. It is said that they sailed all that summer throughout the northern hemisphere, searching for those physicians whom

ok gaf þeim fé til at græða Ála; en enginn þeirra gat þat gǫrt fyrir illum álǫgum Nóttar trǫllkonu.

Ok þá er dróttning hefir kannat alla norðrhálfuna, ok hafði engan þann fengit, at Ála gæti læknat, heldr nú sínum skipum út í Affrícam, ok kannar þat allt, en fekk þó engan þann, er Ála ynni bót. Þar er dróttning tvá vetr. Áli geriz nú banvænn. Enginn af mǫnnum dróttningar þolir at þjóna honum fyrir þeim óþef, er af Ála gekk, nema Þornbjǫrg dróttning.

At liðnum tveimr vetrum býr dróttning ferð sína út í Ásíam, ok kemr við Indíaland. Þar réð fyrir Álfr jarl, sem fyrr var sagt. En er hann vissi, at Þornbjǫrg dróttning var þar komin, gengr hann sjálfr ofan til strandar með sína menn, ok er hann finnr Ála ok dróttningu, fagnar hann þeim vel ok verðr þó hryggr við þat at Áli er svá litt haldinn.

Hann býðr þeim til sín með alla sína menn. Eru þau þar um vetrinn; veitti jarlinn þeim vel ok skǫrugliga. Dróttning spurði, ef hann vissi nǫkkura brœðr Nóttar trǫllkonu á lífi vera. Jarl svarar þá:

'Ek veit víst', segir hann, 'at hon á þrjá brœðr á lífi, er heita Jǫtunoxi, Leggr ok Liðr, ok er Jǫtunoxi langt fyrir þeim, ok þjóna þeir báðir honum. Þeir brœðr Leggr ok Liðr eiga svá góð smyrsl, at allt mega græða, þat er lífs verðr auðit; en enga menn þora þeir at græða, nema Jǫtunoxi skipi þeim. En þó at ek hafa þetta fyrir þér rœtt', segir jarl, 'þá er þér þat þó til enskis bata.'

'Hversu má þat vera?' segir dróttning.

'Þat má ek segja þér', segir hann. 'Jǫtunoxi ræðr fyrir því landi, er allt er út við heimsendann, ok þangat getr þú hann aldri sótt.'

'Þat skal þó prófa!' segir dróttning.

'Þat máttu ok', segir hann, 'en þat má ek segja þér af þessu landi, at þar eru engir menn nema jǫtnar[94] ok flagðkonur. Þar er jafnríkt nótt ok dagr. Þar eru flest illkvikendi ok eitrkvikendi.'

Dróttning segiz þó fara skyldu eigi at síðr. Jarl segiz þá ok eigi mundu letja hana; kvað henni várkunn á vera, ef hennar harmr mætti þar nǫkkut bœtaz— 'skal ek ok allan mik til leggja.' Dróttning þakkar honum fyrir sín heit; skilja þau nú sitt tal. Er dróttning með jarli um vetrinn vel haldin ok hennar menn.

Chapter 15

En at sumrinu komnu bjóz dróttning í burt af Indíalandi. Álfr jarl býðr at fara með henni, en hon biðr hann at veita sér þat lið, at koma til móts við sik, þá er vika væri af vetri; en jarl játar því. Heldr dróttning nú í burt af Indíalandi, ok er eigi sagt af hennar ferð fyrr en hon kemr við land Jǫtunoxa. Ok er hann veit, at tígnir menn eru komnir, lætr hann bjóða þeim heim til veizlu. Dróttning þiggr þat; ok áðr hon gengr heim frá skipum, segir hon sínum mǫnnum, at þeir skulu kalla hana Gunnvǫru ok segja, Ála vera bróðir hennar ok nefna hann Gunnvarð. Þeir játa þessu.

Gengr dróttning nú frá skipum með sínum mǫnnum til hallar Jǫtunoxa, ok tekr hann vel við þeim ok fréttir dróttningu at nafni ok at erendum. En hon sagðiz Gunnvǫr heita ok vera dóttir Gunnbjarnar jarls af Rússía— 'ok fer ek með Gunnvarð, bróður minn mjǫk sáran,

---

[94] The *jǫtnar* are a specific type of giant, and are usually hostile in mythological and legendary sources. This contrasts with the frequent portrayal of the *risar*, another type of giant, as benign beings (although the *risi* that Áli encounters in chapter 17 is entirely hostile).

she knew were the best, and gave them money to heal Áli — but none of them were able to do that, because of the evil curse of Nótt the troll-woman.

And when the queen had explored all of the northern hemisphere and found no one who could heal Áli, she sails her ships out to Africa and searches all of it, but still she found no one who could bring about a cure for Áli. The queen stays there for two winters. Áli now becomes mortally ill. Apart from Queen Þornbjǫrg, none of the queen's men could bear to serve him on account of the stench which emanated from Áli.

At the end of the two winters, the queen prepares for her journey out to Asia, and arrives in India. Earl Álfr ruled over it, as was previously told. And when he learned that Queen Þornbjǫrg had arrived, he himself goes down to the shore with his men, and when he meets Áli and the queen, he greets them well, but becomes distressed that Áli was in such a bad way.

He invites them to stay with him, along with all her men. They stay there during the winter. The earl treated them well and fittingly. The queen asked if he knew whether certain brothers of Nótt the troll-woman were alive. The earl replies:

'I know for sure', he says, 'that she has three living brothers, who are called Jǫtunoxi, Leggr and Liðr — Jǫtunoxi is foremost among them, and the others both serve him. The brothers Leggr and Liðr have such a good ointment that it can heal everything that is destined to live, but they don't dare to heal anyone unless Jǫtunoxi orders them to. But though I have told you this', says the earl, 'it will not be to your advantage in any way.'

'Why might that be?' says the queen.

'I can tell you this', he says. 'Jǫtunoxi rules over the land which is all the way out at the world's end, and you will never be able to find him there.'

'That will nevertheless be tested', says the queen.

'You might do that', he says, 'but I can tell you this about that land: that there are no men there except giants and ogresses. There, night and day are equally powerful. The most evil and poisonous creatures reside there.'

The queen says that she must go nonetheless. The earl says that he would not dissuade her, saying that she might be excused if it might lessen her grief somewhat — 'and I will contribute all that I can.' The queen thanks him for his promise. They now end their conversation. The queen and her men stay with the earl in comfort during the winter.

Chapter 15

And at the coming of summer, the queen prepared to go away from India. Earl Álfr offers to go with her, but she asks him to grant her assistance by coming to meet her when a week of winter had passed, and the earl agreed to this. Now the queen sails away from India, and nothing is said of her journey until she arrives in Jǫtunoxi's land. When he discovered that honourable people had arrived, he has them invited to his home for a feast. The queen accepts, but before she departs from the ships, she tells her men that they should call her 'Gunnvǫr' and say that Áli was her brother and that he was called 'Gunnvarðr'. They agree to this.

Now the queen goes from the ships with her men to Jǫtunoxi's hall, and he receives them well and asks the queen for her name and mission. And she said that she was called Gunnvǫr and that she was the daughter of Gunnbjǫrn, earl of Russia — 'and I come with Gunnvarðr, my sorely wounded brother, and I have not met anyone who could bring about a cure for him.

ok hefi ek engan þann hitt, at hann hafi læknat getat. Nú hefi ek heyrt, at þér eigið tvá brœðr, þá er allt mega grœða þat er lífs verðr auðit. Nú er ek því hér komin, at ek vænti at þér munið bróður minn láta grœða til fullra peninga.'

Jǫtunoxi svarar svá máli dróttningar: 'Með því einu', segir hann, 'læt ek grœða bróður þinn, at þú játir at vera mín dróttning.'

'Því skal ek játa', segir hon, 'ok þó með því, at þú drepir áðr Nótt trǫllkonu.'

'Þat skal ek til vinna', segir Jǫtunoxi, 'þótt hon sé systir mín; erum vit ok ekki skaplík.'

Jǫtunoxi kallar þá á sína menn, ok biðr þá heyra þeirra tal, ok segir þá, hvat þau hafa við talaz, ok kemr allt ásamt með þeim. Jǫtunoxi sendi þá tvá menn af sínum mǫnnum með Ála til brœðra sinna, at þeir grœði hann at heilu. Þessir menn hétu Mandan ok Andan. Þeir koma fyrir þá Legg ok Lið, ok bera framm orðsending Jǫtunoxa. Þeir brœðr taka Ála ok grœða hann; en sendimenn fara aptr til Jǫtunoxa.

Chapter 16

Nú býz Jǫtunoxi heiman til fundar við Nótt trǫllkonu einn saman. Eigi er mér sagt, hverju faraldi hann fór; en eitt kveld kemr hann í helli Nóttar systur sinnar. Hon var þá við soðketil ok át þar ór mannkjǫt ok hrossa.

Jǫtunoxi tekr þá í herðar henni ok fellir hana á bak aptr. En er hon sér bróður sinn, heilsar hon honum; en hann svarar engu, ok greyfiz niðr at henni ok bítr í sundr í henni barkann ok drekkr ór henni blóðit, ok lætr hon svá sitt ljóta líf. Síðan tekr hann sér eld, ok brennir hana til kola. Síðan býz hann í burt, ok fimm nóttum síðarr kemr hann heim í sitt ríki, ok segir þá allt frá ferðum sínum.

Dróttning lætr vel yfir ok segir, at hon vill láta senda eptir Gunnvarði bróður sínum. Hann segir svá vera skyldu, ok sendir þá Mandan ok Andan at sœkja hann. Þeir koma til þeirra brœðra; var þeim þar vel fagnat. Gunnvarðr var þá gróinn, ok fór þaðan með þeim. Ok einn dag, er þeir ríða úti, tekr Andan til orða:

'Gjarna vilda ek fá mér annan lánardróttin en Jǫtunoxa.'

'Svá vilda ek ok', segir Mandan.

Gunnvarðr mælti þá: 'Vili þit, góðir drengir! at vér sverjumz í fóstbrœðralag?' Ok þeir játa því, ok þar í stað sverjaz þeir í fóstbrœðralag. Síðan segir Áli þeim nafn sitt ok ætt, ok þat með, at hann ætlar at drepa Jǫtunoxa. En þeir láta vel yfir því, ok segja sik nauðga honum þjónat hafa— 'eru hér ok eigi fleiri mennskir en vit', segja þeir. 'En Jǫtunoxi hertók okkr frá Polloníu jarli, feðr okkrum.'

Eptir þetta þeirra tal koma þeir heim til Jǫtunoxa, ok tekr hann vel við þeim ok einna bezt við Gunnvarði. Síðan segir hann Gunnvǫru, at hann ætlar til veizlu at búa— 'ok ætla ek at drekka brúðlaup til þín.' Hon kvað þat vel fallit. Jǫtunoxi lætr til bjóða þessarrar veizlu tveimr hundruðum flagða. En at þeim samankomnum ǫllum flǫgðunum verðr mikill glaumr í borg Jǫtunoxa. Ok it fyrsta kveld veizlunnar mælti Gunnvǫr til Jǫtunoxa:

'Nú skulum vér hafa þann sið, sem hafðr er í váru landi.'

'Hverr er sá?' segir Jǫtunoxi.

'Brúðr skal skenkja brúðguma', segir hon, 'ok þeir með henni, sem hon vill.'

'Þat líkar mér vel', segir hann.

Now I have heard that you have two brothers, who can heal everything that is destined to live. I have come here now because I hope that you will have my brother healed, for full payment.'

Jǫtunoxi answers the queen's words in this way: 'On this condition alone', he says, 'will I have your brother healed: that you agree to be my queen.'

'I will accept that', she says, 'on this condition: that you first kill Nótt the troll-woman.'

'I will do that', says Jǫtunoxi, 'even though she is my sister. We are not alike in character.'

Then Jǫtunoxi summons his men and asks them to listen to their conversation, and tells them what they had discussed, and all is agreed among them. Jǫtunoxi sends two of his men with Áli to his brothers, so that they could restore him to health. These men were called Mandan and Andan. They come before Leggr and Liðr and deliver Jǫtunoxi's message. The brothers take Áli and heal him, and the messengers go back to Jǫtunoxi.

Chapter 16

Now Jǫtunoxi prepares to depart to meet Nótt the troll-woman alone. Nothing is told to me concerning the means by which he travelled, but one night he arrives in the cave of his sister Nótt. She was by the cooking-kettle and ate from it man-flesh and horse-flesh.

Jǫtunoxi takes her by the shoulders and trips her backwards. When she sees her brother, she greets him but he does not reply. He bends down over her, bites open her windpipe and drinks her blood out of it, and thus she loses her loathsome life. Afterwards he takes some fire and burns her to cinders. Then he prepares to depart, and five nights later he arrives home to his kingdom and recounts everything about his journey.

The queen expresses approval of it and says that she wants to have her brother Gunnvarðr sent for. Jǫtunoxi says that it would be so, and sends Mandan and Andan to fetch him. They come to the brothers and were greeted well there. Gunnvarðr was healed by then, and left with them. And one day, when they ride out, Andan begins to speak:

'I desperately want a master other than Jǫtunoxi.'

'I also want that', says Mandan.

Gunnvarðr spoke: 'Good men, would you like us to swear oaths of foster-brotherhood?' They agree to this, and there, on the spot, they swear oaths of foster-brotherhood. Afterwards, Áli tells them his name and lineage, and also that he intends to kill Jǫtunoxi. And they express approval of this, and declare that they had served him unwillingly — 'there are no humans here apart from the two of us', they say. 'But Jǫtunoxi captured the two of us from Earl Polloníus, our father.'

After their conversation, they arrive home to Jǫtunoxi, and he receives them well, and Gunnvarðr best of all. He then tells Gunnvǫr that he intends to prepare a feast — 'and I intend to drink a bridal-toast to you.' She said that was quite appropriate. Jǫtunoxi has two hundred ogresses invited to the feast. At their gathering, all of the ogresses caused great revelry in Jǫtunoxi's city. And on the first evening of the feast, Gunnvǫr said to Jǫtunoxi:

'Now we shall follow that custom which we have in our land.'

'What is that?' says Jǫtunoxi.

'The bride will pour out a drink for the bridegroom', she says, 'and with her those whom she chooses.'

'That pleases me well', he says.

Hon tekr nú at skenkja ok þeir allir Mandan ok Andan. Bera þau nú ákaft ǫlit, ok verða flǫgðin ǫll mjǫk drukkin, en gefa sínum mǫnnum lítit ǫl.

Í þessu kemr í hǫllina einn maðr ok talar einmæli við dróttningu Gunnvǫru, en gengr burt síðan. Litlu síðarr gengr dróttning í burt ór hǫllinni — þeir Mandan ok Andan ganga ok með henni — ok er hon kom út af hǫllinni, sér hon Álf jarl, ok verðr þar fagnafundr, ok segir jarl henni, at hann er nú kominn at veita henni lið með fimm hundruð manna. Hon sagðiz þat þiggja mundu— 'vil ek nú, at þér veitið flǫgðunum atgǫngu með eldi ok vápnum!'

Þeir bera nú eld at hǫllinni, ok logar hon skjótt. Jǫtunoxi verðr nú varr við ófriðinn ok þykkiz nú sjá allt eptir út í gegnum, ok gengr til hallardyra ok mælti:

'Svá mjǫk hefir jarl blindat sjónir fyrir mér, því at gǫrla kenni ek þik, Áli flekkr! ok svá þik, Þornbjǫrg dróttning! Hefir þú ok áðr drepit tvau systkin mín, ok þat líkast, at af þínum vǫldum láta ek lífit. En þat þyl ek, ok þat mæli ek um, at þá er þú ferr héðan, þolir þú hvergi kyrr, fyrr en þú finnr Hlaðgerði, þá er þú fannt í dyngjunni.'

Þá mælti Mandan: 'Látum hann nú eigi fleira rausa!'

Hleypr hann þá inn í eldinn, ok hafði í hendi bjarnsviðu, ok lagði til Jǫtunoxa utan á þunnvembit ok þar á hol; en er Jǫtunoxi fekk lagit, greip hann Mandan, ok sviptir honum undir sik. Þat sá Áli, ok snaraz inn í hǫllina, ok hjó á hálsinn Jǫtunoxa með mæki, svá at af tók hǫfuðit, ok lét hann svá lífit. En Mandan stóð þá upp, ok eigi léttu þeir fyrr, en þeir hǫfðu brent ǫll flǫgðin. En síðan tóku þeir allt þat er fémætt var, ok bera á skip sín; halda síðan á burt. Þakkar Þornbjǫrg dróttning nú Álfi jarli sína liðveizlu. Áli fekk þat sverð þar, er Bremill hét, ok var allra sverða bezt. Þau koma nú heim til Indíalands, ok eru þar ǫll um vetrinn í góðum fagnaði ok í boði jarls ǫll vel haldin.

Chapter 17

Litlu eptir þetta, er nú var frá sagt, hverfr Áli í burt af Indíalandi einn saman, leitandi eptir Hlaðgerði. Ferr hann ýmist á skipum eða á hestum. Fimm vetr leitar hann hennar framm ok aptr, ok finnr hana ekki; í þessarri ferð þolði hann margar þrautir. Einn tíma kom hann í þat land, er Svena heitir; en þat er á vára tungu Svíþjóð in mikla. En þá er Áli fór um þann skóg, er heitir Myrkviðr — sá skógr er furðuliga mikill — þar finnr hann einn risa, þann er Kolr hét. Hann hafði stóra stǫng í hendi. En er hann sér Ála, mælti hann:

'Far burt, maðr! ok aptr inn sama veg', segir hann, 'ef þú vilt halda þínu lífi!'

Áli svarar: 'Eigi mun ek aptr hverfa at ǫllu óreyndu.'

Ok er risinn heyrði orð hans, reiddiz hann mjǫk ok grípr sína stǫng ok ætlaði at slá Ála; en hann skýtr sér undan, en stǫngin hleypr niðr í vǫllinn allt upp at hǫndum risanum. Hann lýtr þá eptir hǫgginu; þat sér Áli, ok bregðr skjótt sínu sverði ok hǫggr til risans um þvert bakit, ok tók risann í sundr, ok lætr hann svá sitt líf.

Eptir þetta gengr Áli burt á skóginn; ok at kveldi dags kemr Áli af skóginum at einum litlum bœ. Þar klappar hann á dyrr, ok gengr út skeggjaðr maðr, lágr vexti. Hann mælti til þess er úti var:

'Mál er þér at ganga inn ok hvíla þik, þvíat þú munt langt hafa til gengit!'

Now she begins to pour out the drinks, along with Mandan and Andan. They serve the ale eagerly, and all the ogresses become very drunk, but they give their own men little ale. At that moment, a man arrives in the hall and speaks privately with Queen Gunnvǫr, and goes away afterwards. A little later, the queen departs from the hall, and Mandan and Andan go with her. And when she came out of the hall, she sees Earl Álfr, and they had a joyful meeting there, and the earl tells her that he has now come to grant her assistance with five hundred men. She said that she would accept that — 'now I want you to attack the ogresses with fire and weapons!'

They set fire to the hall, and it burns quickly. Jǫtunoxi becomes aware of the hostilities, and he now thinks that he can see through it all, and he goes to the hall-door and spoke:

'The earl has thoroughly deceived me, because I now fully recognise you, Áli flekkr, and you too, Queen Þornbjǫrg! You have already killed my two siblings, and it's most likely that I will lose my life through your actions. But this I chant, and this I pronounce: that when you go from here, you will have no peace until you find Hlaðgerðr, whom you met in the bower.'

Mandan spoke: 'Don't let him speak anymore!'

Then he leaps into the fire. He had a bear-hunting knife and struck at Jǫtunoxi in the abdomen and up into the chest cavity, and when Jǫtunoxi received the thrust, he grabbed Mandan and sweeps him under himself. Áli saw that and rushes into the hall, and hewed at Jǫtunoxi's neck with a sword, such that he took off his head, and so Jǫtunoxi ended his life. Then Mandan got up, and they did not let up until they had burnt all of the ogresses. Afterwards, they took everything that was valuable and carry it onto their ships, then sail away. Queen Þornbjǫrg thanks Earl Álfr for his support. Áli got the sword called Bremill there, and it was the best of all swords. They now arrive back in India, and they all stay there over the winter in comfort and good cheer at the earl's invitation.

Chapter 17

A little while after that which was just related, Áli departed from India alone, looking for Hlaðgerðr. He travels both by ship and by horse. He wanders back and forth searching for her for five winters, but he does not find her. On this journey he suffered many hardships. One time, he came to that land which is called 'Svena', but it is called Scythia in our tongue. And when Áli went through the forest which is called Mirkwood — that forest is exceedingly large — he encounters a giant called Kolr. He had a large staff in his hand. And when he sees Áli, he spoke:

'Go away, man, back the same way you came', he says, 'if you want to keep your life!'

Áli replies: 'I will not turn back without trying.'

And when the giant heard his words, he became very angry and gripped his staff, intending to strike Áli, but he darts under him, and the staff plunges down into the field, all the way up to the giant's hand. The giant bends over with the strike. Áli sees that, draws his sword quickly and strikes the giant across the back, and splits the giant asunder, and so he loses his life.

After that, Áli walks into the forest, and in the evening, he comes from the forest to a little farmstead. He knocks on the door, and out comes a bearded man, short in stature. He spoke to the one who was outside:

'It is time for you to go inside and rest, because you must have travelled a long way.'

Áli gerir svá; þar gengr hann eptir, sem inn ferr undan, til þess er þeir koma í stofu. Þar sér Áli sitja tvær konur á palli. Þær heilsa báðar fǫður sínum, en hann tekr vel kveðju þeirra. Hann biðr Ála sitja hjá sér. Hann gerir svá, ok frétti hann at nafni; en hann sagðiz Bárðr heita. Áli spurði, hverr konungr væri yfir því landi, er hann væri í kominn. Bárðr kvað hann Eireik heita.

'Er hér nǫkkur ókunnig kona komin?' segir Áli.

'At vísu er þat', segir Bárðr, 'ok nefniz hon Hlaðgerðr, ok er hon hjá konungi, ok ætlar hann at láta brenna hana í eldi, þvíat hann ætlar, at hon sé trǫllkona, ok á morgin skal þetta frammgengt verða.'

Áli biðr hann at fylgja sér at morni til konungshallarinnar. Hann játar því. Skilja þeir þetta tal. Litlu síðarr kemr innarr húsfreyja, ok heilsar hon Bárði ok svá þeim er hjá honum sat. Síðan er upp tekit borð ok á borinn matr. Þvínæst koma inn verkmenn bónda, ok setjaz undir borð. Bóndi sez í ǫndvegi, ok sitr Áli it næsta honum. Ok þá er þeir hǫfðu etit ok drukkit sem á lysti, var framm borin fæðan ok ofan tekinn borðbúnaðr, ok fóru menn at sofa. Áli lá einn saman.

Um morguninn stóð Bárðr upp snemma ok vekr Ála. Hann stendr upp ok býr sik, ok fara síðan til konungshallar. Ok er þeir koma á eitt stræti, sjá þeir þar marga menn ok stóra elda tvá, ok í milli þeirra elda sjá þeir eina konu á stóli.[95] Áli þekkir þegar Hlaðgerði. Hann hleypr þegar framm at stólinum, ok berr hana út af mannhringnum ok til Bárðar, ok bað hann geyma Hlaðgerði, en sagðiz skyldu ganga fyrir konung. Bárðr tók við henni, en Áli gekk fyrir konung ok kveðr hann. Konungr tekr honum vel, ok frétti hann at nafni; en hann nefndiz Áli ok kvaz vera sonr Ríkarðs konungs af Englandi.

'Gǫrla þekki ek þína ætt', segir konungr, 'ok erum vit frændr; eðr því tóktu konu þessa ór várri geymslu?'

Áli svarar: 'Því tók ek hana, at hon var annarstaðar betr komin, en þar sem þér létuð hana.'

'Veiztu nǫkkur deili á henni?' segir konungr.

'Satt er þat', segir Áli. 'Hon er at ǫllu því vel fallin, er hon má at gera, þó at ætt hennar sum sé eigi góð. En ek vil þat þiggja af yðr, konungr! at þér látið hana fara í friði, hvert er hon vill.'

'Því vil ek játa þér', sagði konungr, 'en þú ver hér með oss svá lengi sem þér líkar!'

Áli þakkar nú konungi ok gengr til þeirra Bárðar ok Hlaðgerðar. Skiljaz þeir nú Bárðr ok Áli. Fór Bárðr heim á sinn garð, en þau Áli ok Hlaðgerðr fara til konungshallar, ok fagnar konungr þeim vel.

Chapter 18

Konungr hefir þá uppi orð sín ok bað Hlaðgerðar sér til handa. Hon sagði, at Áli skyldi hennar giptingarmaðr vera. Konungr talar þá þetta mál við Ála, en hann svarar því vel, ok svá lýkr því máli, at Eireikr konungr fastnar sér Hlaðgerði með hennar samþykki ok fulltingi Ála. Er nú búit til brúðlaups, ok er til boðit ǫllum þeim beztu mǫnnum, sem í váru ríkinu, ok stendr veizlan sjau nætr. Ok at henni liðinni fóru boðsmenn heim. Gaf konungr mǫrgum góðar gjafir. Ála gaf hann knǫrr með góðum farmi, ok eitt ess brúnt at lit, er Krákr hét. Áli þakkar honum vel þessar gjafir. Heldr Áli nú þaðan, ok skiljaz með kærleikum.

---

[95] Punishments involving being placed between two fires are also found in the eddic poem *Grímnismál* and in *Þjalar-Jóns saga*.

Áli does so. He follows close behind the man until they come into a sitting-room. Áli sees two women sitting on a step there. They both greet their father, and he welcomes their greeting. He asks Áli to sit next to him. He does so, and asks him his name, and he said that he was called Bárðr. Áli asked who the king of the land into which he had arrived might be. Bárðr said that he was called Eireikr.

'Has an unfamiliar woman come here?' says Áli.

'Certainly', says Bárðr, 'and she is called Hlaðgerðr. She is with the king, and he intends to have her burned in fire, because he thinks that she is a troll-woman, and it will be carried out in the morning.'

Áli asks him to accompany him in the morning to the king's hall. He agrees to that. They end their conversation. A little later, the housewife enters and greets Bárðr and the man sitting next to him. Afterwards, the table is set and food is brought. Next, the farmer's labourers come in and sit at the table. The farmer sits in the high-seat, and Áli sits nearest to him. And when they had eaten and drunk as they wished, the food was taken away and the tableware was removed, and the men went to sleep. Áli lay alone.

In the morning, Bárðr got up early and wakes Áli. He gets up and prepares himself, and then they depart to the king's hall. And when they arrive at a certain street, they see many men and two great fires there, and between the fires, they see a woman on a chair. Áli recognises Hlaðgerðr at once. Immediately, he runs forward to the chair and carries her out of the circle of men to Bárðr, asking him to look after Hlaðgerðr and saying that he must go before the king. Bárðr takes her, and Áli went before the king and greets him. The king receives him well and asked him his name, and he named himself as Áli and said that he was the son of Ríkarðr, king of England.

'Certainly I recognise your lineage', says the king, 'and we are kinsmen — but why did you take this woman out of our custody?'

Áli replies: 'I took her because she was better-placed elsewhere than where you set her.'

'Do you know anything about her?' says the king.

'Certainly', says Áli. 'She is capable in all that she is able to do, though some of her lineage is not good. But I wish to receive this from you, king: that you let her go in peace, wherever she wishes.'

'I will grant you this', said the king, 'and you must stay here with us as long as you like.'

Áli now thanks the king and goes to Bárðr and Hlaðgerðr. Bárðr and Áli take their leave of each other. Bárðr went home to his farmstead, but Áli and Hlaðgerðr go to the king's hall, and the king greets them well.

Chapter 18

The king then begins to speak and asked Hlaðgerðr for her hand in marriage. She said that Áli should be her bride-giver. The king discusses the matter with Áli, and he responds positively, and so the matter is decided, such that King Eireikr betrothes himself to Hlaðgerðr with her agreement and Áli's support. The wedding is now prepared, and all the foremost people in the kingdom are invited, and the feast continues for seven nights. And when it ended, the guests went home. The king gave many people good gifts. He gave Áli a merchant-ship with a good cargo, and a black steed, which was called Krákr. Áli thanks him warmly for these gifts. Áli now journeys away, and they part in friendship.

Ferr Áli þá heim til Englands með heilu ok hǫldnu, ok ríðr heim til borgar frá skipi; en menn hans váru þar eptir hjá skipi. En er Áli kom heim, varð honum hverr maðr feginn. Var þar þá komin Þornbjǫrg dróttning með sínum mǫnnum, ok varð hon Ála allfegin ok hvárt þeirra ǫðru. Hann lét þá ryðja knǫrrinn, en lætr búa langskip með góðum fjárhlut, ok sendir Eireiki konungi þat heim til Svíþjóðar með hans mǫnnum, þeim er Ála hǫfðu þangat fylgt.

Áli gerir þá brúðlaup sitt til Þornbjargar dróttningar, ok var þat veitt með inum mesta prís, ok þar váru allir inir beztu menn, er í váru ríkinu. Ok at því enduðu gefr Áli sínum mǫnnum góðar gjafir, ok fóru þeir heim til sinna heimkynna. Þau Áli ok dróttning unnuz stórliga mikit.

Chapter 19

Skjótt eptir þetta deyr Ríkarðr konungr, en Áli tók ríkit, ok gefa landsmenn honum ko-nungsnafn yfir ǫllu Englandi. Hann var vinsæll af sínum mǫnnum. Áli konungr lagði undir sik Valland ok Saxland. Hann átti tvá sonu við dróttingu sinni. Hét annarr Vilhjálmr en annarr Ríkarðr. Vilhjálm setti hann konung yfir Valland, en Ríkarð yfir Saxland. Váru þeir báðir inir mestu menn, ok er mikill ættbogi frá þeim kominn í þeim lǫndum. Áli gat son í elli sinni, er Óláfr hét. Hann var mestr sona Ála.

En þá er Áli konungr var gamall, dó hann af elli, ok svá Þornbjǫrg dróttning. En Óláfr var tekinn til konungs yfir allt England. Hann fekk sér fríða dróttningu ok af góðum ættum, ok þótti hann mǫrgum mikill konungr ok ágætr bæði at viti ok ríkdómi. Hann var mildr af fé við sína þegna, ok því var hann mjǫk ástúðigr ǫllu landsfólkinu. Hann ríkti lengi í Englandi, ok jók þar sína ætt; enda er hér endir á sǫgu Ála flekks; hafi þeir þǫkk, er hlýddu, en inir skǫmm, er óhljóð gerðu.

Áli then travels home to England safe and sound and rides home to the city from the ship, but his men stayed behind at the ship. And when Áli came home, everyone was happy to see him. Queen Þornbjǫrg had arrived with her men, and she was delighted to see Áli; each was happy to see the other. He then had the merchant-ship unloaded, and has a longship loaded with valuable property and sends it back to King Eireikr to Scythia with those of his men who had accompanied Áli there.

Then Áli has his wedding with Queen Þornbjǫrg, and it was held with the greatest pomp, and all of the foremost people in the kingdom were there. And when it ended, Áli gives his people good gifts, and they went home to their households. Áli and the queen loved each other greatly.

Chapter 19

Shortly after this, King Ríkarðr dies, and Áli took the kingdom, and his countrymen give him the title of king over all England. He was popular with his men. King Áli brought Gaul and Saxony under his rule. He had two sons with his queen. One was called Vilhjálmr, and the other Ríkarðr. He set Vilhjálmr as king over Gaul, and Ríkarðr over Saxony. They were both the greatest men, and a great lineage is descended from them in those lands. Áli had a son in his old age, who was called Óláfr. He was the greatest of Áli's sons.

And when King Áli was elderly, he died of old age, and so did Queen Þornbjǫrg. And Óláfr was taken as king over all England. He married a queen who was beautiful and of good lineage, and he seemed to many a great king and excellent in both wisdom and authority. He was generous with his wealth toward his liegemen, and because of this, he was greatly beloved by all his countrymen. He ruled over England for a long time, and increased his progeny there. And so, here ends the saga of Áli flekkr. Thanks to those who listened, and shame to those who interrupted.

Ála flekks saga: A Snow White Variant from Late Medieval Iceland

Jonathan Y. H. Hui, Caitlin Ellis, James McIntosh and Katherine Marie Olley[1]

1. Background

There has been very little scholarship on the transmission of the Snow White tale-type in medieval Icelandic literature, or in any pre-modern literature.[2] Scholarship on most folktale-types tends to focus on modern variants, with particular attention usually paid to a variant which has come to be seen as the 'standard' version of the tale-type. In the case of Snow White, tale-type number 709 under the Aarne-Thompson-Uther classification system, the 'standard' version is the 1857 edition of the Grimm Brothers' *Sneewittchen*, published in their influential collection of fairytales;[3] it was on this version that Disney would base their 1937 animated film *Snow White and the Seven Dwarfs*, the cultural impact of which continues to the present day. Not all variants of the tale-type will have the very same motifs as the Grimms' version, of course, as is evident from the variation within the fifty-seven tales found in Ernst Böklen's 1910 collection of Snow White variants.[4] In particular, ancient and medieval variants of well-known fairytales need not bear immediately recognisable similarities to the 'standard' versions

---

[1] This article supplements the authors' text and translation of *Ála flekks saga*, which also appears in this issue: Jonathan Y. H. Hui, Caitlin Ellis, James McIntosh, Katherine Marie Olley, William Norman and Kimberly Anderson, '*Ála flekks saga*: A Text and Translation', *Leeds Studies in English*, 49 (2018), 1–43.

[2] Although several pre-modern texts, which will be discussed in this article, have been shown to contain a noteworthy number of Snow White motifs, scholars have tended to consider these early texts not to adhere closely enough to the structure of the tale-type to be considered full literary versions of Snow White. Thus, Charlotte Artese considers Shakespeare's *Cymbeline*, composed in the early seventeenth century, to be the 'earliest known literary version' of Snow White (*Shakespeare's Folktale Sources* (Newark: University of Delaware Press, 2015), p. 175; *Cymbeline*'s Snow White affinities were first pointed out in Karl Schenkl, 'Das Märchen von Sneewittchen und Shakespeare's *Cymbeline*', *Germania*, 9 (1864), 458–60), while Christine Shojaei Kawan, rejecting *Cymbeline*, considers a Russian tale first published in 1795 to be 'the first authentic version of *Snow White* at all known to date' ('A Brief Literary History of *Snow White*', *Fabula*, 49 (2008), 325–42 (pp. 337–38)).

[3] The Grimm Brothers first published *Sneewittchen* in 1812, but it underwent several revisions between 1812 and 1857; see Kay Stone, 'Three Transformations of Snow White', in *The Brothers Grimm and Folktale*, ed. by James M. McGlathery (Urbana: University of Illinois Press, 1988), pp. 52–65 (pp. 57–58). For the ATU classification, see Hans-Jörg Uther, *The Types of International Folktales: A Classification and Bibliography. Based on the system of Antti Aarne and Stith Thompson*, FF Communications, 284–86, 3 vols (Helsinki: Suomalainen Tiedeakatemia, 2004).

[4] Ernst Böklen, *Sneewittchenstudien: Erster Teil, Fünfundsiebzig Varianten im engern Sinn* (Leipzig: Hinrichs, 1910).

of the fairytale that we know today, firstly because different variants of the same tale-type will often be dressed in generically different clothing corresponding to contemporary literary trends, and secondly because, unlike many younger variants, an ancient or medieval variant could not have been based on a modern 'standard' variant as we know it.

Any identification of a folktale variant is ultimately based on that variant's adherence to the structure of the tale-type. With regard to Snow White, the most comprehensive work on the tale-type's structure has been done by Steven Swann Jones. Seeking to amend the motif-specific Aarne-Thompson structure of the tale-type, which comprised five steps ('Snow-White and her Stepmother'; 'Snow-White's Rescue'; 'The Poisoning'; 'Help of the Dwarfs'; and 'Her Revival'),[5] Jones outlined nine key episodes, in two parts, as follows:[6]

Part 1:

1. Origin: the specific circumstances of the heroine's creation or conception.

2. Jealousy: the persecutor becomes jealous of the heroine.

3. Expulsion: the persecutor orders the heroine's death or has her expelled from the household, but she does not die, sometimes thanks to a compassionate executioner.

4. Adoption: the now-homeless heroine finds a house, and its occupants let her stay.

Part 2:

5. Renewed Jealousy: the persecutor hears of the heroine's survival, often through a specific allomotif (such as the magic mirror).

6. Death: the persecutor apparently kills the heroine, either with one attack or with multiple.

7. Exhibition: the heroine's companions exhibit her body in a coffin, which may be placed near a distinct natural feature (for instance hung from a tree, cast out to sea or placed on a mountain).

8. Resuscitation: the heroine is revived, often by the fortuitous removal of the magic object upon moving the coffin or inspecting the 'corpse'.

9. Resolution: the heroine's marriage and the persecutor's punishment.

The purpose of this article is to draw attention to the close correspondences that *Ála flekks saga* ('the saga of Áli flekkr'), an entertaining Icelandic saga probably written in the early fifteenth century, has with the key structural aspects of the Snow White tale-type. Although its Snow White connection has previously gone unnoticed, the saga seems to be the clearest Snow

---

[5]   Antti Aarne, *The Types of the Folktale: A Classification and Bibliography*, trans. and rev. by Stith Thompson, 2nd edn, FF Communications, 184 (Helsinki: Academia Scientiarum Fennica, 1961), p. 245.

[6]   Steven Swann Jones, 'The Structure of *Snow White*', in *Fairy Tales and Society: Illusion, Allusion, and Paradigm*, ed. by Ruth B. Bottigheimer (Philadelphia: University of Philadelphia Press, 1986), pp. 165–84. This chapter was a slightly expanded reprint of Jones' article of the same name in *Fabula*, 24 (1983), 56–71, and the same material appears as part of a wider discussion in Jones' *The New Comparative Method: Structural and Symbolic Analysis of the Allomotifs of Snow White*, FF Communications, 247 (Helsinki: Academia Scientiarum Fennica, 1990).

White variant in the corpus of extant medieval Icelandic literature. Because this discussion will involve a close structural analysis of the saga, a short plot summary will be provided here, but the reader may first wish to read the saga in its entirety: a text and translation can be found in this issue.[7]

Áli, the saga hero and an English prince, is exposed as a child on his father's instruction. After being adopted by a poor couple, he returns to the royal court, where he is recognised and reincorporated into the royal family. He is cursed by a troll-woman, Blátǫnn, to marry her sister, Nótt, but with the help of Nótt's half-human daughter Hlaðgerðr, he escapes and wanders to Tartary. There, he wins the favour of the maiden-king Þornbjǫrg through his military defence of her kingdom, and they marry. On their wedding night, he is cursed for a second time, by Blátǫnn's brother Glóðarauga, to transform into a wolf and kill livestock in both Tartary and England. After some time, he is freed from this curse by his foster-mother. He is then cursed for a third time, by Nótt, who appears to him in a dream and inflicts debilitating wounds on him which can only be healed by her brother, Jǫtunoxi. With the incapacitated Áli in tow, Þornbjǫrg infiltrates Jǫtunoxi's court and agrees to marry him if he has Áli healed. After this is done, they instead burn Jǫtunoxi's hall, but with his dying breath, he inflicts a fourth curse on Áli, condemning him never to find peace until he locates Hlaðgerðr. He eventually finds her in Scythia, saves her life and marries her to the Scythian king. Afterwards, he returns to England and lives happily ever after with Þornbjǫrg.

While the plot of the saga bears little superficial resemblance to the story of Snow White, further analysis reveals convincing underlying similarities. *Ála flekks saga*'s affinity with the Snow White tale-type comes not simply in the form of several familiar Snow White motifs, nor even solely in the strong resonances with the individual episodes listed above, but also in the fact that the narrative structure is tightly sequenced around the typological structure of the Snow White tale-type laid out by Jones.[8] Before our structural analysis, however, brief introduction will be made of the few Snow White connections previously identified in Old Norse literature, in order to contextualise properly *Ála flekks saga*'s affinity with the tale-type.

2. The Snow White tradition in medieval Iceland

Compared to the Cinderella tale-type (ATU 510A), of which the fourteenth-century *Hálfdanar saga Eysteinssonar* and *Vilmundar saga viðutan* have been demonstrated to be clear variants,[9] far fewer traces of the Snow White tale-type have been identified in Old Norse

---

[7] Hui and others, '*Ála flekks saga*'.

[8] Although we do not find in Böklen's collection any single variant with an obvious connection to *Ála flekks saga*, which is unsurprising, we might nonetheless note an intriguing parallel in the two Norwegian versions of Snow White which he denotes *norw. 1.* and *norw. 2.* In these tales, the heroine takes refuge with a household of princes who are cursed to become bears during the day, a motif also found in *Hrólfs saga kraka*. Unusually for a Snow White tale, in *norw. 1.* the protagonist falls in love with one of those who takes her in, and lifts his curse by stealing the transformational bear-skin from under him when he sleeps (Böklen, *Sneewittchenstudien*, pp. 15–17). Although the narrative is significantly different to that of the werewolf episode in *Ála flekks saga*, it is nonetheless interesting that there are western Scandinavian Snow White variants in which animal-transformation curses and skins appear.

[9] *Hálfdanar saga Eysteinssonar*, ed. by Franz R. Schröder (Halle (Saale): Niemeyer, 1917), pp. 27–28; Einar Sigurðsson, '*Vilmundar saga viðutan*' (unpublished master's thesis, University of Iceland, 1962), pp. 69–110; '*Vilmundar saga viðutan*': The Saga of Vilmundur the Outsider, ed. and trans. by Jonathan Y. H. Hui (London: Viking Society for Northern Research, forthcoming); and Jonathan Y. H. Hui, 'Cinderella in Old Norse Literature', *Folklore*, 129 (2018), 353–74.

literature. The suggestion has been made by Christine Shojaei Kawan that aspects of the tradition are reflected in the figure of Snjófríðr, the Lappish princess and daughter of a sorcerer, whose marriage to the Norwegian king Haraldr hárfagri (Haraldr 'fair-hair') is recounted in the late twelfth-century *Ágrip af Nóregskonungasögum*,[10] *Haralds saga hárfagra* in Snorri Sturluson's thirteenth-century *Heimskringla* (in which she is called Snæfríðr, a variant form of the name 'Snjófríðr'),[11] and the fourteenth-century *Flateyjarbók*.[12] These accounts tell that, from Haraldr's first meeting with Snjófríðr all the way through their marriage until her death, he is so infatuated with her that he neglects his kingdom. Even after her death, Haraldr mourns over her corpse for three years, and the paranormality of this obsession is confirmed when Þorleifr spaki moves her from the bed: foul stenches arise, the corpse blackens and worms, frogs and maggots stream forth from it. Noting that Snjófríðr has a snow-name (literally meaning 'Snow-beautiful'), Shojaei Kawan cites the Snjófríðr story as an example of the prince's mourning that is found in some Snow White variants,[13] but it must be stressed that the resonances of the Snow White tale-type in the Snjófríðr story are minimal: she has a snow-name;[14] she is mourned obsessively by the king; and her body is placed on exhibition after her death. The crucial Jealousy, Persecution and Resuscitation aspects of the tale-type are missing, and the story cannot therefore be considered a Snow White variant, but this does not rule out the possibility that the relevant aspects of the Snjófríðr story could have drawn on a pre-existing Snow White tale or tradition that was known in Iceland at the time.

A closer parallel to the Snow White structure can be found in the wolf-transformation episode in *Völsunga saga*. In this episode, Sigmundr, having gravely (perhaps mortally) wounded Sinfjötli by biting him on the neck while in wolf-form, spots a weasel biting another weasel in the same way. The aggressor weasel fetches a leaf and lays it over the wound, healing the assaulted weasel. Sigmundr is brought a leaf by a raven, applies it to Sinfjötli's wound, and the latter recovers immediately.[15]

Carol Clover has pointed out the clear parallels between the strikingly specific resuscitation rituals in *Völsunga saga* and *Eliduc*, one of the twelfth-century Breton *lais* of Marie de France.[16] In the Old French *lai*, Guilliadun, the lover of the married knight Eliduc, falls into a deathly faint upon hearing that Eliduc is married. Eliduc leaves her body in a chapel and returns home, but remains affected by this, and his wife Guildelüec deduces that something is wrong. Finding Guilliadun's body before her burial, Guildelüec understands the situation.

[10] *Ágrip af Nóregskonungasögum*, ed. and trans. by Matthew J. Driscoll, 2nd edn (London: Viking Society for Northern Research, 2008), pp. 4–6.

[11] *Heimskringla*, ed. by Bjarni Aðalbjarnarson, Íslenzk fornrit, 26–28, 3 vols (Reykjavik: Hið Íslenzka Fornritafélag, 1941), I, 125–27.

[12] *Flateyjarbok: En samling af Norske Konge-saegar*, ed. by Guðbrandur Vigfússon and Carl R. Unger, 3 vols (Christiania (Oslo): Malling, 1860–68), I, 582.

[13] Shojaei Kawan, 'A Brief Literary History of *Snow White*', pp. 329–30.

[14] It is not even clear that much Snow White significance can be read into Snjófríðr's name, given that the snow-element may simply be a natural extension, for a country abundant in snow, of the idea of a light complexion as a sign of beauty (which is also expressed in names such as Svanhvít, 'Swan-white', in *Hrómundar saga Gripssonar*).

[15] *Völsunga saga*, ch. 8, in *Fornaldar sögur Norðurlanda*, ed. by Guðni Jónsson, 4 vols (Akureyri: Íslendingasag-naútgáfan, 1954–59), I, 124–25. All references to *fornaldarsögur* will be to this edition, which will subsequently be abbreviated as *FAS*.

[16] Carol Clover, '*Vǫlsunga saga* and the Missing Lai of Marie de France', in *Sagnaskemmtun: Studies in Honour of Hermann Pálsson*, ed. by Rudolf Simek, Jónas Kristjánsson and Hans Bekker-Nielsen (Vienna: Böhlaus, 1986), pp. 79–84. Another saga episode with a number of similarities to *Eliduc* can be found in the fourteenth-century *riddarasaga Dámusta saga*, in which Princess Gratíana's 'death' is engineered by the demonic Alheimr, whom Dámusti defeats with the support of the Virgin Mary; Gratíana is revived by being given a drink, and the process

Inside the chapel, she then sees a weasel heal its dead mate by placing a red flower inside its mouth. Guildelüec then places the same flower inside Guilliadun's mouth and revives her.[17] Clover summarises the similarities with *Völsunga saga* as follows:

> We have in both cases not only the resuscitation of an apparently dead person through the use of a certain plant, but the revelation of the means of healing through an instructional drama in the animal world — a drama that moreover mirrors the situation in the human world. The animal is in both cases a weasel […][18]

While a number of Marie's *lais* were translated into Old Norse at the court of the Norwegian king Hákon IV, forming the compilation we now call *Strengleikar*, *Eliduc* is not among them. But although there is no (surviving) Norse translation of it, the above parallel with *Völsunga saga* suggests that the Eliduc story was known in medieval Iceland. This is interesting because a connection between *Eliduc* and the Snow White tale-type was suggested by Alfred Nutt back in 1892.[19] Although *Eliduc* is not especially reminiscent of the Snow White tale-type beyond Guilliadun's death and resuscitation, Nutt identified an undeniably close relationship between the *lai* and the Scottish folktale 'Gold-Tree and Silver-Tree', which is clearly a Snow White variant.[20] Nutt's ambitious argument holds that *Eliduc* represents a modified version of a pre-existing folktale whose original form must have looked something like 'Gold-Tree and Silver-Tree', that is, potentially a recognisable Snow White variant. Therefore, if we accept Nutt's hypothesis, we have in *Völsunga saga* an episode derived from a *lai* based on a Snow White tale.

3. *Álög*

While the Snow White parallels in the characters of Snjófríðr and Sinfjötli are relatively self-contained elements in their wider narratives, the parallels in *Ála flekks saga* are more fundamental to the narrative. Much of this closer structural affinity is due to the extensive use of the *álög* ('curse') motif. The prevalence of this motif in late medieval Icelandic literature necessitates the introduction of the wider *álög* tradition, in order to contextualise the saga's uses of curses.

The relationship between the Icelandic *álög* and the Irish *geis* has long been recognised by scholars. The primary meaning of *geis* (plural *gessi* or *geisi*, later *geasa*) in Middle Irish is 'a prohibited act or person, a tabu, a prohibition'.[21] The prohibited acts can seem fairly practical and common-sense, for example that a king should not be away from his kingdom

---

of resuscitation is concluded with the removal from under her tongue of a leek, which Alheimr had placed there to prevent her from actually dying from a lack of food while buried (*Dámusta saga*, ch. 14, in *Þjalar-Jóns saga; Dámusta saga: I. Texten*, ed. by Louisa Fredrika Tan-Haverhorst (Haarlem: Tjeenk Willink & Zoon, 1939), pp. 93–100). While a very close parallel to this episode has been identified in the Old French romance *Amadas et Idoine* (Margaret Schlauch, 'The *Dámusta saga* and French Romance', *Modern Philology*, 35 (1937), 1–13, (pp. 6–8)), the use of a love triangle as the cause of the 'death' scene and the use of a plant to effect the revival are reminiscent of *Eliduc*.

[17] Jean Rychner, *Les lais de Marie de France* (Paris: Champion, 1968), pp. 187–88.

[18] Clover, '*Völsunga saga* and the Missing Lai of Marie de France', p. 83.

[19] Alfred Nutt, 'The Lai of Eliduc and the Märchen of Little Snow-White', *Folklore*, 3 (1892), 26–48.

[20] Nutt, 'The Lai of Eliduc', pp. 31–34. The folktale can be found in Joseph Jacobs, *Celtic Fairy Tales* (London: Nutt, 1892), pp. 88–92, and in all subsequent editions.

[21] eDIL, s.v. *geis* (http://www.dil.ie/25555). For discussion of the word's semantics and its overlap with similar concepts see Thomas Charles-Edwards, 'Geis, Prophecy, Omen, and Oath', *Celtica*, 23 (1999), 38–59. See also the

for too long; but they are often very specific and seem strange and arbitrary to the modern reader. The latter category, combined with the fact that these strictures are usually placed on a protagonist by a supernatural or otherworldly figure, led to scholarly speculations on the possibly mythic or magical origins of *gessi*.[22] It has more recently been argued that associating *geis* with the concept of taboo can be unhelpful, and instead we should simply view it as a literary device.[23] Regardless of their untraceable origin, *gessi* can play a crucial role in the narrative. A *geis* imposed on the warrior Fergus mac Róich that he cannot refuse an invitation to a feast, for instance, is used against him in *Longes mac nUislenn* ('The exile of the sons of Uisliu'), forcing him to abandon the eponymous men under his protection, which leads to their deaths, in order to fulfil his obligation to attend a feast. In the most recent discussion of the topic, Ralph O'Connor notes that the *gessi* placed on King Conaire in *Togail Bruidne Dá Derga* ('The destruction of Dá Derga's hostel') are used by the author to great structural effect.[24] A *geis* often serves a similar narrative role to a prophecy in foreshadowing later events and building tension: 'the audience will naturally suspect that the king will somehow fall foul of it in the end'.[25] *Togail Bruidne Dá Derga* is the text in which *gessi* are most prominent and, according to Thomas Charles-Edwards, the 'most obviously deterministic'.[26]

The compelling interest of a *geis*, often imposed at birth or even conception, is when it comes into conflict with a character's other social obligations, which are of course felt particularly acutely by heroes and kings. Conaire is a prime example of this, as in *Togail Bruidne Dá Derga* he faces several such dilemmas in succession and knowingly violates all his *gessi* in turn. Although there is a *geis* against him admitting a lone woman after dark, he gives way to a woman insulting his hospitality rather than have his honour slighted. He flouts another *geis* against settling a quarrel between two of his clients, but he does so to prevent bloodshed and preserve the peace, as a king should. It is the emphasis on impossible choices between contradictory obligations which makes the *Togail*, in Philip O'Leary's words, 'truly tragic'.[27]

The relationship between *geis* and *álög* has been used as a case study in the wider debate about the relationship between Norse and Irish literature. It was first raised by Einar Ólafur Sveinsson,[28] and it features briefly in Gísli Sigurðsson's classic statement of the case for Gaelic contribution to Icelandic literature.[29] Rosemary Power argues that they use a similar formula,

---

etymological discussion in Tom Sjöblom, *Early Irish Taboos: A Study in Cognitive History*, Comparative Religion, 5 (Helsinki: University of Helsinki, 2000), pp. 51–56; Sjöblom further contends that *geis* has been overused in scholarship, obscuring other related vocabulary and sometimes resulting in the identification of taboo in literary episodes where it was not necessarily intended.

[22] David Greene, 'Tabu in Early Irish Narrative', in *Medieval Narrative: A Symposium*, ed. by H. Bekker-Nielsen and others (Odense: Odense University Press, 1979), pp. 9–19. The usage of *geis* seems to have spread and its meaning widened, and is also applied to situations in later versions of a story where the term does not feature in the early version (Charles-Edwards, 'Geis', pp. 57–58).

[23] Qiu Fangzhe, '*Geis*, a Literary Motif in Early Irish Literature', *St Anne's Academic Review*, 2 (2010), 13–16 (p. 13).

[24] Ralph O'Connor, *The Destruction of Da Derga's Hostel: Kingship and Narrative Artistry in a Mediaeval Irish Saga* (Oxford: Oxford University Press, 2013), pp. 72–81.

[25] O'Connor, *The Destruction of Da Derga's Hostel*, p. 74.

[26] Charles-Edwards, 'Geis', p. 39.

[27] Philip O'Leary, 'Honour-Bound: The Social Context of Early Irish Heroic *Geis*', *Celtica*, 20 (1988), 85–107 (p. 88).

[28] Einar Ól. Sveinsson, 'Celtic Elements in Icelandic Tradition', *Béaloideas*, 25 (1957), 3–24 (pp. 19–20).

[29] Gísli Sigurðsson, *Gaelic Influence in Iceland: Historical and Literary Contacts. A Survey of Research*, 2nd edn (Reykjavik: University of Iceland Press, 2010), pp. 67–70.

but finds greater correspondences between *álög* and *geis* in more modern Gaelic folktales, rather than *geis* in medieval Irish literature. Despite this, she suggests that the motif in Norse can be traced to Gaelic oral tales reaching Iceland during the Viking Age.[30]

In medieval Icelandic literature, the *álög* motif is predominantly found in the young romances, both in *fornaldarsögur* and *riddarasögur*. Along with *Ála flekks saga*, which Alaric Hall, Steven D. P. Richardson and Haukur Þorgeirsson labelled 'the pre-eminent Old Icelandic example of an *álög* tale',[31] scholars have noted that the motif is also to be found in *Svipdagsmál* (which is made up of two eddic poems), *Hálfdanar saga Eysteinssonar*, *Hjálmþés rímur* and *Hjálmþés saga*, *Illuga saga Gríðarfóstra*, *Sigrgarðs saga frækna* and *Vilhjálms saga sjóðs*.[32] To this list we might also add a relatively little-known narrative tradition, *Haralds rímur Hringsbana*, a medieval Icelandic ballad probably based on a lost *fornaldarsaga*, **Haralds saga Hringsbana*.[33] Here are summaries of each of these instances of *álög*:

- In the two poems that form *Svipdagsmál*, Svipdagr states that he was compelled by his stepmother to go and find Menglöð.

- In *Hálfdanar saga Eysteinssonar*, the Russian princess Ingigerðr, disguised as 'Grímr', curses the protagonist Hálfdan never to have peace until her hand, glove and ring are freely given to him, before departing.[34]

- In *Hjálmþés saga ok Ölvis*, Hjálmþér rejects his wicked stepmother Lúða's sexual advances, and she later curses him to have no peace until he finds Hervör Hundingsdóttir. He counter-curses that her jaws will gape open (rendering her incapable of further curses), and that she will stand with a foot on each cliff with a fire kindled under her, and no food except what ravens bring her.[35] Parallels have been noted in the late Old Irish *Fingal Rónáin* and the Middle Welsh *Culhwch and Olwen*.[36]

- Also in *Hjálmþés saga*, 'Hörðr'/Hringr reveals at the end of the saga that he too had rejected Lúða's advances, and that she had responded by cursing him and his sisters Álsól and Hildisif to transform into monstrous creatures who could only be released from those forms once specific conditions had been fulfilled.[37]

- In *Illuga saga Gríðarfóstra*, 'Gríðr' reveals to Illugi at the end of the saga that she had once been Princess Signý, and that she had been married and had a daughter called Hildr. Signý's wicked stepmother Grímhildr cursed Signý to become a troll-wife, giving no explicit reason but presumably to eliminate the step-sibling of her own

---

[30] Rosemary Power, '*Geasa* and *Álög*: Magic Formulae and Perilous Quests in Gaelic and Norse', *Scottish Studies*, 28 (1987), 69–89 (p. 84).

[31] Alaric Hall, Steven D. P. Richardson and Haukur Þorgeirsson, '*Sigrgarðs saga frækna*: A Normalised Text, Translation, and Introduction', *Scandinavian-Canadian Studies*, 21 (2013), 80–155 (p. 88).

[32] Einar Ól. Sveinsson, 'Svipdag's Long Journey: Some Observations on Grógaldr and Fjölsvinnsmál', *Béaloideas*, 39/41 (1971–73), 298–319; Power, '*Geasa* and *Álög*', pp. 76–83.

[33] Stephen A. Mitchell, *Heroic Sagas and Ballads* (Ithaca, NY: Cornell University Press, 1991), pp. 171, 185.

[34] *Hálfdanar saga Eysteinssonar*, ch. 8, in *FAS*, IV, 258.

[35] *Hjálmþés saga ok Ölvis*, ch. 8–11, in *FAS*, IV, 194–204.

[36] The *Culhwch and Olwen* connection was first raised by Sven Grundtvig, in his introduction to the ballad of Ungen Svendal in *Danmarks gamle folkeviser*, ed. by Sven Grundtvig and Axel Olrik, 12 vols (Copenhagen: Samfundet til den Danske Literaturs Fremme, 1853–1976), II, 239. On the *Fingal Rónáin* connection, see Ralph O'Connor, '"Stepmother Sagas": An Irish Analogue for *Hjálmþérs saga ok Ölvérs*', *Scandinavian Studies*, 72 (2000), 1–48.

[37] *Hjálmþés saga ok Ölvis*, ch. 22, in *FAS*, IV, 240–41.

seven daughters. Part of this curse was that all men would fall in love with Hildr but be murdered by Gríðr. Hildr counter-cursed on her mother's behalf, cursing Grímhildr to stand with feet greatly apart, with a fire kindled under her, into which she would fall and burn to death if Signý and Hildr were to escape her curse.[38]

- In *Sigrgarðs saga frækna*, Princess Ingigerðr of Tartary rejects the offer of her wicked stepmother Hlégerðr to have her two sisters marry Hlégerðr's brothers. Hlégerðr curses her three stepdaughters, two to turn into animals to be abused, and the third, Ingigerðr, to become faithless and greedy. Ingigerðr counters by saying that those will be Hlégerðr's last ever words.[39]

- In *Vilhjálms saga sjóðs*, Vilhjálmr loses a board-game match to a giant after being distracted by the giant's daughter, who had disguised herself as a beautiful woman. Vilhjálmr is ordered to find the giant's lair within three years, during which time he must discover the names of the ninety trolls in the lair.[40]

- In *Haralds rímur Hringsbana*, a warrior called Hermóðr is duelling the protagonist Haraldr. Haraldr sustains a head injury, but wins the duel by cutting off Hermóðr's leg. Before executing Hermóðr, the latter curses Haraldr never to have his head-wound healed except by Hermóðr's haughty sister, who, he says, will have Haraldr hanged.[41]

In order to contextualise the curses in *Ála flekks saga* within the discussion of the *álög* motif, they are listed overleaf, in a table reproduced from John Roberts' discussion on the saga in his doctoral thesis.[42]

Rosemary Power identifies three variants of the *álög* motif in Icelandic literature based on the identity of the curser. The first, which she considers to have been a late development, involves a non-stepmother-figure imposing the curse on the hero.[43] Power notes that it may be preceded by a game between the two, and her main Icelandic example is *Vilhjálms saga*. We might add *Haralds rímur*, which has a duel before the curse, to this category. Power also suggests that the curses in *Ála flekks saga* fall under this category, albeit without the game motif.

[38] *Illuga saga Gríðarfóstra*, ch. 5, in *FAS*, III, 420–22.

[39] Hall, Richardson and Haukur Þorgeirsson, 'Sigrgarðs saga frækna', pp. 107–8.

[40] *Vilhjálms saga sjóðs*, ch. 10, in *Late Medieval Icelandic Romances*, ed. by Agnete Loth, 5 vols (Copenhagen: Munksgaard, 1962–64), IV, 22.

[41] *Haralds rímur Hringsbana*, ed. by Ólafur Halldórsson, Íslenzkar miðaldarímur, 1/Rit, 3 (Reykjavik: Stofnun Árna Magnússonar á Íslandi, 1973), p. 48.

[42] John J. Roberts, 'Dreams and Visions in Medieval Icelandic Romance' (unpublished Ph.D. thesis, University of Leeds, 2007), p. 180. We are grateful to Dr Roberts for granting us permission to reproduce this table.

[43] Power, 'Geasa and Álög', pp. 76–78.

	Curser	Victim	Curse	Justification	Retaliation	Remedy
1	Blátǫnn	Áli	To go into the forest and become Nótt's husband	Áli never greeted Blátǫnn kindly	Curse 2	Hlaðgerðr's assistance
2	Áli	Blátǫnn	To become a stone slab in the kitchen and break apart if Áli escapes from Nótt	Retaliation for curse 1	Curse 3(a)	None
3(a)	Glóðarauga	Áli	To become a wolf and kill men and livestock, in particular Þornbjǫrg's	Retaliation for curse 2	Curse 4	See remedy for curse 3(b)
4	Áli	Glóðarauga	To sit on a chest and yell constantly until Áli is released from his curse; then he will be hanged	Retaliation for curse 3(a)	Curse 3(b)	None
3(b)	Glóðarauga	Áli	When Áli has destroyed all Þornbjǫrg's livestock, he must do the same in his father's kingdom; he will not be released unless a woman pleads for his life	Extension of curse 3(a) in retaliation for curse 4	No specific retaliation; curse 4 applies	Assistance of Hildr, who begs for Áli to be spared
5	Nótt	Áli	Áli's wounds can only be cured by her brothers, and if this is not done within ten years, he will die	Escaping from Nótt (curse 1) and killing her brother	Nótt's death at the hands of her brother by means of trickery	Cure by Nótt's brothers, achieved by means of trickery
6	Jǫtunoxi	Áli	Áli must go and have no peace until he finds Hlaðgerðr	Pre-emptive strike before he is killed	Killing of Jǫtunoxi	Áli finds and rescues Hlaðgerðr

The second variant has a stepmother impose the quest on the hero.[44] Occasionally, this is a direct retaliation for the hero spurning her sexual advances, which Power refers to as the 'Phædra motif', referring to the Greek mythological character who fell in love with Hippolytus, her husband Theseus' son by another woman. The 'Phædra motif' is found in *Hjálmþés saga* (Lúda and Hjálmþér) and is present in modified form in *Sigrgarðs saga* (in which the wicked stepmother Hlégerðr attempts and fails to arrange marriages between her two brothers and two of her stepdaughters). We cannot be sure if the 'Phædra motif' was present in the *Svipdagsmál* tradition, since the poems do not tell us why Svipdagr's stepmother sent him on his quest. Within this second variant, we also have several examples in which the stepmother-imposed curse is on her stepchildren, who are not the saga heroes. In these cases, the curse is only revealed and explained by the stepchildren themselves towards the end of the saga, after the heroes have freed them. The stepchildren had invariably been transformed into monstrous animals or creatures, and it is in this form that the heroes first encounter them. Examples are found in *Hjálmþés saga* ('Hörðr'/Hringr, 'Álsól'/Vargeisa and 'Hildisif'/Skinnhúfa), *Illuga saga* and *Sigrgarðs saga*.

In the third variant, 'the lady herself puts the hero under *geasa* or *álög* to search for her'.[45] This is much rarer in medieval Icelandic literature, and the only such example that Power provides is *Hálfdanar saga Eysteinssonar*.

Power's subdivision of these variants of the *álög* motif is not entirely clear-cut, because there are strong overlaps between these categories. Áli's counter-curse to Blátǫnn (number 2 in the table) involves flames being kindled on her after her transformation into a stone; this mirrors the fate of the wicked stepmothers in *Hjálmþés saga* and *Illuga saga*, who are both cursed to have fires lit under them.[46] The fact that Blátǫnn is also turned into a stone and Glóðarauga is later cursed to yell ceaselessly (number 4) denies both of them the faculty of speech, and therefore the ability to utter any further curses, something that is manifested overtly in *Hjálmþés saga* and *Sigrgarðs saga*. Glóðarauga's initial curse on Áli (number 3(a)) transforms him into a monstrous creature, mirroring a common curse on protagonistic characters by wicked stepmothers within the second variant (*Hjálmþés saga*, *Illuga saga* and *Sigrgarðs saga*). Jǫtunoxi's curse (number 6) imposes the very same quest on Áli as is found in Power's second and third variants (*Hjálmþés saga* and *Hálfdanar saga Eysteinssonar* respectively), namely to have no peace until he finds a certain lady, although in all three variants, the curser has a different relationship to the hero.

Fuller discussion of the dream-aspect of Nótt's curse on Áli (number 5) can be found in the introduction to our translation of the saga,[47] but particular mention must be made of the similarity of the *álög*-driven quest to *Haralds rímur Hringsbana*. In both cases, the hero is cursed to be unable to recover from certain wounds unless he locates the only person with the power to heal him. In both cases, the hero has already made an enemy of at least one sibling of this healer's siblings (Áli has had Blátǫnn and Glóðarauga killed; Haraldr is about to kill Hermóðr). In both cases, some sort of trickery or coercion is required to have the hero healed: Áli and Þornbjǫrg disguise themselves to trick Jǫtunoxi; while Haraldr uses cunning and disguise to find his way to Hermóðr's sister, eventually forcing her to heal him under

---

[44] Power, '*Geasa* and *Álög*', pp. 78–82.
[45] Power, '*Geasa* and *Álög*', pp. 82–83.
[46] See motif M431.6 in Inger M. Boberg, *Motif-Index of Early Icelandic Literature*, Bibliotheca Arnamagnæana, 27 (Copenhagen: Munksgaard, 1966), p. 197.
[47] Hui and others, '*Ála flekks saga*', pp. 9–10.

threat of rape.[48] One other potentially important similarity is the fact that both Áli and Haraldr assume aliases after wandering through a forest (Haraldr goes by 'Dulinn', 'the disguised one'), but the two stories share little else in common. On this evidence, it must remain a possibility that Áli's quest to find Jǫtunoxi was directly influenced by the Haraldr Hringsbani tradition.

In *Ála flekks saga*, then, we have not only the largest number of *álög* in any extant medieval Icelandic text, but also a range of manifestations, with clear parallels in other roughly contemporary legendary sagas. Indeed, almost all of the *álög* in the other sagas listed above find a strong parallel with at least one of the curses in *Ála flekks saga*. It does not seem as though the author of *Ála flekks saga* was simply attempting to craft a saga shaped around numerous and varied *álög*; rather the framing and sequencing of the *álög* shows them to be important structural and thematic units in the saga. Their central role can be demonstrated through their facilitation of the saga's adherence to the structure of the Snow White tale-type, which, along with other relevant structural and narrative elements of the saga, will now be discussed.

4. Structure

4.i. Structure: Origins

The parallels with Snow White are apparent from the very outset of the saga in Áli's Origin episode, which emphasises the unusual circumstances of his birth and childhood. It is tempting to read into King Ríkarðr's powers of foresight, and possibly the king and queen's sudden conception of a child after an unspecified period of childlessness, the supernatural element that generally accompanies the conception of Snow White. Additionally, Ríkarðr's foresighted injunction, that his child must be exposed if it is male, might also reflect a common aspect of the rivalry between Snow White and her persecutor which leads to the Jealousy episode. Where Snow White variants frequently set up a sexual rivalry between two women, here an implicit male rivalry might be reflected in Ríkarðr's rejection of Áli, who, as a male heir, might one day be a source of conflict to his father. His father's insistence on Áli being exposed is similar to the jealous (step-)mother's insistence on the same fate for the younger, more beautiful Snow White, especially given that in some variants the father is party to this and abandons his daughter himself.

Though convenient, such an explanation for Áli's exposure is not overly convincing, due to the lack of any Oedipal aspect in medieval Icelandic versions of the child exposure motif, that is, versions of the motif in which the child is exposed because he represents a future threat to his father.[49] Infant exposure is a fairly commonplace event in the Icelandic sagas and, while Sean Lawing considers that 'little reason needed to be given', most sagas mention some specific motivation, whether it be illegitimacy, revenge or a negative premonition about the infant's future, as in *Ála flekks saga*.[50] Of course, these literary instances should not be

---

[48] *Haralds rímur Hringsbana*, pp. 49–59.

[49] In the child exposure episode in *Samsons saga fagra*, the child's inheritance is a factor in the father's decision to have him exposed, although (as in *Ála flekks saga*) the exposure is well-intended in this case, because Sigurðr, as Goðmundr's bastard son, is said not to be entitled to any inheritance according to the laws of Glæsisvellir, and would instead have to live out his life as a slave; see *Samsons saga fagra*, ed. by John Wilson, Samfund til udgivelse af gammel nordisk litteratur, 65 (Copenhagen: Jørgensen, 1953), ch. 17, p. 33.

[50] Sean B. Lawing, 'The Place of the Evil: Infant Abandonment in Old Norse Society', *Scandinavian Studies*, 85 (2013), 133–50 (p. 136). Not all these motivations are to be considered equal, however. *Finnboga saga, Gunnlaugs*

taken as an accurate reflection of the historical practice.[51] Most children exposed were unlikely to survive whereas the exposure of Áli principally serves to mark his birth and early childhood as exceptional or memorable; his survival is never seriously in doubt.[52]

As in many Snow White variants, the task of exposing the child is assigned to servants, who fail to kill the child, although in the case of *Ála flekks saga* they do technically fulfil their orders. In another feature common to many Snow White tales, the child is taken in by people that live on the edge of human society: in this case the impoverished Gunni and his wife Hildr, whose low social status is denoted by their outermost position during feasts. Áli's forced departure from the royal, courtly milieu and incorporation into their family seems to represent a mini Expulsion and Adoption episode within the Origins section as a whole, complete with compassionate executioners in the slaves who lie about having killed him.[53] The compassionate executioner is 'not a compulsory figure' in Snow White variants,[54] but the servants do seem to fulfil just such a function. The order to expose a child does not necessarily encompass the active killing of the child, but the fact that the slaves lie about it is reminiscent of the compassionate executioner's choice to defy the (actual) kill-order and allow the hero or heroine to live. As in Snow White variants both with and without the motif, the protagonist is then forced to gain a new identity in a lower social circle, which in *Ála flekks saga* is achieved through Áli's adoption by Gunni and Hildr.

The ritual of birth which follows Áli's rescue, in which Hildr lies on the floor and pretends to give birth to Áli, constitutes a physical re-enactment of labour and clearly functions as a way for Hildr and Gunni to claim Áli as their own. The ritual can also be understood as an attempt by Hildr to restore to the child the sense of personhood and the legal rights which exposure denied it.[55] Abandonment places the infant in a liminal position where it is neither living nor dead, not unlike the unborn child: hence it must be born again in order to be reincorporated

---

saga ormstungu and *Þorsteins þáttr uxafóts* all include comments emphasising that infant abandonment was only considered acceptable for those who could not afford to raise the child, suggesting other justifications were open to criticism.

[51] Infant abandonment was an accepted part of Old Norse pre-Christian society, one of two traditions (along with the eating of horse-flesh) that was briefly maintained after the Conversion in 1000 AD (*Íslendingabók*, ch. 7, in *Íslendingabók. Landnámabók*, ed. by Jakob Benediktsson, Íslenzk fornrit, 1 (Reykjavik: Hið Íslenzka Fornritafélag, 1986), p. 17). However, the Church was quick to proscribe the practice except in exceptional cases of severe deformity, though the existence of 'strongly worded laws' regarding the practice after Conversion have been taken by Sean Lawing as evidence 'that infant abandonment was sufficiently established to persist beyond its post-conversion ban' (Lawing, 'The Place of the Evil', p. 137).

[52] The child's rescue is a motif common from folklore (R131ff.), and rescue by a peasant a recognised sub-motif within that category (R131.6). Stith Thompson, *Motif-Index of Folk-Literature: A Classification of Narrative Elements in Folktales, Ballads, Myths, Fables, Mediaeval Romances, Exempla, Fabliaux, Jest-Books and Local Legends*, rev. and enl. edn, 6 vols (Bloomington: Indiana University Press, 1955–58), v, 279–81. See also motif R131 in Boberg, *Motif-Index of Early Icelandic Literature*, p. 231.

[53] Instances of the compassionate executioner motif are also found elsewhere in Old Norse literature. Several Snow White variants extend the motif to involve the substitution of animal viscera as proof of the heroine's supposed death (see footnote 57 below), and in *Drauma-Jóns saga* we find a clear parallel to this, in Ingibjörg's decision not to kill Jón and instead substitute a dog's heart as proof of his supposed death. In the chivalric *Bevers saga*, we find the hero's clothes dipped in pig's blood for similar purposes, and in *Þjalar-Jóns saga*, the hero's clothes are dipped in his own blood.

[54] See motif K152 in Boberg, *Motif-Index of Early Icelandic Literature*, p. 170, and Shojaei Kawan, 'A Brief Literary History of *Snow White*', p. 326.

[55] Lawing ('The Place of the Evil', pp. 136–37) points out that '[i]nfants appear to have lacked legal status in pre-Christian law — something that was gained only after an infant had been sprinkled with water (*ausa vatn*), named or given food'.

into society. The noted inability of any name to stick to the child afterwards problematises the success of the ritual in *Ála flekks saga* and further reveals the scene as part of the couple's struggle to give the child a sure identity. That the bestowal of a name customarily provided protection from the threat of abandonment makes Áli's initial lack of a name,[56] even after the birth ritual, all the more problematic and his abandonment and rebirth thus sets the scene for his continual struggle with recognition and identity, through further cycles of Jealousy, Expulsion and Adoption.

4.ii. Structure: Cycles of Jealousy, Expulsion and Adoption

The persecution proper, however, does not begin until the first curse against Áli. The reason that Blátǫnn explicitly supplies for cursing Áli is that he never greeted her 'með góðum orðum' ('with kind words').[57] It is not the most obvious manifestation of Jealousy, but the implication is that Blátǫnn feels slighted by perceived inequity. Two things are notable about Blátǫnn's reason: firstly, it seems jarringly contrived in terms of the construction of the saga, in that we are never even told that Áli has ever met Blátǫnn, let alone snubbed her; and secondly, the Jealousy does not take place within the familial sphere. Although it is common in Snow White variants for the persecutor to be within the family unit, the fact that Blátǫnn has no familial relationship with Áli need not be problematic, as Graham Anderson notes in his discussion of ancient Snow White variants that '[c]lose family tensions tend to be toned down in the romances, and their role supplied by external rivals instead'.[58] Indeed, Blátǫnn's equivalents in another variant of the *álög* motif are stepmothers (in *Hjálmþés rímur*/*Hjálmþés saga* and *Sigrgarðs saga*). Blátǫnn's accusation of impoliteness is reminiscent of the actual disdain shown to Lúða and Hlégerðr respectively, immediately before their curses — and both of these cursers are the victims' stepmothers. We may therefore detect in Blátǫnn traces of the wicked-stepmother-as-curser motif, which fills the same functional role as the wicked stepmother motif commonly found in Snow White variants. That this is a Jealousy episode is implied by the narrative artificiality of Blátǫnn's reason for her curse.

We must, however, be wary of reading too much Snow White significance into the Blátǫnn-Áli interaction on its own. Wicked stepmothers are found in many other tale-types, and we have already seen in Section 3 that *Ála flekks saga* has common substance with the 'stepmother sagas' such as *Hjálmþés saga* and *Sigrgarðs saga*, a category independent of the Snow White tale-type. However, if we accept the possibility that Blátǫnn's curse represents a Jealousy episode, it is important that it directly triggers an incontrovertible Expulsion episode. Blátǫnn's curse expels Áli from the civilisation of his father's royal court into the wilderness; more specifically, Áli is explicitly sent into a forest, and implicitly, by being sent to Nótt, into a cave afterwards. Forests appear as places into which the protagonist is expelled in some twenty-five of the variants listed by Böklen, while the cave into which he is sent to take on a pseudo-domestic role as Nótt's husband could be seen as an ironic subversion of the Adoption episode before his Adoption proper.

---

[56] Juha Pentikäinen suggests that the 'decision as to whether a child was to be kept or abandoned [...] was actualized, at the latest, at the moment of name-giving or baptism' (*The Nordic Dead-Child Tradition: Nordic Dead-Child Beings. A Study in Comparative Religion*, trans. by Antony Landon, FF Communications, 202 (Helsinki: Academia Scientiarum Fennica, 1968), p. 74).

[57] Hui and others, '*Ála flekks saga*', p. 21.

[58] Graham Anderson, *Fairytale in the Ancient World* (London: Routledge, 2000), p. 53.

The dog which Hlaðgerðr sends to help Áli escape from Nótt's cave may also be posited as a feature of significance to the discussion of Snow White parallels in the saga. Boberg categorises this dog under the motifs 'Dog as Messenger' and 'Helpful dog',[59] but one specific aspect of its appearance remains difficult to explain, namely the full purpose of the pork that it brings to Áli. In her instructions to Áli, Hlaðgerðr states that cutting up this pork and leaving it on the path behind him will prevent Nótt from pursuing him. Though Hlaðgerðr does not explain how it will do so, one possibility is that the dog — whose ability to break through the wall of Nótt's cave with its muzzle is an indication of its formidable physicality — would linger on the path to eat the pork, and that Nótt would be deterred by its presence there.[60] The appearance of a dog with the primary function of obstructing an antagonist's pursuit of the protagonist finds broad resonance in several other Snow White variants, though this is usually manifested in one of two ways: the compassionate executioner's killing of the dog in place of the heroine;[61] or the consumption of poisoned food by the dog instead of the heroine.[62] This latter manifestation is of particular interest, even though a connection may not be immediately apparent due to the lack of harmful food in the saga episode. During his identification of the *Ephesiaca*, written by Xenophon of Ephesus in the second century, as a Snow White variant, Graham Anderson suggested that an episode from this ancient tale, involving the heroine Anthia surviving her imprisonment in a pit with several dangerous dogs thanks to the regular feeding of the dogs by a sympathetic captor, shared a specific function with the instances in Böklen's collection of the consumption of poisoned food by a dog.[63] Even though the *Ephesiaca* episode does not involve the self-sacrificing consumption of harmful food, and even though its dogs are more dangerous than those found in Böklen's variants, Anderson considered these narratives to share the same underlying idea: the dog must be fed, or dire consequences will follow. Anderson regarded this shared idea as a significant piece of evidence for the affinity of the *Ephesiaca* with the Snow White folktale, and his suggestion is important for our discussion because it raises the possibility that this same idea underpins Hlaðgerðr's instructions to Áli regarding her dog; in Áli's case, failure to leave the pork behind on the path for the dog to eat would lead to Nótt being able to pursue him.[64] This would account for the significance of the otherwise unexplained pork, and reinforce the implication that Hlaðgerðr's dog, like the dogs in the *Ephesiaca* episode, can be dangerous. Hlaðgerðr's dog may therefore be a version of a Snow White element that stems back to the second century at the latest, and is also found, in a very different form, in some more modern Snow White variants.

After Áli's escape from Nótt's cave, he enters the kingdom of Tartary for the first time. This constitutes entry into a new social sphere, and a strong case can be made for it as an Adoption episode, not least because a change in 'situation, status, and environment' is crucial

---

[59] See motifs B291.2.2 and B421 in Boberg, *Motif-Index of Early Icelandic Literature*, pp. 46, 47.

[60] If the pork is intended to be consumed, it is unlikely to be by Nótt, whose diet is shown to consist of the flesh of horses and humans.

[61] Böklen's collection contains ten variants in which a dog fulfils this function. These variants come from Scandinavia (*dän.*, *norw. 2.*, *schwed.*, *isl.*), the Iberian peninsula (*port. 3.*, *cat.*), Italy (*lig.*, *tosc. 2.*, *abruzz.*) and Romania (*rum. 2.*). Different animals sometimes fulfil this function in other variants, but dogs are by far the most common.

[62] In the Polish and Russian variants in Böklen's collection (*poln.* and *russ.* respectively), an enchanted apple meant for the princess is eaten by a loyal dog. A Sicilian variant (*sic. 2.*) also contains this motif, but in that tale, the animal is a cat and the poisoned item of food is a cake.

[63] Anderson, *Fairytale in the Ancient World*, pp. 52, 55. The *Ephesiaca* episode can be found in *Longus: Daphnis and Chloe. Xenophon of Ephesus: Anthia and Habrocomes*, ed. and trans. by Jeffrey Henderson (Cambridge, MA: Harvard University Press, 2009), pp. 318–21 [IV.6.1–7].

[64] It is perhaps no coincidence that Nótt later lays her curse on Áli by reaching him in a dream, rather than in person.

to the heroine's escape from hostility in both Part 1 and Part 2 — the Adoption episode being, according to Jones' structure, the heroine's only escape in Part 1.[65] It is in this Tartary episode that Áli constructs a new identity for himself and adopts the name *Stutthéðinn*, meaning 'Short-Pelt' or 'Short-Cloak', possibly foreshadowing the animalistic transformation yet to come. He is accepted in the court and soon proves his worth by leading Þornbjǫrg's army to victory over the invading Indian force. In so doing, he gains Þornbjǫrg's hand in marriage. The military role for which Áli volunteers is a demonstration of the proof of his worth, not dissimilar to how the Grimms' Sneewittchen makes herself useful by doing the housework for the dwarfs whose house she discovers. A hero leading an army to victory on behalf of a king or queen (whose kingdom the hero does not necessarily need to be from) is not in itself an unusual course of action for a hero in medieval romance, but its functional significance — and by extension the plausibility of reading Áli's entry into Tartary as an Adoption episode — is heightened by the fact that it immediately follows the episodes of Jealousy and Expulsion.

At the pinnacle of Áli's adoption into Tartary, the night of his wedding to its maiden-king, Þornbjǫrg, he is cursed for a second time. Though the persecutor this time is Blátǫnn's brother Glóðarauga, it may still be viewed as the first step in a Renewed Jealousy episode. The reason for Glóðarauga's curse is in fact the same as Blátǫnn's, albeit with much stronger grounds — namely Áli's mistreatment of Blátǫnn (through his fatal counter-curse) — and this new curse may be read as a dramatic continuation of the first, as it puts Áli in greater physical danger, due to his being hunted as a wolf. Similarly, the wolf-transformation must be considered to constitute a third Expulsion episode; in line with the general affinity of wolves with outlaws,[66] Áli is this time driven out of human society altogether, not just the English court. He is rescued and adopted for a second time by his foster-mother, Hildr, when she recognises his eyes in those of the wolf cornered by King Ríkarðr's hunters, saves his life and brings him home. When he subsequently emerges from the wolf-skin, rather like a child released from the womb, it is tempting to read the episode as a deliberate evocation of Hildr's ritual labour earlier in the saga, when the adoption motif appeared for the first time.

4.iii. Structure: Renewed Jealousy, Expulsion and Death

This same generic pattern, of combined Jealousy and Expulsion with ever-higher stakes, is also applied to Nótt's curse. Nótt's motivation is stronger than Blátǫnn's and Glóðarauga's, as she claims revenge for two perceived wrongs: for Áli's earlier escape from her and for his mistreatment of Glóðarauga (again through his fatal counter-curse). The Expulsion aspect of Nótt's curse is once again clear in two ways: in social terms, he is shunned by most humans on account of his stench; and in geographical terms, the search for the cure takes him through Africa and Asia to Jǫtunoxi's kingdom at the extreme fringes of the world. The manifestation of Nótt's hostility also raises the stakes once again: while Áli faced the threat

---

[65] Jones, 'The Structure of *Snow White*', p. 173. Áli's visit to Hlaðgerðr's cottage, which takes place after he is expelled but before he reaches Nótt, might seem like an Adoption episode at first glance, but he does not stay there for any meaningful period of time. His entry to Tartary is a far more plausible alternative.

[66] See, for instance, Eleanor Rosamund Barraclough, 'Inside Outlawry in *Grettis saga Ásmundarsonar* and *Gísla saga Súrssonar*: Landscape in the Outlaw Sagas', *Scandinavian Studies*, 82 (2010), 365–88 (p. 367), and Marion Poilvez, 'Access to the Margins, Outlawry and Narrative Spaces in Medieval Icelandic Outlaw Sagas', *Brathair*, 12 (2012), 115–36 (pp. 121–22). On the connection between the connected social and geographic aspects of outlawry more widely, see, for instance, Kirsten Hastrup, *Culture and History in Medieval Iceland: An Anthropological Analysis of Structure and Change* (Oxford: Clarendon, 1985).

of death while in wolf-form, Nótt's curse makes his death inevitable should he fail to escape within ten years. On top of this, Áli's immobile and festering state during his incapacitation reinforces the likelihood that this represents a Death episode. Despite the fact that Áli neither dies nor becomes comatose, his physical state mirrors that of the corpse of Snjófríðr, who was discussed in Section 2: both are said to rot with a great *ópefr* ('stench').[67] In other words, Áli's deteriorating illness has physical symptoms that are associated with death elsewhere in Old Norse literature, reinforcing the likelihood that his illness was an adequate allomotif for the theme of death.

The escalation of threat is an important part of the repetition of attacks on the hero or heroine in Snow White variants, given that one of the later attacks must cause the Death episode. Because of the strong generic similarities between the curses of Blátǫnn, Glóðarauga and Nótt, any differences between them are all the more pronounced. We have already seen the increase in the curser's motivation, but another key pattern is the diminishing power of Áli's counter-curses: against Blátǫnn he issues a successful counter-curse; against Glóðarauga he issues a successful counter-curse which results in a counter-counter-curse on him; and against Nótt in his dream, he can make no reply at all. Nótt's curse catches Áli at a moment of uttermost vulnerability; he is unable to avoid her paranormal attack or to articulate a reply in his state of slumber. In terms of narrative construction, these different sets of markers feeding into the progression of the three generically similar curses are indications of deliberate literary craft, and may also be reflective of the strong familiarity that the saga author had with the Snow White tale-type, as well as his confidence in adapting it. Steven Swann Jones, commenting on variants which contain an additional cycle of persecution after the heroine's revival, remarks that 'these longer versions, by incorporating a third cycle of persecution, further support the idea that these cycles of persecution are units of dramatic structure apparent to narrators, who may double or treble them in the story'.[68] *Ála flekks saga* does in fact have an additional post-revival curse which will be discussed below, but here it is sufficient to note Jones' acknowledgement of the structural flexibility that different Snow White variants can have. In essence, Glóðarauga's curse may be read as 'Renewed Jealousy, Expulsion and Adoption', while Nótt's curse may be read as a 'Renewed Jealousy, Expulsion and Death' episode, and this repetition of the same 'units of dramatic structure' seems to be part of the deliberate adaptation of the tale-type.

Alongside this structural repetition, Jǫtunoxi could be considered a second manifestation of the compassionate executioner motif. The wounds that Nótt inflicts on Áli in his dream can only be healed by her brothers, one of whom, Jǫtunoxi, holds utter dominion over the other two, who possess the healing ointment and only apply it at his command. The implicit assumption behind the escape clause that Nótt puts in her curse seems to be that Jǫtunoxi will never agree to heal Áli, presumably because Áli has already had two of their trollish siblings killed, a point Jǫtunoxi raises when he finally realises Áli's identity in chapter 16. In other words, Nótt's curse holds the implicit intention for Jǫtunoxi to be Áli's executioner, whether actively or by simply refusing to heal him before his life expires.[69] In choosing to grant Áli life, he fulfils the specific function of a compassionate executioner, even though compassion is technically never a motivation for his actions.

---

[67] *Ágrip af Nóregskonungasögum*, p. 6.
[68] Jones, 'The Structure of *Snow White*', pp. 173, 176–77.
[69] A parallel can be drawn here with *Haralds rímur Hringsbana*, in which Jǫtunoxi's equivalent figure — the only one who is able to heal the hero's wounds, according to the curse — is Hermóðr's sister. In that tale, Hermóðr

4.iv. Structure: Exhibition and Resuscitation

Probably one of the most significant reasons that the saga's relationship with the Snow White tale-type has previously gone unnoticed is the lack of an obvious Exhibition episode, which is the most recognisable and iconic feature of the tale-type. Although Áli lies helpless throughout his protracted Death episode, the saga contains little overt indication that he is ever on display. However, it is intriguing that Nótt's curse forces Þornbjǫrg to travel so widely in search of a cure, scouring first the northern hemisphere, then Africa and finally Asia, all the while with Áli in tow.[70] Áli is thus implicitly exhibited to the whole of the known world whilst in his death-like state. Indeed, though he emits so foul a stench that only Þornbjǫrg can bear to attend to him, there is no indication that Áli is hidden away during their travels. On the contrary, when the couple arrives in India, its ruler, Earl Álfr, goes down to the shore to meet them, and, after greeting both Áli and Þornbjǫrg, we are told that he 'verðr þó hryggr við þat at Áli er svá litt haldinn' ('becomes distressed that Áli was in such a bad way'). In other words, the earl learns of Áli's condition not through a description or report, but by actually seeing him. Furthermore, the travels of the incapacitated Áli also fulfil a fundamental aspect of the Exhibition episode, namely that the Exhibition is inevitably tied to the Death episode by its very nature as a public display of the protagonist's ongoing state of death. The search for a cure for Áli, with Áli himself in tow, places primary emphasis on his ongoing state of death. There are hints, then, that the travels of Þornbjǫrg and Áli might constitute a reflex of an Exhibition episode, even if it is treated rather briefly and obliquely.

Áli's Resuscitation is similarly understated, to the point of being cursory. Few details are provided about his healing process, other than that the cure is an ointment possessed by Leggr and Liðr, two of the troll-family's siblings who are otherwise entirely insignificant (and the only two who are not killed, because their role is so minor that they are never hostile to Áli). It is unclear how long the healing process takes, but it does not appear to be very long. There is little more that needs to be said about this episode other than that Áli becomes a fully active character again afterwards — he participates in the attack on Jǫtunoxi's hall not long after he is healed — thereby emphasising, by contradistinction, his utter lack of agency in his earlier state of incapacitation.

Following Áli's revival, Jǫtunoxi places the saga's sixth curse on him. This curse seems to be the most out-of-place, as it breaks the pattern of increasing peril. It is, as discussed in Section 3, a different sort of curse to the other three, rather more similar to the curses in *Hálfdanar saga Eysteinssonar* and *Hjálmþés saga*, in which a hero will have no peace until he finds a certain woman. In terms of the Snow White typology, it is in fact not problematic; as mentioned earlier, Jones notes that that some Snow White variants contain another cycle

---

explicitly states his expectation that she will have Haraldr hanged (in other words, playing the role of executioner), though, as in *Ála flekks saga*, Haraldr uses disguise and trickery to get himself healed (as well as threat of rape, something Áli does not do).

[70] In medieval cosmography, the known world was often represented according to a tripartite division — Europe, Africa and Asia; this idea was derived from classical tradition. This tripartite division is visually encoded in one particular type of map which is found in medieval manuscripts from many European countries, including Iceland; this map is referred to as the 'T-O map', so called because, within the circular representation of the world, the three continents are approximately depicted as one semi-circle (Asia) and two quadrants (Europe and Africa), with the three bodies of water dividing the continents (the Mediterranean, the Nile and the Don) collectively forming a 'T' shape. For a detailed study of cosmographical thought in medieval Norway and Iceland, see Rudolf Simek, *Altnordische Kosmographie: Studien und Quellen zu Weltbild und Weltbeschreibung in Norwegen und Island vom 12. bis zum 14. Jahrhundert* (Berlin: de Gruyter, 1990).

Curse number	Relation to Marriage
1	Blátǫnn curses Áli to be married to the troll-wife Nótt.
3(a), 3(b)	Glóðaraugr curses Áli on his wedding night, before he can consummate his marriage.
5	While Áli is incapacitated by Nótt's curse, his wife Þornbjǫrg travels the world to find a cure. The cure is secured by Þornbjǫrg, under a pseudonym, offering herself to Jǫtunoxi in marriage; his slaying of Nótt, his sister and the performer of the curse, is one of the conditions of their marriage.
6	Jǫtunoxi curses Áli when his wedding-feast is turned into a hall-burning. The curse involves inflicting Áli with a wanderlust that separates him from his wife, and is lifted when Áli finds Hlaðgerðr and acts as her marriage-giver.

of persecution after the heroine's revival, representing additional manifestations of 'units of dramatic structure apparent to narrators'.[71] Furthermore, although the sixth curse feels out-of-place with the rest of the tightly structured saga — including, for instance, Áli's isolated fight against a giant[72] — it may in fact have a deeper thematic meaning. Jones notes that

> the structural pattern of episodes in "Snow White" recapitulates the personal development of the heroine; in other words, the sequence of episodes is structured to correspond to the basic trials and transitions of the maturing young woman in order to illustrate for the audience the process of maturation.[73]

The three main watersheds are adolescence, leaving home and marriage.[74] In other words, Jones suggests that structural repetition — a dominant narrative feature in *Ála flekks saga* — is interlinked with the theme of maturation. It is therefore appropriate that in *Ála flekks saga*, all four curses upon Áli relate in some way to marriage, either as part of the motivation, the resolution or the curse itself, as can be seen in the table above (with curse numbers corresponding to Roberts' table in Section 3).

The manifestation of Jǫtunoxi's curse, though awkward in generic terms, makes some sense in thematic terms. While the first curse threatens Áli with an undesirable marriage and the third and fifth curses test his marriage to Þornbjǫrg, the sixth curse does not put Áli in a marriage situation at all. Instead, it sees Áli essentially assuming the role of substitute father in marrying Hlaðgerðr off, marking the first time he plays a parental function in the saga. This prefigures his eventual succession in the final chapter of the saga, which forms part of the Resolution episode.

---

[71] Jones, 'The Structure of *Snow White*', pp. 173, 176–77. One such text containing an additional post-revival persecution is Böklen's *norw. 1.*, which, as noted in footnote 6 above, also contains animal-transformations through the use of skins.

[72] The fact that this giant is named Kolr ('Coal') is perhaps reflective of another deep-rooted Snow White connection, especially given that another minor character in the saga has the name 'Rauðr' ('Red'). The colours red and black, as well as white, are of great symbolic importance in many Snow White variants. Anderson has also noted that names relating to two of these colours, this time white and red, are found in the *Ephesiaca* (Anderson, *Fairytale in the Ancient World*, p. 51), in the form of the servants Leucon ('White') and Rhode ('Rose').

[73] Jones, 'The Structure of *Snow White*', p. 177.

[74] Jones, 'The Structure of *Snow White*', pp. 177–79.

4.v. Structure: Resolution

The Resolution episode of *Ála flekks saga* is straightforward, describing the happy ending of the protagonist's marriage that is customary in both fairy-tales and medieval romances, and the description of their royal progeny that is customary in the latter. In *Ála flekks saga*, the Resolution is compounded by the odd fact that Áli and Þornbjǫrg get married again in chapter 18, despite having already done so in chapter 8, when they had formalised everything but their marital consummation. It is possible that their first marriage was considered incomplete because they did not consummate it, but in any case, it is striking that they hold what seem to be the same wedding celebrations again, albeit in England rather than in Tartary this time. It gives Áli the rare distinction of experiencing major life events twice, with one forming a full experience and the other an incomplete version of that experience; he has two births (one regular, the other re-enacted), two weddings (one unconsummated, the other properly consummated) and, eventually, two deaths (one a prolonged state of near-death, the other, at the very end of the saga, a natural death).

5. Conclusion

The sum of the above structural analysis is outlined in the table below, with the saga's particular modifications to the Snow White structure in square brackets. Taking the saga as a whole, then, there can be little doubt that the entire narrative tightly follows Jones' nine-episode typological structure. This is emphasised by the fact that not only do all the nine episodes appear in *Ála flekks saga*, but they do so in exactly the same sequence as they are outlined in Jones' structure. In view of this, as well as the methodical use of the *álög* motif, it is extremely unlikely that *Ála flekks saga*'s close adherence to the Snow White tale-type is coincidental. Although the most recognisable episodes depicting the protagonist's Exhibition and Resuscitation are treated rather perfunctorily, this may simply suggest that Snow White tales circulating in Iceland in the late medieval period treated the death-and-resuscitation arc in very general terms. Therefore, because of its close and numerous structural parallels to the Snow White tale-type, *Ála flekks saga* must be considered to represent the clearest Snow White variant in the extant corpus of medieval Icelandic literature. Furthermore, the saga must also be regarded as one of the earliest known literary Snow White variants in the world, and it serves as a *terminus ante quem* for the transmission of the Snow White tale-type into Iceland; the tale-type must have entered Iceland, whether in oral or literary form, by the time the saga was composed in the late fourteenth or early fifteenth century.

Snow White episode	Event in *Ála flekks saga*	Chapter nos in *Ála flekk saga*
1. Origin	Áli's conception, exposure and return to the English court	1–3
2. Jealousy	Blátǫnn's curse	4
3. Expulsion	Consequent departure from the English court to the wild to find Nótt	5
4. Adoption	New identity in Tartary	6–8
5. Renewed Jealousy [Expulsion and Adoption]	Gloðarauga's curse and consequent wolf-transformation	8–11
6. [Renewed Jealousy, Expulsion and] Death	Nótt's curse and Áli's consequent physical decay	12–15
7. Exhibition	Þornbjǫrg's travels across the world in search of a cure, with Áli in tow	14
8. Resuscitation	Áli healed by Leggr and Liðr	15
(Extra cycle of persecution)	Jǫtunoxi's curse and Áli's consequent departure to Scythia to find Hlaðgerðr	16–17
9. Resolution	Marriages and descendants	18–19

Wise Aggressors and Steadfast Victims:
The Shift in Christian Feminine Ideals from Old to Middle English Religious Poetry

Judith Kaup

Introduction

In this essay I explore the shift in the depiction of ideal Christian feminine virtues which takes place in the transition from Old to Middle English religious poetry. A brief analysis of the Old English poems *Judith*, *Elene*, and *Juliana* illustrates emerging differences in the treatment of the topics of group identity, the common good, and the relationship between worldly and spiritual power.[1] Further examination of these topics with regard to the virgin martyr legends that gained popularity in the Middle English period reveals a trend in the depiction of saintly women. The politically influential and temporally powerful female saints of the heroic tradition are superseded by equally strong but unworldly holy women. I propose that this shift is connected to a broader change in ideals of Christian living, which first emerged in the Benedictine reform movement and was further enhanced in the Gregorian reform.

Judith, *Elene* and *Juliana* are representative of two types of Christian narratives, one presenting a world where natural kin and kin in faith are identical, and where power and worldly authority reside with this kin-group; the other a situation where the only possibility to achieve Christian perfection lies outside all worldly spheres and ties. While the first type shows close affinity to the heroic tradition and represents pre-reform ideals, the latter strictly distinguishes religious and secular ideals in accordance with the ideology of the reform movement. Though the dating of all three poems is notoriously difficult, it is likely that the Cynewulfian poems *Elene* and *Juliana* were composed some time between 750 and 850, while *Judith* is probably of a slightly later date.[2] Therefore, I do not intend to establish a strictly linear development from one type of Christian narrative to the other within the Old English period. Instead, it seems prudent to present the differences between these texts as examples of

---

[1] Unless otherwise stated, quotations of Old English poetry are from *The Anglo-Saxon Poetic Records: A Collective Edition*, ed. by George Philip Krapp and Elliott Van Kirk Dobbie, 6 vols (New York: Columbia University Press, 1931–53): *Juliana*, ASPR, III, 113–33; *Elene*, ASPR, II, 67–102. *Judith*, ed. by Mark Griffith (Exeter: Exeter University Press, 1997).

[2] R. D. Fulk, *A History of Old English Metre* (Philadelphia: University of Pennsylvania Press, 1992), p. 368, reaches the conclusion that Cynewulf must have composed between 750 and 850. *Judith*, ed. by Griffith, pp. 44-47, suggests a late ninth- to early tenth-century date for *Judith*.

synchronic cultural variation which nevertheless herald a trend in religious poetry. This trend later becomes predominant and manifest in the rising popularity of narratives of the virgin martyr type in late eleventh- and early twelfth-century England.

Unlike most scholarship on the role of women in the religious life of Anglo-Saxon and Norman England, my essay sets out from an analysis of the crucial elements of religious narrative which shed light on underlying beliefs and concepts of Christian perfection. Though my focus is on female Christian ideals, observations regarding the evaluation of worldly power, kinship ties, and virginity as a way of distancing oneself from the world, show trends in religious observance that hold true for both men and women. The changing ideals of religious life are reflected in the literary presentations of female Christian virtues and the portrayal of exemplary, saintly Christian women. This change is closely related to a wider tendency to strictly differentiate between institutionalised religious living and religious devotion within a secular setting, which started with the Benedictine reform in the late tenth century and gained momentum after the Gregorian reform in the late eleventh century. I start with a few observations on the development of women's religious lives in Anglo-Saxon England, pointing out their relevance for my discussion of *Judith*, *Juliana* and *Elene*. After that I close with a glance at the virgin martyr tales and suggest reasons for the genre's rise in popularity in the Early Middle English period.

Developments in the Religious Life of Women in Anglo-Saxon England

In the Anglo-Saxon period, different models of religious life for women coexisted. However, Foot observes how a clear distinction was drawn between cloistered religious and those living in the world after the monastic revolution of Edgar's reign.[3] Vernacular texts highlight this distinction by using different terms for cloistered women (*mynecena*) on the one hand, and on the other vowesses (*nunnan*) who remained in the secular sphere but devoted their lives to spiritual endeavours.[4] The desire to clearly differentiate between these categories of religious life is in line with the reformers' intention to highlight the superiority of the monastic life. They wanted to make clear whether a woman belongs to the more prestigious category of *mynecena* or not. The concept of the cloistered woman is 'an invention of tenth-century circumstances, arising from the novel imposition of Benedictine ideals, notably [...] the separation and claustration of women'.[5] Cubitt also stresses the far-reaching implications of the Benedictine reform movement and proposes that Ælfric's writings attempted to impose monastic standards upon the whole of society.[6] If monastic standards were supposed to serve as a model even for the laity, it is clear that anyone aspiring to religious perfection would necessarily have to do so in a monastic setting. This devaluation of alternative Christian lifestyles is at odds with heroic Christian role models as presented in *Judith* and *Elene*. Cubitt also suggests that 'the reformers were less interested in promoting women's religious life than in controlling it'. Such a climate would obviously favour cloistered female devotion, as it ensures regulation and control over devout women. Strong, powerful, independent and, most importantly, worldly women as role models would counteract this purpose. Furthermore, the

---

[3] Sarah Foot, *Veiled Women*, 2 vols (Aldershot: Ashgate, 2000), I, 101.
[4] Foot, *Veiled Women*, I, 200.
[5] Foot, *Veiled Women*, I, 203.
[6] Catherine Cubitt, 'Virginity and Misogyny in Tenth- and Eleventh-Century England', *Gender and History*, 12 (2000), 1-32 (p. 2).

idea of spiritual kindred, which is so important in *Juliana*, is also propagated by Ælfric. It is closely connected to the ideology of virginity, which naturally inhibits worldly kinship ties.[7] A virgin martyr, disconnected from her natural family and opposed to forming worldly ties by marriage, is of course a perfect representation of these ideals. Virginity gains additional value in the discourse of the Benedictine reform. Though always the height of Christian perfection and deserving the hundred-fold heavenly reward, it now also signifies the monastic life. The separation of the virgin from all things worldly, including natural kinship ties, becomes at least as important as her bodily purity. This new use and interpretation of virginity in the reform context clearly differs from the pre-reform situation, when the divide between secular and monastic devotion was not as deep. A monastic, possibly virginal, life was only one of various ways to lead an exemplary Christian life. Luecke points out that neither Bede nor Aldhelm spoke derogatively of nuns who were not virgins.[8] Although Aldhelm's work on virginity was to be very influential in the Benedictine reform[9] and probably used to propagate the aforementioned Benedictine ideal of virginal female religious in a regulated, cloistered setting, Luecke observes how Aldhelm, though valuing virginity higher than chastity in principle, still stresses that a devout chaste nun may actually achieve greater holiness than her proud virginal sister.[10] When Aldhelm addresses the nuns of Barking as his equals in religious devotion in his preface to the prose *De Virginitate* and sees them as fellow fighters in the struggle for the evangelisation of England, this suggests that an active involvement of the nuns in affairs outside their convent was welcomed in the seventh century.[11] Total disentanglement from all worldly matters was not yet the ideal, even for a virgin.

Let us keep the developments briefly sketched here in mind, and turn to the analysis of the three Old English poems and determine their relationship to the reform movements.

Judith, Juliana, and Elene — Female Saints Grounded in the Heroic Tradition

Here, I analyse the poems with a view to their evaluation of power, kinship, and violence. The treatment of these crucial topics reveals the poems' relationships to ideals of Christian living, showing clearly whether Christian perfection can be achieved in a secular setting or depends on total renunciation of all worldly ties and values.

Judith is portrayed as wise, divinely chosen, and a responsible leader of the Hebrews. The repeated emphasis on her wisdom and good counsel make her a paragon of Anglo-Saxon feminine virtues.[12] This, together with her special connection to the divine and the fact that her

---

[7]   Cubitt, 'Virginity and Misogyny', p. 18.

[8]   Janemarie Luecke, 'The Unique Experience of Anglo-Saxon Nuns', in *Medieval Religious Women. Volume 2: Peaceweavers*, ed. by Lillian Thomas Shank and John A. Nichols (Kalamazoo: Cistercian Publications, 1987), pp. 55–65 (p. 56).

[9]   Mechthild Gretsch, *The Intellectual Foundations of the Benedictine Reform*, Cambridge Studies in Anglo-Saxon England, 25 (Cambridge: Cambridge University Press, 1999), p. 184, shows the immense influence of Aldhelm, particularly of his *De Virginitate*, on members of the Benedictine reform movement.

[10] Luecke, 'Unique Experience', p. 61.

[11] Christine Fell, *Women in Anglo-Saxon England* (Oxford: Blackwell, 1984), p. 109; Sarah Foot, '*Flores ecclesiae*: Women in Early Anglo-Saxon Monasticism', in *Female 'Vita Religiosa' between Late Antiquity and the High Middle Ages: Structures, Developments and Spatial Contexts*, ed. by Gert Melville and Anne Müller, Vita regularis. Abhandlungen, 47 (Zürich: Lit, 2011), pp. 173–86 (p. 173).

[12] Cf. the ideal as described in *Maxims I*, ASPR, iii, 156–62, ll. 84b–92b: 'ond wif geþeon leof mid hyre

actions always aim at the common good of her people,[13] makes her a representative of a 'hero of the tribe', that is a 'figure who is marked by extraordinary power and therefore functions as a mediator between the categories of human and divine'.[14] The aspect of usefulness for and inclusion in one's society which is expressed in the categories 'hero of the tribe' and 'hero outside the tribe' is also a crucial distinctive feature of the protagonists in the religious poetry surveyed here. Judith, although exceptional in her unfaltering trust and belief in God and the resulting courage and determination, is firmly situated within the social network of her people. Her killing of Holofernes is an act of salvation on behalf of all the Bethulians, and her deed not only heralds but brings about the Hebrews' victory over the Assyrians. Her success is proof that God cares for his people, as is made visible by the token of Holofernes' head. Bourquin sees Judith's actions as an example of a heroic chain structure, where the hero serves to catalyse the heroic potential of her/his community. As the hero heroises others, they can in turn heroise yet more people, resulting in a heroic chain which perpetuates the original courage of the hero.[15] However, the Bethulians are already called *sigefolc* (l. 152a) immediately after Judith's return and before they actually achieve victory on the battlefield, which makes the exemplary function of Judith's deed secondary. Furthermore, Judith addresses the men as *sigerofe hæleð* (l. 177b). While this could be interpreted as simple encouragement, she also explains (ll. 195b-198a) that:

> Fynd syndon eowere,
> gedemed to deaðe   ond ge dom agon,
> tir æt tohtan,   swa eow getacned hafað
> mihtig dryhten   þurh mine hand.

([The] enemies are yours, condemned to death, and you shall have fame, glory in battle, as has shown you [the] mighty lord through my hand.)

---

leodum, leohtmod wesan, rune healdan, rumheort beon meorum ond maþmum, meodorædenne for gesiðmægen symle æghwær eodor æþelinga ærest gegretan, forman fulle to frean hond ricene geræcan, ond him ræd witan boldagendum þæm ætsomne' ('and a woman shall thrive beloved amongst her people, be light-hearted, keep counsel, be generous with horses and treasures, at the mead-drinking always and everywhere in front of the warrior-band first greet the protector of nobles, put the first cup in the lord's hand, and know counsel for the both of them, the hall-rulers'). Note that the importance of counsel is mentioned twice. See also Elaine Tuttle Hansen, 'Women in Old English Poetry Reconsidered', *Michigan Academician*, 9 (1976), 109–17 (pp. 111–12) for women's role as counsellors. Cf. Fred C. Robinson, 'The Prescient Woman in Old English Literature', in *The Tomb of Beowulf and Other Essays on Old English*, ed. by Fred C. Robinson (Oxford: Blackwell, 1993), pp. 155–63 (pp. 157 on female counsel and 160 on Judith's depiction as typical Germanic wise woman).

[13] Hansen, 'Women in Old English Poetry', p. 111, observes that 'the queen's value is reflected in her noble conduct towards others' and highlights the importance of women for the stabilisation of society.

[14] Joseph F. Nagy, 'Beowulf and Fergus: Heroes of Their Tribes?', in *Connections Between Old English and Medieval Celtic Literature*, ed. by Patrick Ford and Karen G. Borst, Old English Colloquium Series, 2 (Berkeley: University of California, 1983), pp. 31–44 (p. 34). The term was originally coined by Marie-Louise Sjoestedt, *Dieux et Héros des Celts* (Paris: Leroux, 1940), pp. 79–121, and taken up by Nagy in his study of the Old English hero Beowulf and the early Irish hero Fergus.

[15] Guy Bourquin, 'The Lexis and Deixis of the Hero in Old English Poetry', in *Heroes and Heroines in Medieval English Literature*, ed. by Leo Carruthers (Cambridge: Brewer, 1994), pp. 1–18 (p. 10), explains the concept of the heroic chain: 'the Dobest of the genuine hero(ine) is his/her heroizing of fellow creatures (*Judith* 150–58, 171–79, 195–98): such heroizing takes heroism one step onwards beyond simply acting heroically for the sake of others (the heroic Dowel). Heroizing one's neighbours (heroic Dobest) means prodding them, through one's own example, to take their fate into their own hands, avail themselves of their own heroic aptitudes and become in their turn exemplary to still others. That the heroic chain is a circular one becomes still clearer at the end of the poem when the semiotic process works backwards: the warriors bring a complementary token back to Judith who in her turn attributes the glory of everything to God's own glory (332–46)'.

The statement clearly does not refer to a possibility or a likely event but is asserting that victory is already gained. While both *sigefolc* and *sigerofe* could be seen simply as conventional terms, the poet's careful and conscious use of epithets and terms throughout the poem suggests the relevance of his choice here as well. The military action is a fulfilment of the logic set in train by Judith's deed, not an imitation of her example. Judith's example does not call for courageous imitation — her deed has already demonstrated God's support for his people, and the victory on the battlefield has to be claimed, not won, by the Bethulians.

While Irving also observes the operation of a double structure (the exemplary deed of a hero leads to the subsequent following of his heroic example) in Old English, Middle High German and medieval Spanish literature,[16] he stresses how the 'continuity and transmission of heroic values'[17] is thematised in the poems he studies. In *Judith* the virtue transmitted by the heroine's deed is faith rather than heroic courage, as her people, once they have regained faith in God, can be certain of victory. Notwithstanding Judith's exemplary courage, the more important revelation for the Bethulians is God's unfaltering support of His people. Judith's announcement that God is gracious to them (l. 154) already results in an outburst of ecstatic joy before she even reveals Holofernes' head and shows the token of her heroic deed. It was their trust in God and subsequently in their own abilities that needed to be renewed. In the poem's effect on its audience, however, the exemplary function is paramount: the text demonstrates that a people that trusts in God's help will inevitably achieve victory. The point is brought home with utmost effectiveness by the double structure of the narrative (Judith kills Holofernes — the Bethulians kill the Assyrians), which shows that once firm trust in God's help is established, victory is already achieved. The message to the audience is an exhortation to have true faith in God. True faith can lead to heroic courage in battle, but the moral of the poem is also applicable to other spheres in life. Faith enables the believer to cope with the struggles of this world.

The absolute superiority of God's followers over the infidel is also apparent in the direction of violence in the poem. Contrary to the expectations raised by the initial depiction, which presents Holofernes and his men as aggressors, they are never given a chance to make good their threat against the Bethulians. Violence is a positive force, used to destroy God's enemies. Judith and her people wield the power to control the direction of violence. Violence thus features in the sense of the Old English noun *geweald* or the cognate German term *Gewalt*, which can express the power to direct or control action. This aspect is also present in the poem in the verb *gewealdan*, which is used to describe Judith's handling of Holofernes immediately before the fatal blows.[18] In this scene the power relations of the poem seem to be reversed: Judith, the intended victim, does with the former aggressor Holofernes as she pleases. He is in her power, an expression which uses *geweald~Gewalt* in both German and Old English.[19]

16 Edward B. Irving, Jr., 'Heroic Role-Models: Beowulf and Others', in *New Readings on Women in Old English Literature*, ed. by Helen Damico and A. Hennessey Olsen (Bloomington and Indianapolis: Indiana University Press, 1990), pp. 347–72.

17 Irving, 'Heroic Role Models', p. 370.

18 Cf. Joseph Bosworth and T. Northcote Toller, *An Anglo-Saxon Dictionary* (London: Oxford University Press, 1898), s. v. *geweald*: 'power, strength, might, efficacy'. Friedrich Kluge, *Etymologisches Wörterbuch der Deutschen Sprache*, 24th edn, rev. by Elmar Seebold (Berlin: de Gruyter, 2002), explains German *Gewalt* as an abstract verbal noun of the verb *walten*, a cognate of OE *wealdan*, going back to a Common Germanic root *wal-* with the meaning 'to be strong, to rule'.

19 Cf. *Elene*, ll. 610a–11a ('he wæs on þære cwene geweealdum'; 'he was in the power of the queen') and the German idiom *jemanden in der Gewalt haben* ('to have someone in one's power').

In fact, it is not a reversal but an epiphany of the power balance which was in operation all along. God is the 'highest judge', the supreme ruler, whose people can only be harmed by their own inadequacy, that is through a lack of belief and trust. To belong to God's people results in worldly as well as spiritual power and superiority. In *Judith*, group identity is not a complicated issue: the right group with respect to faith and power matches with Judith's kin group, the Hebrews.

Power also resides with the faithful in Cynewulf's *Elene*. The connection of worldly power and Christian faith is already established in the introductory sequence, which deals with the Emperor Constantine's conversion to Christianity. Faced with a large army of Huns, who far outnumber his troops, Constantine receives a vision of the cross, telling him to carry this 'sigores tacen' (l. 85a, 'sign of victory') into battle.[20] He follows this advice, whereupon the Roman troops achieve a miraculous victory. After learning about the Christian faith, the Emperor entrusts his mother Elene with leading a mission to the Holy Land to discover the cross of Christ. The main part of the poem is concerned with Elene's dealings with the Jew Judas, who at first stubbornly denies his knowledge of the whereabouts of the cross and has to be forced into co-operation. Once forcibly persuaded he is readily converted and becomes a fervent Christian. Elene names him Cyriacus and has him made bishop of Jerusalem. Judas' conversion is a central theme of the poem, and it has been suggested that *Elene* should really be renamed.[21] Schrader is convinced that Elene 'is not the central figure in the poem, despite its customary title. The actual hero is Judas Cyriacus, and the poem is about him in the way *Juliana* is about Juliana'.[22] In addition, Regan observes that 'Judas is clearly the poem's most complex character, and for modern readers nourished on psychological subtlety in characterisation he is probably the most attractive'.[23] Though true to an extent, such evaluations overlook Elene's essential importance as the initiator of most of the narrative's actions and the driving force behind Judas' conversion. However interesting Judas may be, he only exemplifies Elene's power to achieve her goals — without her determined and forceful treatment of him, he would not have accepted Christianity. Elene's role is indispensable and in line with her presentation as a type of *Ecclesia*.[24] Furthermore, her depiction as a strong, determined and authoritative figure underlines her regal character. The fact that she is a woman does not play an important role in the narrative, though it has some relevance for its typological reading, as women were viewed as best suited to being a type of the church. Elene's mission, which links two peoples across the sea, is reminiscent of the important role

---

[20] Note how the sign of Christ's spiritual victory becomes a sign of worldly, military victory. The easy conflation of both spheres, the spiritual and the worldly, is typical for the poem and others of its type.

[21] Rosemary Woolf, 'Saints' Lives', in *Continuations and Beginnings: Studies in Old English Literature*, ed. by Eric G. Stanley (London: Nelson, 1966), pp. 37–66 (p. 46). Jackson J. Campbell, 'Cynewulf's Multiple Revelations', in *The Cynewulf Reader*, ed. by Robert E. Bjork (New York: Routledge, 2001), pp. 229–50 (p. 229) states that 'it has been recognized by a number of people for a number of years that this arbitrary yet persistent title [i.e. *Elene*] is a grave misnomer. After absorbing the full impact of all 1300-odd lines of the poem, we are conscious that it is not a poem about Queen Elene at all, however important she may be as a part of the total structure. It is hoped that its next editor will have the courage to call it the *Invention of the Cross*, or something more appropriate'.

[22] Richard J. Schrader, *God's Handiwork: Images of Women in Early Germanic Literature* (London: Greenwood, 1983), p. 18.

[23] Catherine A. Regan, 'Evangelicism as the Informing Principle of Cynewulf's *Elene*', in *The Cynewulf Reader*, ed. by Robert E. Bjork (New York: Routledge, 2001), pp. 251–80 (p. 257) [first publ. *Traditio*, 29 (1973), 27–52].

[24] Stacy S. Klein, 'Reading Queenship in Cynewulf's *Elene*', *Journal of Medieval and Early Modern Studies*, 33 (2003), 47–89 (p. 49) mentions Elene's interpretation as a type of *Ecclesia* as the predominant critical reading. See also pp. 57 and 61.

of women in creating family bonds among different kin groups. Her description is typical of Old English queens and noblewomen. Her external appearance is not mentioned beyond ornamental attributes, which serve to highlight her regal status and by implication represent the power of her people and the orderly state of her society.[25] Elene is, like Judith, a leading figure and also holds a firmly established position within her society. She is Constantine's mother ('his modor', l. 214b), the 'kinswoman of the emperor' (l. 330b and l. 997a, 'caseres mæg'). Some critics have taken the stress on her kinship with Constantine and the frequent reference to her son in the poem as an attempt to diminish her importance, as it would portray her as a surrogate for Constantine.[26] However, Klein observes that it is part of a more general tendency of Cynewulf's to describe Elene as embedded within a firm network of social relations: 'with her son frequently in her thoughts, her own men always around her, and her regular correspondence with the imperial court, Elene is hardly ever alone or lacking in company'.[27] Far from diminishing her role, Cynewulf thus shows Elene to be in accord with Anglo-Saxon ideals, endowed with qualities desirable in an Anglo-Saxon queen. Klein points out that Cynewulf's preference for naming his female protagonist by the generic terms *cwen* or *hlæfdige* as opposed to the personal name *Elene* (which is most often used in the source) also suggests an interest in transforming Elene from a particular queen into a more generic exemplar of queenship, an image of female royalty whom Anglo-Saxon readers might view not simply as a phenomenon of a bygone Roman past but as a figure who might be found within their own Germanic world.[28]

This technique heightens the exemplary effect of the narrative, as it reduces the distance of the Anglo-Saxon audience from the historical plot. Elene is a good queen, always surrounded by and mindful of her kin and people. What is more, all her actions are driven by a concern for the greater good of her community, which by extension includes all Christians.[29] Terms underscoring her regal authority predominate: she is the *cwen* ('queen'),[30] *guðcwen* ('battle-queen'),[31] *sigecwen* ('victory-queen')[32] and *þeodcwen* ('queen of the people').[33] Her authority clearly extends to sovereign power even in Jerusalem, where her orders are obeyed immediately upon her arrival.

> Heht ða gebeodan   burgsittendum
> þam snoterestum   side ond wide
> geond Iudeas,   gumena gehwylcum

---

[25] I have discussed how Old English poetry uses the figure of the gold-adorned woman to represent intact social order and a thriving community in an as yet unpublished article, 'The Gold-Adorned Woman as a Symbol of Social Order'.

[26] Earl R. Anderson, 'Cynewulf's *Elene*: Manuscript Divisions and Structural Symmetry', *Modern Philology*, 72 (1974), 111–22 (p. 118); Gordon E. Whatley, 'The Figure of Constantine the Great', *Traditio*, 36 (1981), 161–202 (pp. 175–77).

[27] Klein, 'Reading Queenship', p. 69.

[28] Klein, 'Reading Queenship', p. 56.

[29] Campbell, 'Multiple Revelations', pp. 234–35, interprets her introduction in terms of her relationship to Constantine, and the stress on her queenship and absolute dedication to her mission as elements which enhance the 'feeling [...] that this "queen of Christians" is acting not for her own benefit or from personal motives but as an agent of divine power'.

[30] Lines 275b, 324a, 378b, 384b, 411b, 416b, 551b, 558b, 587b, 605a, 610b, 662a, 715b, 848b, 979b, 1017a, 1068a, 1129a, 1135a, 1151b, 1169a, 1204b.

[31] Lines 254a, 331a.

[32] Lines 260a, 997a.

[33] Line 1155b.

meðelhegende,   on gemot cuman
þa ðe deoplicost   dryhtnes geryno
þurh rihte æ   reccan cuðon.
Ða wæs gesamnod   of sidwegum
mægum unlytel,   þa ðe Moyses æ
reccan cuðon.

(Then she ordered the citizens to be bidden, the wisest far and wide throughout Judea, each one of the men, to be assembled, to come to a council, who most deeply knew the mysteries of the Lord by rightly interpreting the scriptures.)[34]

The way she is described when she awaits the assembly of wise men highlights all the essential features displaying her authority:

þrungon þa on þreate   þær on þrymme bad
in cynestole   caseres mæg,
geatolic guðcwen   golde gehyrsted.

(Then they thronged in a band where in power and authority on a throne the kinswoman of the emperor awaited them, the stately battle-queen, adorned with gold.)[35]

The passage unites regal attire, aspects of kinship, and the control of power and violence implicit in the term 'battle-queen' to present Elene as an embodiment of the perfect ruler. Epithets accentuating her power and regal appearance abound,[36] and there are additional descriptive references to her powerful status: she is 'sio rice cwen bald in burgum' (ll. 411b-412a, 'the powerful queen, ruling in cities'); 'sio þær hæleðum scead' (ll. 709b-710a, 'she ruled there over warriors'); and Judas is 'on þære cwene gewealdum' (ll. 610b, 'in the queen's power'). In addition, her actions also emphasise her authoritative position: she orders,[37] speaks[38] and teaches.[39] She also dispenses treasures to her 'new' people, thus cementing the bond between ruler and retainer.[40] Her ensuing exhortation to worship the true God shows how the act of treasure-giving, a typical feature of heroic society, is transferred to a Christian context. Here, the receiving of treasure calls for religious observance, not brave deeds of war. Her depiction as regal and community-minded is thus also in keeping with a typological reading. It is fitting that Elene as a type of *Ecclesia* should demand religious duties in exchange for the treasures. All her actions are directed at the furthering of the Christian faith, increasing her community and shielding it against the threats of the opposing forces. Her mission to discover the true cross of Christ is an act designed for the common good of all Christians, and the bit she has fashioned for her son's horse in accordance with Judas Cyriacus' advice is also an instrument furthering the forces of the righteous in their battle against evil.[41]

Elene uses violence, in the aforementioned sense of wielding her power to direct action, to achieve her aims when she orders the Jews to answer her questions. She has the authority to

---

[34] Lines 276a–84a.
[35] Lines 229a–331b.
[36] For example *ðære æðelan* (l. 545a, 'the noble one'); *tireeadig cwen* (l. 605a, 'glorious queen'); *arwyðan cwen* (ll. 1128b–29a, 'venerable queen'); *seo æðele* (l. 1130b, 'the noble one'); *cwen seleste* (l. 1169a, 'best queen').
[37] For example lines 276a, 278b, 412b.
[38] Examples being lines 285a, 287b, 332a–b, 403a–6a, 642a–b, 662a–b, 669a, 685a–b.
[39] For instance l. 1205a.
[40] Lines 1217b–26a.
[41] Lines 1173b–86a; ll. 1196a–1200b.

criticise their failure to accept the Messiah,[42] and she causes them confusion and distress by her anger and insistence on discovering the hiding place of the cross. The number of wise men thought to be competent to answer the queen's question dwindles, and the fear and confusion of the Jews grow until they finally hand over Judas as the most knowledgeable member of their community. Woolf sees it as a weakness of the narrative that Elene's treatment of Judas recalls the typical scenery of a passion and suggests that Judas' 'resistance, which is structurally that of a martyr, may arouse an unintended sympathy'.[43]

Regan questions Woolf's assumption that the sympathy the audience may feel for Judas is unintended, and offers a plausible reason for the parallels to a passion:

> in the traditional passion, the punishment meted out to the prisoner by the ruler is the prisoner's means of gaining sainthood. The same relationship between ruler and prisoner exists in the poem. Judas is a potential saint and Elene's punishment is the means by which he comes to acknowledge the Cross and thereby achieve sanctity.[44]

I believe the audience's possible sympathy with Judas is indeed intended and a vital element in furthering the didactic purpose of the poem, as he serves as a positive role model. His conflict exemplifies problems of group identity, which become especially visible in what I would define as a phase of transition from the kinship bonds constituting a heroic society to the spiritual bond prevalent in religious communities. Unlike in *Judith*, where these commitments are not in conflict, *Elene* addresses this problem, showing an awareness of possible difficulties posed by the concept of spiritual kinship. Judas' loyalty to his people — 'he fears that if the truth were known, the lineage (*æðelu*, 433) and religion of Israel would no longer rule the world'[45] — conflicts with his knowledge of the truth, which makes him a potential member of the spiritual community of Christians. Whereas in *Judith* the identity of the kinship group and the religious community overlap — the Hebrews are God's people and the Assyrians are God's enemies — *Elene* thematises the possibility that one has to forsake one's kin group in order to become a member of the — superior — spiritual community of Christians.[46]

In *Elene*, the Christian community is portrayed as superior in worldly as well as spiritual matters. All instances of violence in the poem, including the initial battle of Constantine against the Huns, yield positive results and promote the advancement of the Christian faith. As in *Judith*, violence is exclusively carried out against the unbelievers. A marked difference between the two texts is the effect violent action has on those afflicted: in *Elene*, the unbelievers are given a second chance, because they have the option to discover and embrace the true faith and thus become part of the community of Christians. The aim of violence is not the destruction but the conversion of the opposing party.[47] While they can initially belong to the 'right' or the 'wrong' group, just as in *Judith*, group identity in *Elene* is flexible, as it is

---

[42] Lines 288a–312b.

[43] Woolf, 'Saints' Lives', pp. 46–47.

[44] Regan, 'Evangelicism', pp. 258–59.

[45] Richard J. Schrader, *Old English Poetry and the Genealogy of Events*, Medieval Texts and Studies, 12 (East Lansing, Michigan: Colleagues Press, 1993), p. 45.

[46] We will see shortly how the prevalent importance of spiritual kinship in the family of Christ is already firmly established in *Juliana*, where the saint's loyalty towards her father or the obligations of the society she lives in are irrelevant when confronted with the demands of her identity as a Christian.

[47] Klein, 'Reading Queenship', p. 62, points out that 'the particular tactics that Elene uses to convert the Jews — the verbal denigration of their community and intellectual traditions, and the actual physical torture of their leader, Judas — is also implacably anchored in a sentiment that was widespread throughout Anglo-Saxon England: that violence was both a precondition for and an intrinsic part of strengthening and extending Christian *imperium*'.

defined solely by acceptance or rejection of the Christian faith. This aspect is highlighted by using the term *þeodcwen* (l. 1155b, 'queen of the people') for Elene towards the end of the poem, when at least a substantial number of Jews have been converted. It is employed in the passage which relates how Elene reflects upon the best use for the newly discovered nails of the cross:

> þeodcwen ongan
> þurh gastes gife   georne secan
> nearwe geneahhe,   to hwan hio þa næglas selost
> ond deorlicost gedon meahte,   dugoðum to hroðer,
> hwæt þæs wære dryhtnes willa.

(The queen of the people by the grace of the spirit eagerly pondered exactly to what purpose she could best and most worthily put the nails, for the good of the people, [and] what would be God's will with regard to that.)[48]

While the term *þeodcwen* may not necessarily carry strong associations with 'people' and *þeod* can also be a simple intensifier, I suggest it is used purposefully here. As the scene stresses Elene's concern with the common good of her people, it seems fitting to call her the 'people's queen'. In addition, the frequent use of the term 'the people' with reference to the converted Jews in the last passage of the poem also suggests a conscious employment of *þeod* to define the newly forged spiritual kin of believers. Elene's people are defined in accordance with their religious beliefs. They are not an ethnically defined group but include everyone who belongs to the community of the faithful. Thus, all Christians belong to Elene's people, which is true both on a historical and a tropological level, concurrently reflecting her roles as worldly queen and type of *Ecclesia*.

Like *Judith*, *Elene* thematises group identity and leadership. However, whereas good and bad leadership are exemplified in *Judith* by Judith and Holofernes respectively, *Elene* features only positive leading figures: the Christian queen who embodies an ideal Anglo-Saxon noblewoman and her son, the willingly converted Emperor Constantine. The opposing side is depicted as lacking any authoritative leader at all. Bjork observes 'a confusion or lack of focus in the *dryht* of hell'[49] as a typical feature in its description in Old English verse saints' lives. This concept is employed to some extent in the description of both the Huns and the Jews. The king of the Huns remains a shadowy figure in the background who lacks distinctive features.[50] The Jews are portrayed as a rather disorganised group without a distinguishable leader. Only after Judas' conversion, when he takes on a leading role as bishop Cyriacus, is order achieved.[51] The chaotic state of a pre-conversion society is replaced by the functional structures of the Christian community. The fault of the Jews is their stubborn refusal to join what they should recognise as the right group. This is made clear by the example of Judas, who needs Elene's aggressive conversion approach to accept what he has known to be the truth all along.

[48] Lines 1155b–59b.
[49] Robert E. Bjork, *The Old English Verse Saints' Lives* (Toronto: University of Toronto Press, 1985), p. 127.
[50] Lines 32b, 49b.
[51] The distribution of order and disorder is also visible in the speech patterns of the respective parties. Carol Braun Pasternack, *The Textuality of Old English Poetry*, Cambridge Studies in Anglo-Saxon England, 13 (Cambridge: Cambridge University Press: 1995), p. 105, points out how 'the contrast between Judas's and the devil's speech pattern' in the confrontation between Judas and the devil in ll. 902a–52a 'is the contrast between the disorder of evil and the clarity of good'.

It is worth noting that all the actions in *Elene* are significant in matters of group identity, group formation and the achievement of a common good. Bourquin recognises a heroic chain structure in *Elene* and specifies that each of Constantine, Elene and Cyriacus 'is made to develop his own capabilities to the full but is also recaptured at a higher level in a communal process where each hero is generated by some other and generates the next in succession'.[52] Only as a functional member or leader of a group can the individual Christian in the poem develop his or her full potential. Constantine achieves victory for his army under the sign of the cross and then strives to help the community of Christians by sending Elene on a mission to discover the true cross. Elene is the protagonist in which responsibility for kin group and Christian community merge. Though at first glance Judas' conversion seems to be an individual act, it is really an event serving the common good. Elene forces Judas to reveal the location of the cross in order to advance the good of all Christians, and her desire to do so is initially caused by her kinship with Constantine. The action is thus motivated by the demands of her natural group and her spiritual community. Judas' conversion results in a positive effect on his ethnic kin (the conversion of the Jews is a positive effect within the logic of the narrative), and his subsequent role as bishop is one of responsibility for his new spiritual group. The Christian faith is a unifying force which not only enhances social order and group coherence but also endows its members with the power to direct action, and perpetuates itself by communal actions. In *Elene*, the community of Christians is identical with the worldly social group of Elene. Of course on an allegorical level this is only natural, as the queen is a type of *Ecclesia*. However, it is still important that even on a strictly historical level of interpretation there is total agreement of the dominant worldly power with the divine power. To be a Christian means to be part of a community desirable in all regards, worldly and spiritual.

The exemplary character of *Elene* is directed predominantly at the audience. The Christians are portrayed as the good, functional group which operates according to the patterns familiar to the audience, thus making it easier to embrace the values transmitted. The merging of ideals and structures of heroic society with Christian values is clearly visible.

Cynewulf's virgin martyr tale *Juliana* introduces a shift from the easy conflation of worldly and spiritual power and the conciliation of heroic and Christian values. *Juliana* is, on the one hand, still grounded in heroic tradition, but is on the other hand critical of the values of traditional heroic narrative. Magennis highlights how *Juliana* exploits the language of Germanic heroism only to denounce it and show the audience the superior value of Christian ideals.[53] Cynewulf's poem is the first vernacular English example of a virgin martyr tale.[54] It is representative of a type of religious narrative in England which propagates very different values of Christian living from those illustrated in the religious poems of the heroic tradition. This type of narrative, which puts its saintly protagonist squarely outside of the secular world, was to become the predominant model in the Middle English period. The treatment of topics such as group identity, the common good, power relationships and the exertion of violence in

---

[52] Bourquin, 'Lexis and Deixis', pp. 10–11.

[53] Hugh Magennis, *Images of Community in Old English Poetry*, Cambridge Studies in Anglo-Saxon England, 18 (Cambridge: Cambridge University Press, 1996), p. 86.

[54] Margaret Enid Bridges, *Generic Contrast in Old English Hagiographical Poetry*, Anglistica, 12 (Copenhagen: Roskilde and Bagger, 1984), p. 13: 'in the virgin-martyr passion — of which *Juliana* is the first known vernacular example and which becomes very popular in the late Old English and early Middle English periods — the persecution is sexual as well as religious'. It is debatable whether the differentiation of 'sexual' and 'religious' is applicable for these passions, as the sexual violation of the Christian virgin is so closely connected to her spiritual corruption. The symbolic value of pure virginity cannot be detached from its religious significance.

Juliana differs strikingly from their evaluation in *Judith* and *Elene*.[55] While both Judith and Elene perform acts of salvation on behalf of their communities and hold respected positions within these communities, Juliana does not belong to her worldly community. Her separation from her father, who is representative of kinship bonds, and from Eleusius, who represents the worldly community both as her suitor and as prefect, is visible in the terms applied to her. Initially, possessive pronouns and terms of kinship dominate,[56] but soon give way to epithets and terms stressing her fearlessness, purity and holiness.[57] Abraham discusses the question of how community inclusion is defined in *Juliana* with a focus on legal terminology. On account of the terminology used in the context of sacrifice, she concludes that the crucial question dealt with in *Juliana* is a legal matter — that is, whether tribute should be rightfully paid to the gods of Eleusius or to the Christian god — not a question of religious truth.[58] Though I believe matters of religious truth and judicial matters can easily and purposefully overlap, Abraham's astute observations regarding the terminology employed are revealing. They show that Cynewulf consciously drew on contemporary legal practices and customs in the composition of the poem and must have had a purpose for doing so. I believe this technique highlights how the saint's isolation from her community is absolutely inevitable, not only spiritually but also legally. If Juliana pays tribute to a different ruler, she obviously belongs to a different community. It is in line with the critical stance Cynewulf takes towards traditional heroic society to thus bring home the point that one cannot be a Christian and a member of a heathen community.[59] Furthermore, Abraham shows how the theme of guardianship (*mundbyrd*) becomes more central in Cynewulf's poem in contrast to the Latin legend.[60] Thus, the message that Juliana belongs to a different community and follows different laws is enforced continuously throughout the poem. This alienation of the saint from her worldly community is a typical feature of the *passio*.[61]

Especially when Juliana is compared with the heroines Judith and Elene, it becomes clear that we are dealing with a very different kind of heroism. The isolation of the saint from her worldly community naturally affects the nature of her heroism, which has no immediate positive effect for anyone else but her. What Juliana achieves is first and foremost her own

[55] Cf. Magennis, *Community*, p. 90: 'in contrast to its [the hall and feasting imagery's] effect in endorsing Germanic communal values in *Judith*, this imagery contributes in *Juliana* to the expression of moral hostility with which Cynewulf views the values of the secular world'.

[56] Line 41a 'bryd' ('bride'); l. 61b 'haligre fæder' ('father of the holy one'; the expression, though not applied to Juliana herself, defines her within family bonds); l. 68b 'þin dohtor' ('your daughter'); l. 79a 'fæmnan fæder' ('the women's father'; cf. l. 61b); ll. 93a–96a 'þu eart dohtor min seo dyreste ond seo sweteste in sefan minum ange for eorþan, minra eagna leoht Juliana!' ('you are my daughter, the dearest and the sweetest in my heart, the only one upon earth, light of my eyes Juliana!'); l. 141b 'dehter' ('daughter'); ll. 166a–67a, 'min se swetesta sunnan scina, Juliana!' ('my sweetest ray of the sun, Juliana!').

[57] For example l. 147a 'seo unforhte' ('the unafraid one'); l. 175a 'seo æþele mæg' ('the noble maiden'); l. 209a-b, 'æþele mod unforht' ('the noble one, with unafraid heart'); l. 454 'seo wlitescyne wuldres condel' ('the splendidly shining candle of glory'); l. 315b, l. 345a, l. 589b, 'seo halge' ('the holy one').

[58] Lenore MacGaffey Abraham, 'Cynewulf's *Juliana*: A Case at Law', in *The Cynewulf Reader*, ed. by Robert E. Bjork (New York: Routledge, 2001), pp. 171–92 (p. 175).

[59] The notion of two separate spheres which do not interfere with regard to the paying of tribute expressed in Matthew 22.21 is not relevant here. The poem clearly stresses the opposition of worldly and spiritual sphere and does not allow for reconciliation.

[60] Abraham, 'A Case at Law', p. 176.

[61] Magennis, *Community*, p. 169: 'the saint who aspires to and represents an ideal of heavenly community, is isolated in a hostile and obdurate earthly community. The individual *passio* is a version of an archetypal conflict rather than a dramatization of a unique event'.

salvation. Her refusal to marry a heathen and her steadfast endurance of all tortures only achieves a positive effect for other people by giving an example which can inspire others to toil for Christian perfection. Her actions are exemplary both within the narrative and with respect to the poem's effect on its audience. She sets an example and is an ideal to be aspired to. The principle of contrast employed in the *passio* serves to achieve unequivocal support for the ideals the saint embodies as well as clear rejection of the worldly values he or she eschews. Bridges proposes two essential kinds of contrast in the *passio*:

> if the diametrical mode of contrast involves a clash of opposites, the gradational mode of contrast marks the varying degrees to which characters either approximate or fall short of an ideal. The latter mode is characteristic of such traditional categories of speech as the farewell address and the prayer, which the *passio* may have borrowed from the *vita*. Insofar as they contain exhortations to imitation (addressed to the sympathetic audience) and requests for intercession or elevation, these speeches imply gradational contrast along a continuous scale separating yet linking the imperfect mimetic Christian and his exemplary ideal (Christ and the translated saints).[62]

In *Juliana*, then, diametrical contrast is employed in the depiction of the heroine and her heathen persecutors, and made even more pointed by the stress on the irreconcilable nature of the Christian and worldly communities. Her parting speech, which is highly didactic, explains how every Christian can aspire to the ideal presented by the saint, thus bridging the gap between sainthood and 'ordinary' Christian conduct.

The direction of violence in *Juliana* also sets the poem apart from *Judith* and *Elene*. Here, only the heathens exert violence, but to no avail.[63] Juliana's strength lies in the unmoving resistance she displays in the face of violence directed against her — thus demonstrating the futility of worldly power against the power of faith. Whereas Judith and Elene possess the strength to move and display the power to direct action, the virgin martyr has the strength to remain unmoved and the power to resist action. There is also one instance in *Juliana* where violence directed against her is reflected back upon her persecutors: the bath of boiling lead prepared for the saint does not harm her but instead spurts out and kills 75 heathens nearby.[64] The worldly power of the prefect cannot reach Juliana, who wields the superior spiritual power. Moreover, her victory over the devil is clearly depicted as a result of spiritual strength. It demonstrates that the predominant danger for the Christian lies in being deceived by the forces of evil. Juliana is wise enough to suspect the trap and thus able to overcome the devil. Bzdyl points out that 'in *Juliana*, Cynewulf's subject is the true nature of reality; his goal is to win men to salvation by teaching them to see through devilish delusion'.[65] The motif of deceit as the main tool of the devil is elaborated on in the devil's account of his evil deeds, which focuses on his attempt to mislead rather than simply tempt man into committing sins and acquiring vices.[66] Wittig highlights how exemplary and didactic purposes are met in the

---

[62] Bridges, *Generic Contrast*, pp. 14–15.

[63] The death of Eleusius and his men at sea may be regarded as an instance of an act of violence by God. The notion that the sea passes divine judgement is reminiscent of the scene where the lead 'acts' to protect Juliana and punish the heathens (ll. 384b–589a). Note also that Eleusius' sea voyage lacks any logical motivation and appears to be an action caused by his overwhelming anger at his defeat by Juliana. Thus, his irresponsible and uncontrolled wrath drives him out to sea, where he and his men are destroyed by divine power.

[64] Lines 384b–589a.

[65] D. G. Bzdyl, '*Juliana*: Cynewulf's Dispeller of Delusion', in *The Cynewulf Reader*, ed. by Robert E. Bjork (New York: Routledge, 2001), pp. 193–206 (p. 194) [first publ. *Neuphilologische Mitteilungen*, 86 (1985), 165–75].

[66] For example ll. 325b–27a, 'þæt we soðfæstra þurh misgedwield mod oncyrren, ahwyrfen from halor' ('so that we

heroine's encounter with the devil: while Juliana's behaviour is exemplary in its Christ-like strength, the devil's confession contains homiletic elements as it explains the psychology of temptation, thus making the faithful aware of the devil's techniques.[67]

The comparison of the three poems illuminates the religious values of their intended audiences. If we look at the heroic appeal of poems like *Judith*, *Elene*, *Andreas* and the *Dream of the Rood*, they seem to be written for an audience which cherishes martial success and measures the power of a god in terms of its manifestation in worldly affairs.[68] It is also visible that the common good of the respective heroine's and hero's kin is of predominant importance in these texts. Christian faith functions as a stabilising factor within the society of the heroes and heroines depicted. *Juliana* and other narratives of the virgin martyr tradition put the emphasis on spiritual strength and the salvation of the individual believer who is part of the community of the faithful, which does not coincide with the society one is born into.

Woolf suggests that

> in the Anglo-Saxon period the particular tastes of the ladies of a noble household seem not to have been considered by the authors of secular poetry, but Juliana is unmistakably a religious poem designed for the pleasure and edification of women in a religious community.[69]

It is debatable whether the tastes of the noblewomen would have always differed so much from those of men as long as they shared the same social background. A lady established in the social network and raised according to the values of a society cherishing heroic deeds and often engaged in military conflicts would probably have enjoyed narratives which deal with these topics.[70] However, just as Judith and Elene are more feasible role models for a noblewoman because they adhere to the ideals of an Anglo-Saxon lady and fulfil functions within a worldly society, Juliana is a better model for a nun, who forsook her role within worldly society, possibly even against the wishes of her kin group, in order to become part of a spiritual community.

While *Judith* and *Elene* thus exhibit clear similarities,[71] *Juliana* belongs to a different genre, although traces of the heroic tradition can be found. Magennis rightly points out that a tension between the overt repudiation of heroic values and the poem's strong connection to

---

change the heart of the faithful by deceit, turn them from salvation'); ll. 363b–64b, 'þus ic soðfæstum durh mislic bleo mod oncyrre' ('thus I pervert the heart of the faithful by various shams').

[67] Joseph Wittig, 'Figural Narrative in Cynewulf's *Juliana*', in *The Cynewulf Reader*, ed. by Robert E. Bjork (New York: Routledge, 2001), pp. 147–70 (p. 156) [first publ. *Anglo-Saxon England*, 4 (1975), 37–55].

[68] The Old English *Judith* can be included under 'Christian' as it has been thoroughly adapted to suit a Christian audience and all traces of the heroine's Jewish faith have been removed. Cf. Paul de Lacy, 'Aspects of Christianisation and Cultural Adaptation in the Old English *Judith*', *Neuphilologische Mitteilungen*, 97 (1996), 393–410.

[69] Woolf, 'Saints' Lives', p. 46.

[70] Cf. Schrader, *God's Handiwork*, p. 47.

[71] It should be borne in mind that these similarities also align them with other poems in which heroic tradition and religious motives merge. Poems such as *Andreas*, *Guthlac A* or *The Dream of the Rood* bear clear similarities in style and diction and likewise merge religious topics and heroic tradition. Gordon Hall Gerould, *Saints' Legends* (New York: The Riverside Press, 1916), pp. 61–62, 65, and 79 coins the term 'epic legend' for the poems *Juliana*, *Elene*, *The Fates of the Apostles*, *Guthlac* and *Andreas*. He supposes that they are representative of 'a much larger body of verse, which celebrated the heroes and heroines of the church in true Germanic fashion' (pp. 89–90). He situates the 'epic legend' within a larger tradition (including *Genesis A* and *B*, *Exodus*, *Daniel*, *Christ*, the *Dream of the Rood* and *Judith*), which dealt with religious topics using the established diction and style of heroic epic (pp. 90–91).

the heroic tradition is noticeable.[72] I believe this tension is representative of the poem's status as a transitional work. The introduction of new Christian values and ways to achieve Christian perfection to people still grounded in a different tradition naturally creates this tension. We have seen that *Elene* addresses the tension caused by the competing ties of natural and spiritual kinship. While the topic is not discussed in *Juliana*, the tension between competing values is still felt.

Virgin Martyrs: The Power of Passivity

I now examine more closely the genre of the virgin martyr tale in its relationship to heroic Christian poems and changing feminine ideals in religious poetry. It is beyond the scope of this essay to aim at a complete evaluation of the genre, which remained popular over several centuries.[73] A condensed overview will suffice to specify the essential differences as well as the common features in the portrayal of ideal Christian women in comparison to poems of the heroic tradition.

An emphasis on communal values and the common good, the overlapping of spiritual superiority and worldly power, and the positive role of Christianity in advancing group coherence and the social order are the shared features of the narrative poems *Judith* and *Elene*. The eponymous heroines of these poems present positive feminine role models for Christian conduct within communities adhering to the values of heroic society. *Juliana* differs in all of these respects: the heroine distances herself from her role in society, and her actions are directed at her individual salvation. Her defiance of the obligations of kinship in favour of her Christian identity depicts the Christian faith as incongruent with traditional values. Worldly power and spiritual superiority appear in stark opposition. These differences are due to the genres of the three poems, i.e. to the fact that *Juliana* is, despite its stylistic and lexical proximity to heroic diction, more akin to other virgin martyr tales than to the poems *Judith* and *Elene*. It has been pointed out by many scholars that narratives of the virgin martyr type display striking parallels in plot and also contain recurrent motifs. Winstead explains the deliberate similarity, and occasionally even identical reproduction, of these tales with the desire to show the saints' resemblance to one another and to Christ.[74] It is no surprise, then, that we readily recognise the parallels between the Old English *Juliana* and the Middle English *Sainte Margerete* from the Katherine Group. Both virgins are initially desired by a pagan of worldly standing. Once it becomes clear that marriage is not an option due to the woman's Christian faith, the focus shifts, and the pagan tries to force the virgin to sacrifice to the heathen gods.[75] After a series of tortures, the virgin, who remains steadfast in her faith throughout, is executed. Both virgins also encounter demons while imprisoned, whom they

---

[72] Magennis, *Community*, p. 87.

[73] See Gerould, *Saints' Legends*, pp. 133–34.

[74] Karen A. Winstead, *Virgin Martyrs* (Ithaca, New York: Cornell University Press, 1997), pp. 1-3.

[75] Perhaps it is not really a shift in focus but rather an adjustment of the method — if the virgin can be convinced to give up her faith, she would no longer be betrothed to Christ and therefore free for her heathen suitor. Cf. Jocelyn Wogan-Browne, 'Saints' Lives and the Female Reader', *FORUM for Modern Language Studies*, 27 (1991), 314–32 (p. 321): 'in the legendary lives, there is a certain amount of displacement designed to reveal the ideological force of virginity: the pagan persecutors are often surprisingly willing to accept the saint's refusal of physical favours and they embark at once not on forcible rape but on torture-enforced campaigns for her ideological capitulation'.

successfully force into submission and interrogate. Comparable patterns recur in all tales of the genre.[76]

A brief analysis of the genre's treatment of central topics such as virginity, power and violence in comparison to *Judith* and *Elene* reveals essential differences, but also shared features in the depiction of women.

Virginity or even chastity are never mentioned in *Judith* and *Elene*. The authority of the respective heroines stems from their faith, wisdom, determination and/or social standing, not from virginal purity. Although Judith is presented as especially affiliated with God, the connection is not depicted in marital or erotic terms. She is the handmaid of God, not the bride of Christ. Neither *Judith* nor *Elene* are concerned with the heroines' gendered and sexual identities at all. This is particularly striking in comparison to *Judith*'s biblical source: any trace of Judith's exploitation of her sexual allure to lead Holofernes on is edited out of the poem, as is the exceptional beauty of the protagonist.[77] She is, however, not depicted as virginal either — sexuality is simply not an issue.[78] In the virgin martyr tales on the other hand, virginity is the essential asset of the saintly woman. Her exceptional status and her essential immunity to physical violation are grounded in the sealed perfection of her virginal body. Salih observes that '[the virgin martyrs'] power stems from their virginity; the choice to be a virgin is the originary choice which enables all others'.[79] This choice makes the virgin martyr 'both bride and virago; her desires are directed to Christ and her body is glorified and miraculously impermeable'.[80] The *sponsa Christi* motif also adds a secular dimension to the importance of the saint's virginity: as the bride-to-be, the martyr has to save her virginity for her future husband, a practice also expected of any other betrothed maiden.[81] Several concepts of virginity merge in the figure of the virgin martyr. On the one hand, the Christian

---

[76] See Sarah Salih, *Versions of Virginity in Late Medieval England* (Woodbridge: Brewer, 2001), p. 48; cf. Karl D. Uitti, 'Women Saints, the Vernacular, and History in Early Medieval France', in *Images of Sainthood in Medieval Europe*, ed. by Renate Blumenfeld-Kosinski and Timea Szell (Ithaca, New York: Cornell University Press, 1991), pp. 247–67 (pp. 253–54): 'when we look at the handful of surviving texts devoted to women saints on Gallo-Romance territory from the late ninth century through about 1200 or so, a striking and recurrent narrative pattern manifests itself. I refer to the tale of a holy and beautiful Christian maiden who refuses both the blandishments and the threats of a pagan (usually Roman) ruler, and who maintains her chastity and her status as God's betrothed to the point of accepting extraordinary physical suffering and a martyr's death'. In *Medieval English Prose for Women*, ed. by Bella Millett and Jocelyn Wogan-Browne (Oxford: Clarendon Press, 1990), p. xxi, the editors explain the selection of *Sainte Margerete* for their edition of texts from the Katherine Group by arguing that the 'shared design and purpose make it possible for a single Life to give a good idea of all three'. See also *John Capgrave: The Life of Saint Katherine*, ed. by Karen A. Winstead (Kalamazoo: TEAMS, 1999), p. 1 and Wogan-Browne, 'Saints' Lives', p. 315.

[77] Cf. Hugh Magennis, ' "No Sex Please, We're Anglo-Saxons"? Attitudes to Sexuality in Old English Prose and Poetry', *Leeds Studies in English*, n. s., 26 (1995), 1–27 (pp. 12–13). Magennis sees a twofold reason for the changes applied: 'this is due in part to the Anglo-Saxon discomfort with sexual themes evident too in Ælfric's version of the Judith story (as elsewhere), but it is also a feature of the poet's *Germanizierung* of the biblical material, a is transposed into a type of narrative poetry which traditionally lacks of a sexual dimension' (p. 13).

[78] See my detailed discussion of the opinion that Judith is depicted as a virgin in the Old English poem: Judith Kaup, *The Old English 'Judith': A Study of Poetic Style, Theological Tradition and Anglo-Saxon Christian Concepts* (Lewiston: Mellen, 2013), pp. 279–89.

[79] Salih, *Versions of Virginity*, p. 49.

[80] Salih, *Versions of Virginity*, p. 98. Cf. Sarah Salih, 'Performing Virginity: Sex and Violence in the *Katherine Group*', in *Constructions of Widowhood and Virginity in the Middle Ages*, ed. by Cindy L. Carlson and Angela Jane Weisl (London: St Martin's Press, 1999), pp. 95–112 (p. 100): 'virginity constitutes a "culturally consistent gender", in which the virgin's desire is directed towards God and her body is whole and impenetrable'.

[81] See Felicity Riddy, 'Temporary Virginity and the Everyday Body: *Le Bone Florence of Rome* and Bourgeois Self-making', in *Pulp Fictions of Medieval England*, ed. by Nicola McDonald (Manchester: Manchester University

virgin is a creature of angelic perfection, unblemished by the world, and oblivious to all desires of the flesh.[82] On the other hand, the virgin martyr's relationship with Christ is described in erotic terms. She achieves redemption 'not through her transcendence of earthly desire, but through her transference of physical desire to Christ'.[83] Thus, in contrast to Judith and Elene, whose femininity is hardly noticeable, the corporeality and sexuality of these holy women is of predominant importance for their religious achievement.[84] In addition, her status as the betrothed of Christ puts the virgin martyr under his personal protection, and her violation would constitute an offence against him as her future husband. It is also important to realise that this emphasis on virginity clearly situates these women saints outside secular society. If they are role models at all, they are role models for women who devote their lives entirely to God, namely nuns or anchoresses, who do not fulfil secular female roles in their society.

The issue of power also sets the heroic Christian women apart from the virgin martyrs. Both Judith and Elene are portrayed as powerful and authoritative figures. They are respected and obeyed within their communities and even beyond. They are heroines in a heroic setting, with warriors at their command and equipped with the attributes of worldly power, gold and adornment. At first glance, the typical virgin martyr appears, especially in comparison, absolutely powerless. Nevertheless, while Judith and Elene wield the power to direct action, which could be also described as the power of moving both themselves, as they travel freely across boundaries, and others, whom they order to move, the virgin martyrs possess the power to resist action — to remain unmoved. The virgin martyr Lucy is an especially graphic example, as she literally cannot be moved by any means. Neither magic nor the physical power of a thousand men and a large number of oxen can drag her away when her persecutors want to hand her over to a crowd to be gang-raped to death.[85] In the Old English *Juliana* the heroine

Press, 2004), pp. 197–216 (p. 203), for an evaluation of the relationship of secular and religious virginity. Cf. Jane Tibbetts Schulenburg, 'The Heroics of Virginity: Brides of Christ and Sacrifical Mutilation', in *Women in the Middle Ages and the Renaissance. Literary and Historical Perspectives*, ed. by Mary Beth Rose (Syracuse: Syracuse University Press, 1986), pp. 29–72 (pp. 40–41), on the merging of secular and Christian feminine ideals regarding virginity.

[82] Ruth Evans, 'Virginities', in *The Cambridge Companion to Medieval Women's Writing*, ed. by Carolyn Dinshaw and David Wallace (Cambridge: Cambridge University Press, 2003), pp. 21–39 (p. 25).

[83] Elizabeth Robertson, 'The Corporeality of Female Sanctity in the *Life of Saint Margaret*', in *Images of Sainthood in Medieval Europe*, ed. by Renate Blumenfeld-Kosinski and Timea Szell (Ithaca, New York: Cornell University Press, 1991), pp. 268–87 (p. 269). Cf. Armando Maggi, 'Virgins for the Virgin: The "Imprese" of Three Sixteenth-century Italian Academies and the Gaze of the Holy Mother', *Rivista di Letterature Moderne e Comparate*, 51 (1998), 367–78 (pp. 367–78), who describes practices of male devotion to the Virgin Mary. He argues that the direction of erotic desires towards Mary nullifies them, because the Virgin cannot comprehend them (p. 373).

[84] It is noticeable that the *sponsa Christi* motif is not yet present in the Old English *Juliana*. L. Hödl, 'Jungfräulichkeit', in *Lexikon des Mittelalters* (Stuttgart: Metzler, 1977–99), cols. 808–9, highlights the influence Cistercian spirituality and the commentaries on the Song of Songs in the twelfth century have on the development of the *sponsa Christi* motif. See also Theodor Wolpers, *Die Englische Heiligenlegende des Mittelalters* (Tübingen: Niemeyer, 1964), pp. 158–59: 'das Martyrium kann ohne seine Schrecken als etwas Herbeizusehnendes, als eine Form ekstatischer Liebesvereinigung mit Christus gesehen werden, wie es besonders seit Bernhard v. Clairvaux geschieht. Damit verbindet sich, in den Jungfrauenlegenden, vielfach das Sponsa-Christi-Motiv' ('martyrdom can be viewed without its terror as something desirable, as a kind of ecstatic union with Christ. This has been especially common since Bernard of Clairvaux and often, in the virgin martyr legends, connected with the *sponsa Christi* motif').

[85] 'Life of the Blessed Virgin Lucy', in *The Golden Legend or Lives of the Saints. Compiled by Jacobus de Voragine, Archbishop of Genoa, 1275. First Edition Published 1470. Englished by William Caxton, First Edition 1483*, ed. by F. S. Ellis, Temple Classics, 7 vols (London: Dent, 1900), II, 130–35; see also Kathleen Coyne Kelly, 'Useful Virgins in Medieval Hagiography', in *Constructions of Widowhood and Virginity in the Middle Ages*, ed. by Cindy

is also described in terms stressing her defiance of threat and torture.[86] It is an essential trait of the virgin martyr that she is absolutely unmoveable and indestructible.[87]

Power, often associated with activity, is displayed in passive resistance. However, the active involvement of the virgin martyr in shaping events should not go unnoticed. Salih clarifies:

> the tyrants believe that they are in control of the narrative, that they have the choice of whether to execute or reprieve the heroines, but they are wrong. The virgins take control even of the details of their deaths. Having survived fires, wheels, boiling liquids, etc. by the magical strength of their virginity, the martyrs consent to be beheaded.[88]

A powerful instrument of heroic Christian women and virgin martyrs alike is their tongue. The authority of speech and the superiority that derives from wisdom and understanding, which are associated with the true faith, are important assets of the heroines in both genres. The ability to control the situation, be it actively or by resistance, is due to their superior understanding of the significance of events. Knowledge is a prime asset of the faithful and is set in stark contrast to the ignorance of the heathens. The persecutors of the virgins are unable to decode the meaning of the miraculous events taking place before their very eyes. Their blindness is usually further highlighted by the fact that other pagans witnessing the events understand their significance and convert to Christianity.

While the virgin martyrs cannot directly cause action by means of commands, as the heroic saints do, they still exercise considerable influence by their speech. Their utterances can be divided into two basic types: those which further the action in accordance with the martyr's wishes[89] and those which verbalise their faith, sometimes in the manner of learned discourse, or stress their commitment to their heavenly spouse. Taunting and thus further enraging the potential or active torturer also features prominently in the virgin martyr legends.[90] The display of their broken, tortured bodies in contrast to their unbroken, glorious spirit, manifested in their speech, is the virgins' proof of divinely sanctioned authority. The public torture creates the stage for the virgins' performance of faith.[91] In the virgin martyr legend, the proof of spiritual superiority enables the women to exercise worldly power through their speech. No

---

L. Carlson and Angela Jane Weisl (London: St Martin's Press, 1999), pp. 135–64 (p. 151), and Corinne Saunders, *Rape and Ravishment in the Literature of Medieval England* (Cambridge: Brewer, 2001), p. 130.

[86] She is unafraid and unmoved, e.g. lines 147a, 'seo unforhte' ('the unafraid one'); 209b, 'mod unforht' ('unafraid mind'); 259b, 'seo þe forht ne wæs' ('she, who was not afraid'); 226a–27a 'þæt he ne meahte mod oncyrran, fæmne foreþonc' ('that he could not change the mind, the intention of the woman'); 600b–700a, 'wæs seo wuldres mæg anræd ond unforht' ('the woman of glory was resolute and unafraid').

[87] Evans, 'Virginities', p. 31.

[88] Salih, *Versions of Virginity*, pp. 95–96.

[89] Salih, *Versions of Virginity*, pp. 95–96, points out with reference to the Katherine Group's *Juliana* that she 'helpfully lists the tortures she is prepared to withstand, as if prompting her father, who has not yet begun to torture her, to fulfil his proper role in the narrative. The tyrants never understand that they do not control the narrative but are simply the virgins' instruments'.

[90] While in this discussion I am concerned with medieval English examples only, the basic pattern of these legends stays very much the same from antiquity even to the present day. Cf. Uitti, 'Woman Saints', pp. 253–54; Sheila Delany, *Impolitic Bodies* (New York: Oxford University Press, 1998), p. 191.

[91] Salih, *Versions of Virginity*, pp. 74–98. Katherine J. Lewis, '*Lete me suffre*: Reading the Torture of St Margaret of Antioch in Late Medieval England', in *Medieval Women: Texts and Contexts in Late Medieval Britain. Essays for Felicity Riddy*, ed. by Jocelyn Wogan-Browne, Rosalynn Voaden, Arlyn Diamond, Ann Hutchison, Carol M. Meale, and Lesley Johnson, Medieval Women: Texts and Contexts, 3 (Turnhout: Brepols, 2000), pp. 69–82 (p. 78), analyses the process in the legend of Margaret: the torture 'is intended to silence her, but actually serves to construct an affective and authoritative platform from which to speak and preach. Olibrius seeks to harm and

such proof is necessary in the poems *Judith* and *Elene*, because worldly and spiritual authority are presented as identical. This contrast between the two spheres is also visible in the depiction of violence.

There are usually two types of violent encounters in the virgin martyr tale. While the virgins are the object of violence at the hands of fathers, heathen suitors and persecutors, they are often also portrayed as physically wrestling with demons. The two types can be seen as representing worldly and spiritual combat. The tortures inflicted upon the virgins by the representatives of worldly authority always fail to achieve the desired effect. The virgins are thus presented as beyond the reach of worldly afflictions and temptations — they have already achieved a state of spiritual perfection which manifests itself on the stage prepared for them by their persecutors. The confrontations with demons illustrate that the exceptional virtue of the virgins also enables them to withstand the far more dangerous spiritual onslaughts and inner temptations. Salih suggests that Margaret's encounter with the dragon possibly represents her final rejection of female sexuality and thus all temptations of the flesh.[92] Juliana's demon tries to deceive her in very much the same manner which he later reveals to be one of his favourite tactics in leading Christians astray.[93] Interestingly, the virgins are as physically engaged in these spiritual battles as they are physically unaffected by the worldly violence directed against them. This paradoxical depiction emphasises how much more strength is needed to ward off the more subtle spiritual temptations than the more obvious worldly ones. Therefore, while the virgin martyr legends exemplify the futility of physical violence and worldly power in the face of spiritual superiority, they also show the difficulties involved in attaining such superiority.

Conclusion

It has become clear that the main difference between religious texts of the heroic tradition like *Judith* and *Elene* on the one hand and legends of the virgin martyr genre on the other lies in the evaluation of the relationship between spiritual and worldly power. The virgin martyr legends equate worldly authority with paganism, propagating the rejection of worldly goods and status. Accordingly, an ideal Christian woman can only exist outside the structures of worldly society. In addition, her perpetual virginity, the cornerstone of all her achievements, creates an unbridgeable gap between the virgin martyr and any woman embedded in secular society. A woman cannot hope to achieve Christian perfection without rejecting the world and thus there is no place on earth for the woman saint. The absolute manifestation of feminine Christian perfection is only achieved in death and departure to heaven for the consummation of the holy marriage.[94]

---

correct her, but she turns the punishment back upon him: her ability to withstand sustained and ferocious torture renders him and his people unable to watch, thus destabilizing him from his position of apparent author of the spectacle. Her exemplary suffering further undermines his position and authority by converting thousands of his people, who have read it as confirmation of the truth of Christianity, as she intended, rather than as an exposition of is fallacy, the reading which Olibrius attempts to impose. [...] Margaret, the putative "passive" victim, becomes agent and campaigner, using her bleeding body and her unwavering speech as weapons against Olibrius'.

[92] Salih, *Versions of Virginity*, pp. 88–89.

[93] Disguised as an angel, he attempts to convince her that God does not want her to suffer martyrdom. Interestingly, this is the only point in the poem where Juliana is afraid (ll. 267a–68a), which could be intended to illustrate the dangers of deception, because it illustrates that only deception can frighten the saint.

[94] Salih, *Versions of Virginity*, p. 97.

A powerful queen or a cunning woman who engages in military action is clearly at odds with such an ideal. The Old English heroines Judith and Elene present models of ideal faith that can be lived out within worldly society. The poems' presentation of societies where the common good and worldly power are in harmony with ideal Christian living aligns them with the broader tradition of saints' lives featuring lay protagonists. I have pointed out earlier that already the Benedictine reform deepened the divide between secular and monastic forms of Christian life, favouring monasticism over all other forms of religious devotion. The Gregorian reform in the late eleventh century continued this process and it has been observed that legends about saintly lay people were no longer in line with the dominant church doctrine of that period.[95] Vauchez points out that, even though salvation could be attained by the pious laymen, 'Christian perfection [...] was identified more and more closely with isolation from and contempt of the world'.[96] It is easy to see how the virgin martyr legends fit into this concept of sainthood — and it is equally obvious that narratives about saintly women like Elene or Judith do not adhere to these ideals.[97] In addition, the depiction of powerful worldly women as Christian role models is probably influenced by the realities of the times when the texts were composed.

The idea of the Anglo-Saxon period as a Golden Age for women with the Norman Conquest as a decisive turning point has been rejected or modified in recent scholarship.[98] There is, however, an undeniable decline in female agency in religious life from early to late Anglo-Saxon times, which is connected to the effects of the religious reform movements. Women played an important role in the early monastic foundations in Anglo-Saxon England, with the religious life offering opportunities to exert considerable influence. Neuman de Vegvar stresses female monastics' involvement in shaping events and developments of their day and emphasises the worldly power attained by Anglo-Saxon royal women monastics.[99] This heyday of female monastic power was short-lived and Neuman de Vegvar suggests it was closely tied to the needs of the conversion period.[100] Foot's findings support this opinion as they show that there were fewer nunneries in tenth and eleventh century England than there had been in the seventh and eight centuries.[101] This will have affected the opportunities for women to exercise power and rulership in monastic roles. The decline of the power of female religious in turn influenced modes of female devotion. Schulenburg observes that changing societal realities in the eleventh century occasioned new models of female sanctity

---

[95] André Vauchez, 'Lay People's Sanctity in Western Europe: Evolution of a Pattern (Twelfth and Thirteenth Centuries)', in *Images of Sainthood in Medieval Europe*, ed. by Renate Blumenfeld-Kosinski and Timea Szell (Ithaca, New York: Cornell University Press, 1991), pp. 21–31 (p. 22). The Gregorian reform, named after pope Gregory VII, is an ecclesiastical reform which propagated, *inter alia*, spiritual renewal, celibacy of the clergy and the prohibition of lay investiture. Overall, it also deepened the divide between lay and institutional piety.

[96] Vauchez, 'Lay People's Sanctity', pp. 23–24.

[97] See Wolpers, *Englische Heiligenlegende*, pp. 157–208, for a description of developments in hagiographic writings.

[98] Fell, *Women in Anglo-Saxon England*, is one of the most prominent advocates of the idea of the deterioration of women's rights and social standing after the Norman Conquest. This evaluation is still found in more recent studies, e.g. Laurie A. Finke, *Women's Writings in English: Medieval England* (London: Longman, 1999), esp. p. 23. Pauline Stafford, 'Women and the Norman Conquest', *Transactions of the Royal Historical Society*, 4 (1994), 221–49, refutes the idea and stresses the relative scarcity of evidence for the Anglo-Saxon period and points out how scholars' political agendas have influenced their readings.

[99] Carol Neuman de Vegvar, 'Saints and Companions to Saints: Anglo-Saxon Royal Women Monastics in Context', in *Holy Men and Holy Women. Old English Prose Saints' Lives and Their Contexts*, ed. by Paul E. Szarmach (Albany: State University of New York Press, 1996), pp. 51–93 (pp. 76–77).

[100] Neuman de Vegvar, 'Saints and Companions', p. 77.

[101] Foot, *Veiled Women*, I, 201.

in Europe.[102] McNamara also suggests a direct link between the deterioration in women's economic independence and means of achieving powerful positions within church and society on the one hand and the development of extreme forms of asceticism and devotion amongst religious women on the other.[103] She contrasts the situation from the early days of conversion up to the eleventh century, 'when sainthood continued to reward women who expressed their high status by generosity to the church and to the poor'[104] with the period between 1050 and 1150 when the 'Gregorian church sought to disentangle itself from the power of lay patrons, bringing the system that had produced so many saintly women into disrepute'.[105] McNamara points out that this development coincided with a devaluation of the role of women in twelfth-century society and states:

> as a group, women were being systematically deprived of control over their own wealth and reduced to dependency upon their families or their husbands. Thus, if we divide society into alms givers and alms takers, many women of the ruling classes who had been securely placed among the givers suffered a decisive loss of status and were once more reduced to takers.[106]

Subsequently, women's expressions of their faith and Christian charity took new forms. Service for the poor was soon restricted by church authorities and replaced by spiritual almsgiving. Religious women did not only offer up their prayers but also their fasts and other, more austere forms of self-inflicted suffering for the redemption of souls from purgatory.[107]

At a time where female agency was more restricted, two contradictory reasons for the increasing popularity of the virgin martyr legends seem plausible. On the one hand, the legends may have appealed to a female audience as they offered models of female agency and volition — agency through the power of resistance and examples of the divine protection of female choice.[108] On the other hand, they can be read as prescriptive texts, meant to channel female devotional practices and promote controlled female monasticism. This second reading involves a reception of the texts as more abstract role models, propagating the values of virginity and separation from the world — virtues, which could be imitated in a regulated monastic setting. By contrast with the early Anglo-Saxon situation, where female religious could obtain considerable power and influence through monastic life, hierarchical ecclesiastical order after the Gregorian reform also reaffirmed the gender boundaries and hierarchies, making cloistered women the subject of male control.[109]

On a more general level, affecting the depiction of saintly men as well as women, the Gregorian reform resulted in a more spiritualised view of sainthood, causing a shift in

---

[102] Jane Tibbetts Schulenburg, *Forgetful of Their Sex: Female Sanctity and Society, ca. 500–1100* (Chicago: University of Chicago Press, 1998), p. 7.

[103] Jo Ann McNamara, 'The Need to Give: Suffering and Female Sanctity in the Middle Ages', in *Images of Sainthood in Medieval Europe*, ed. by Renate Blumenfeld-Kosinski and Timea Szell (Ithaca, New York: Cornell University Press, 1991), pp. 199–221.

[104] McNamara, 'The Need to Give', p. 203.

[105] McNamara, 'The Need to Give', p. 202.

[106] McNamara, 'The Need to Give', p. 204.

[107] McNamara, 'The Need to Give', pp. 205–20.

[108] Wogan-Browne, 'Saints' Lives', p. 321, suggests a metonymic link between literary convention and social conditions in twelfth- and thirteenth-century England in the virgin martyr legends.

[109] See, for example, Janet Nelson, 'Women and the Word in the Earlier Middle Ages', *Studies in Church History*, 27 (1990), 53–78 (pp. 77–78). Klein, 'Reading Queenship', p. 74, observes a profound emphasis on hierarchy and boundaries, including gender oppositions, already for the Benedictine reform. This supports my essay's argument that the development started with the Benedictine reform and continued through to the Gregorian reform.

hagiographic production towards legends dealing with saints who clearly rejected all worldly matters. Religious narratives or saints' lives of the heroic tradition, such as *Judith* and *Elene*, are in contrast clearly from a different social and religious era. They are 'outdated' with respect to the models of exemplary, saintly Christian life within the world they represent and also in their depiction of powerful female figures. Both Elene and Judith are portrayed as positive models of Christian rulership.[110] The poems offer examples of Christian living within the world and show the achievement of Christian perfection in a secular setting.[111] To wield worldly power on the basis of strong faith is depicted as a laudable Christian activity. Role models like this were clearly at odds with the ideals of the Benedictine reform and even less acceptable after the Gregorian reform.

Not only the underlying theological ideologies but also the realities of female (Christian) living are reflected in the hagiographic and religious writings of the respective periods. Prior to the Benedictine and Gregorian reforms, when women were participating more actively in secular as well as clerical power, narratives about powerful Christian heroines were at once more credible and more appealing. It should also be noted that Anglo-Saxon ideals greatly favour the individual's positive identification with his or her community.[112] Therefore, the ideal of the virgin martyr, with its stress on the saint's conflict with her worldly community, is considerably less attractive for an Anglo-Saxon audience still grounded in the values of heroic society. However, by the late eleventh century, when the reality of female religious practices and devotion were centred around strict enclosure and distance to worldly affairs, such legends were both prescriptively and descriptively appropriate.

---

[110] Kathryn Powell, 'Meditating on Men and Monsters: A Reconsideration of the Thematic Unity of the *Beowulf* Manuscript', *Review of English Studies*, n. s., 57, no. 228 (2006), 1–15 (p. 10). Marie Nelson, 'Judith: A Story of a Secular Saint', *Germanic Notes and Reviews*, 21 (1990), 12–13, similarly points out that *Judith* is the story of a great war leader who wins a secular fight (p. 13) and stresses that she 'is more a defender of an earthly people than she is a defender of her own eternal soul' (p. 12).

[111] Fell's sentiment that male and female saints in the Anglo-Saxon period are portrayed as 'real people' certainly stems from these saints being part of the secular world: *Women in Anglo-Saxon England*, p. 109.

[112] Magennis, *Community*, p. 105: 'the heroic world is presented as a world of immutable certitude in which one's place is defined and one's obligations are clear. The society is presented as firm and cohesive, and it is this society which gives the individual his or her significance in the world. A message of many poems preserved in the great poetry codices of late Anglo-Saxon England is that life outside the ordered society has neither attraction nor meaning. As suggested in an earlier chapter, this is a message which members of the textual community would have found congenial and pertinent'.

Chaucer's Osewold the Reeve and St Oswald the Bishop (from the *South English Legendary* and Other Sources)

Thomas R. Liszka[1]

Everyone knows Herry Bailly's name. But interestingly, in all of the *Canterbury Tales*, his name is given only once, in the Cook's Prologue (I.4358).[2] Elsewhere, he is called only 'the Host'. Indeed, Chaucer did not give names to most of his Canterbury pilgrims. Of the ten pilgrims to whom Chaucer gave names, the names of five are mentioned only once: those of the Host, the Prioress (Eglentyne, I.121), the Friar (Huberd, I.269), the Miller (Robyn, I.3129), and the Monk (Piers, VII.2792); and two are mentioned twice: those of the Wife of Bath (Alys, III.320, and Alisoun, III.804) and the Nun's Priest (John, VII.2810 and 2820). By contrast, in leading up to the Reeve's Tale, Chaucer works the Reeve's name, 'Osewold', into his narrative three times — once in the Miller's Prologue (I.3151) and twice more in the Reeve's Prologue (I.3860, 3909). It might appear then that the name was a detail of some importance to Chaucer.[3]

J. A. W. Bennett and Susanna Greer Fein both argue for an association of Chaucer's Osewold with St Oswald the Bishop (died 922). Bennett points out that the 'name [...] carries a suggestion of the North' because of its association with the Northumbrian saint whose *vita* was written in Cambridgeshire.[4] And Fein — building on J. A. Burrow's identification of St Oswald as an example of a *puer senex*, a youth deserving the honor of age and demonstrating its wisdom[5] — argues that 'the name's chief importance for Chaucer' was the 'inverted applicability' of that characteristic of the saint for his Reeve. As she puts it, 'the name Oswald

---

[1] I am grateful to Christine Cooper-Rompato, Juris Lidaka, and Sandra Petrulionis for their valuable comments and suggestions on drafts of this article, and to Samuel Findley for his help with the analysis of the translations from Latin. I dedicate this article to Dr. J. I. Miller, who taught me the ways of the world and to whom I owe my career.

[2] All quotations of Chaucer are from *The Wadsworth Chaucer: Formerly The Riverside Chaucer*, ed. by Larry D. Benson, 3rd edn (Boston: Wadsworth, Cengage Learning, 1987) and are cited parenthetically in the text.

[3] Only one pilgrim's name is mentioned more times than the Reeve's in the text proper. The Cook's name is given four times in the prologue to his unfinished tale (Hogge, I.4336, and Roger, I.4345, 4353, and 4356). References to Chaucer the pilgrim's name are difficult to count. It is mentioned explicitly only in the five rubrics to his tales — 'Heere bigynneth Chaucer's Tale of Thopas', etc. The Man of Law refers to Chaucer by name in the text proper while praising his works (II.47), but the reference is possibly to Chaucer the poet. To appreciate the irony, it is not necessary for us to imagine that the Man of Law knows that Chaucer is present. Similarly, the Clerk's Tale ends with the 'Lenvoy de Chaucer', but it is even more doubtful that the reference is to Chaucer the pilgrim, or even that the Clerk makes it.

[4] J. A. W. Bennett, *Chaucer at Oxford and at Cambridge* (Toronto: University of Toronto Press, 1974), p. 87.

[5] J. A. Burrow, *The Ages of Man: A Study in Medieval Writing and Thought* (Oxford: Clarendon Press, 1986), pp.

calls attention to the Reeve's morbid obsession with time, which did not ripen him to early saintliness but left him, with his "olde lemes" and "coltes tooth", decrepit in his veniality'.[6]

As further support of this association of Chaucer's Osewold with St Oswald the Bishop, I would add that Chaucer may have had a particular incident in mind from the life of St Oswald reminiscent of the confusion of beds on which the Reeve's Tale is based. In both the saint's life, as it is recounted in the *South English Legendary* (*SEL*), and in Chaucer's tale, characters get into wrong beds, and consequently demons are encountered (metaphorical ones, in Chaucer's case) and characters are beaten horribly. If Chaucer did have this incident in mind, the link between the tale and its teller, which has appeared weak to many,[7] should appear stronger. The Reeve is telling a tale whose resonances with events from his namesake's life, for those who might recognize them, reflect his desire to embarrass the Miller, in ways beyond those already evident, and whose differences from it reveal his own shortcomings in comparison to the virtues of the bishop and saint.

Oswald's life could have been familiar to Chaucer and his audience from several sources which I will discuss below, but the *SEL* seems the most probable. This was a collection of Old Testament history, narratives from Christ's and Mary's lives, saints' lives, and other related texts, existing in various combinations and current from the second half of the thirteenth through the fifteenth centuries.[8] Oswald's vita in this collection usually extends to 222 lines. While it survives in 18 *SEL* manuscripts, the versions are quite consistent in general content, and there are no significant variant readings among them that would call into question the points I make below.[9] The vita highlights: 1) his close relationships with Saints Oda and Dunstan, Bishop Oskytel, Kings Athelstan and Edgar, and even Pope John; 2) his becoming a canon secular and then his devotion to the monastic life, while taking on the bishoprics of Worcester and York; 3) his several confrontations with the devil; 4) his participation with Bishop-Saints Dunstan and Athelwold in the enforcement of a policy to remove lecherous/*luþer* (married?) priests from their churches and to confiscate their property; 5) several miracles, including one in which a sinking boat loaded with monks who had come to hear him preach is raised from the depths; 6) his practice of housing, feeding, clothing, and washing the feet of twelve poor men each day; and 7) his heroic calm and continued religious activity in the face of old age, sickness, and death.

96–101.

[6] Susanna Greer Fein, '"Lat the Children Pleye": The Game betwixt the Ages in the Reeve's Tale', in *Rebels and Rivals: The Contestive Spirit in 'The Canterbury Tales'*, ed. by Susanna Greer Fein, David Raybin, and Peter C. Braeger (Kalamazoo, MI: Medieval Institute Publications, 1991), pp. 73–104 (p. 79). John Matthews Manly speculated that Chaucer may have had a particular reeve in mind. Indeed, he cites intriguing evidence that someone mismanaged property with which Chaucer was familiar and which may have been in Norfolk. See his 'The Reeve' and 'The Miller', in *Some New Light on Chaucer: Lectures Delivered at the Lowell Institute* (1926; repr. New York: Peter Smith, 1951), pp. 84–101. But unfortunately, Manly was unable to identify his hypothetical 'tricky Reeve of Baldeswelle' by name (p. 93).

[7] See Fein, 'Lat the Children Pleye', p. 74, esp. n. 2.

[8] See especially O. S. Pickering, 'The *Temporale* Narratives of the *South English Legendary*', *Anglia*, 91 (1973), 425–55; Manfred Görlach, *The Textual Tradition of the South English Legendary*, Leeds Texts and Monographs, n. s. 6 (Leeds: University of Leeds, School of English, 1974); O. S. Pickering, 'The Expository *Temporale* Poems of the *South English Legendary*', *Leeds Studies in English*, n. s. 10 (1978), 1–17; Thomas R. Liszka, 'The *South English Legendaries*', in *The North Sea World in the Middle Ages*, ed. by Thomas R. Liszka and Lorna E. M. Walker (Dublin: Four Courts Press, 2001), pp. 243-80; and *Rethinking the 'South English Legendaries'*, ed. by Heather Blurton and Jocelyn Wogan-Browne (Manchester: Manchester University Press, 2011), in which the previous essay is reprinted (pp. 23–65).

[9] See the appended apparatus of all substantive variants among the manuscripts of the two passages from the *SEL*

There are two relevant passages from the *SEL*, both relating to his encounters with the devil. The first establishes that, when Oswald was a monk, the devil often came to him at night to torment him 'wanne he was al one inis bede' (I.73, line 66).[10] The phrase 'inis bede' (italicized in the quote below) was probably originally intended to mean 'in his prayers' or 'in his devotions' — consistent with Charlotte D'Evelyn's gloss for *bede* in the *SEL* edition (III.43) and with the version of the line as it appears in five manuscripts, with readings related to *beodes* rather than *bede*. However, I submit that, given the two references to night in the context (also italicized), the half line, as it appears in most of the manuscripts, could easily have been read or misread as 'when he was alone in his bed'. Indeed, in place of 'wanne he was al one inis bede', one manuscript has the reading 'as he allone in bed lay'. In this episode, the devil would roar, but the good saint could easily defeat him by making the Sign of the Cross:

¶His breþeren were wel glad of him • þo hi vnderȝite
Þat holy lif þat he was on • for noþing hy nolde him lete
In orisons he was *niȝt* & day • & in oþer gode þinge
Þer of þe deuel hadde envie • and þoȝte him þerof bringe
Ofte he com in deorne stude • *biniȝte* him to afere
Wanne he was al one *inis bede* • & made reuful bere
Ac wanne þis holyman hurde him • so deoluoliche rore
Þe signe he made of þe crois • & ne hurde him namore
Þo þe deuel ysey þis • þat he nemiȝte him come wiþinne
He þoȝte mid oþer felonye • þis holyman wynne
(I.73, lines 61-70; emphasis mine)

(His brethren were very happy for him, when they understood the holy life that he was leading. They would not discourage him for anything. He was in prayers, night and day, and performing other good actions. For that reason, the devil had envy, and intended to bring him out of it. Often, he came to his private place at night to frighten him when he was alone in his prayers [or 'in his bed'] and made a dismal outcry. But when this holy man heard him roar so distressfully, he made the Sign of the Cross and heard him no more. When the devil saw this, that he could not possess him, he decided to defeat this holy man with other treachery.)

The second passage contains the parallel to the Reeve's Tale. In this passage, Oswald's 'deorne stude' or private place is unambiguously a bed. While Oswald was praying one night and while all but one of the other monks 'in hore bede lay • aslepe', that last monk, on returning from his bath, accidentally 'lay in seint Oswold is bed'. Four devils accost him, ask him how he could be so bold as to lie in his master's bed, and when the monk does not have a good answer, they beat him until he cries out and makes 'such bere'. Obviously, he is not the match for them that Oswald is. The other monks who come running also chastise the monk for his presumption, but the episode ends happily with shrift, penance, and forgiveness:

As inis pryuey orisons • seint Oswold a niȝt was
& is monekes in hore bede lay • aslepe it biuel bicas

quoted below. And see Görlach, *Textual Tradition*, 146–48, for a discussion of text of the vita as a whole.
[10] All quotations from the *SEL* and the reference to its glossary are from *The South English Legendary: Edited from Corpus Christi College Cambridge MS. 145 and British Museum MS. Harley 2277 with Variants from Bodley MS. Ashmole 43 and British Museum MS. Cotton Julius D. IX*, ed. by Charlotte D'Evelyn and Anna J. Mill, Early

Þ[at] o monk him let baþie • and þo he hadde ydo
He lay in seint Oswold is bed • ac to raþe he com þerto
Vour deuelen come & esste anon • wat he dude þere
In þe bed þat is maister was • & hou he so hardy were
¶Þo he nemiȝte non encheson vinde • faste hi him toke
And bete him so sore þoru þe cri • al þe monkes awoke
And come & holpe him hasteliche • & esste wat him were
And wat he in þulke bedde dude • & wy he made such bere
He was yknewe of al is gult • and among hom al yssriue
And sede is penance was inou • þei is gult were forȝiue
¶Seint Oswold forȝef it him • & bad þe monkes also
By þulke cas ywar hy were • efsone to misdo
(I.76, lines 153–66)

(As Saint Oswald was in his private prayers one night and his monks in their beds lay asleep, it happened by chance that one monk was bathing himself. And when he had finished, he lay in Saint Oswald's bed, but too rashly he came thereto. Four devils came and asked anon what he was doing there in the bed that belonged to his master, and how he could be so presumptuous. When he could not give a reason, they took him fast and beat him so sorely that, because of his cries, all the monks awoke and came hastily and helped him and asked what was happening to him and what he was doing in that bed and why he made such an outcry. He was made aware of his guilt by all and among them all, absolved. And they said he had had penance enough, though his sins had been forgiven. Saint Oswald forgave him for it and bade the monks also that, by that example, they should be wary again to misdo.)

Beyond the setting in a bedroom and the basic plot of someone's entering a wrong bed by mistake and the culmination in a horrible beating, several ideas will be important to note for the Reeve's Tale — especially, the agency of devils in the punishment of the presumptuous, the spiritual superiority of Oswald to the presumptuous monk, and the inevitable, if unstated, hint of sexuality in a story involving a bed, devils, and a naked bather.

Of course, closer sources for the plot of the Reeve's Tale as a whole have long been known and are discussed and edited by Walter Morris Hart and Peter G. Beidler.[11] Indeed, Beidler calls the basic story 'one of the most popular fabliaux in medieval Europe'. However, he argues that, rather than following any one source exclusively, Chaucer 'drew upon his memory of several of them to fashion his own wonderful story'.[12] I would argue that, in this fashioning, while Chaucer took most of the story from the more obvious sources and analogues, once the sexual comedy begins, he focused on the confusion of beds in order to evoke the parallel with the episode from St Oswald's life.

In particular, with respect to the first young man's sleeping with the daughter, an event which does not involve a confusion of beds, Chaucer bypasses content of significant comic and narrative potential available in the sources to achieve his focus. Aleyn's entrance into the daughter's bed begins the comic action, but Chaucer uses only five lines of poetry to tell this

English Text Society, o. s., 235, 236, 244, 3 vols (London: Oxford University Press, 1956–59) and are cited parenthetically in the text. The translations are mine.

[11] W. M. Hart, 'The Reeve's Tale', in *Sources and Analogues of Chaucer's Canterbury Tales*, ed. by W. F. Bryan and Germaine Dempster (New York: Humanities Press, 1958), pp. 124–48 [first publ. 1941]; Peter G. Beidler, 'The Reeve's Tale', in *Sources and Analogues of The Canterbury Tales*, ed. by Robert M. Correale and Mary Hamel, 2 vols (Cambridge: Brewer, 2002–5), I 23–73.

[12] Beidler, 'The Reeve's Tale', 23, 26.

part of the story (I.4193–97). In the comparable parts of both versions of *Le Meunier et Les .II. Clers*, however, after the father locks his daughter in a trunk for her own protection, the clerk who approaches her makes a lover's plea and then wins her love via a trick. He offers her a ring, which he claims is gold and has the magical ability to restore her maidenhead, when in actuality it was something he had taken from an andiron in their fireplace. The narration in both versions, without the locking of the daughter in the trunk, fills approximately 35 lines and is as entertaining as the mistake made by the wife in entering the other clerk's bed. In *Ein Bispel van .ij. Clerken*, the clerk similarly woos the daughter and wins her by giving her a fraudulent golden ring that is really from their fireplace. There is no claim of magic and the daughter sleeps in a conventional bed rather than a trunk; nevertheless, the narration is developed through 30 lines of poetry. In the *Decameron* version (IX.6), Boccaccio may seem to narrate this part of the story as briefly as Chaucer does. From the time all are in their beds to Pinuccio's enjoyment of the daughter only two sentences pass, but really Boccaccio crafts the entire story to culminate in this moment. Because Pinuccio and the daughter had previously fallen in love, Pinuccio plans a way to sleep with her without their reputations' suffering dishonor. He and his companion employ a trick, claiming to be returning from a journey late at night and to require lodging, so that the girl's father will allow Pinuccio the opportunity to sleep in their house. He does not seize an opportunity of the moment as do his companion and all of the men in the other versions of the story.

Chaucer, however, despite these opportunities for development, moves quickly past Aleyn's initial venture to focus on John's crafty shifting of the cradle from the foot of the miller's and his wife's bed to the foot of his own. Thus begin over 100 lines of comedy based on the mistakes and consequences of the wife's and then Aleyn's entering the wrong beds. Chaucer makes significant use of details in the analogues, but he has clearly focused on events reminiscent of the episode from St Oswald's life.

* * *

While Chaucer does nothing to make his readers aware of his borrowings from his other sources, Chaucer invokes the saintly name that he has given his Reeve, Osewold, three times leading up to the tale. Apparently, through this crescendo of allusions, he wished to invite a comparison between Osewold and his bishop namesake, one which I think develops nicely Chaucer's previously well-recognized characterization of the Reeve as someone who inappropriately acts as if he were a priest.[13]

We are told that the Reeve's 'top was dokked lyk a preest biforn' (I.590) and 'tukked he was as is a frere aboute' (I.621). He objects to the tale that the Miller proposes to tell because 'it is a synne and eek a greet folye' (I.3146). And the Host recognizes his exposition of the four embers of old age — boasting, lying, anger, and covetousness — as inappropriate 'sermonyng', then adds, mockingly, 'the devel made a reve for to preche' (I.3883–903).[14] Chaucer has the Miller similarly mock Osewold's pretension in several ways, but especially by

---

[13] See, for example, Jill Mann, *Chaucer and Medieval Estates Satire* (Cambridge: Cambridge University Press, 1973), p. 284 n. 70, and, more recently, Bryan Carella, 'The Social Aspirations and Priestly Pretense of Chaucer's Reeve', *Neophilologus*, 94 (2010), 523–29.

[14] A detail perhaps suggested by St Oswald's reputation as a great preacher. In another episode from his life, both in the *SEL* (I.76, lines 171–72) and in many of the other versions mentioned below, monks come by the boatload, literally, to hear him preach.

having the carpenter in his tale perform a kind of exorcism with botched, nonsensical prayers (I.3479–86).

If the narrative told by Chaucer's would-be priest is compared to the version told about the sainted, super priest, additional mockery of the Reeve becomes apparent, as events seem twisted from the way they should appear. First, in both narratives, persons get into wrong beds. In the saint's life, this is an act of presumption which culminates in the beating of the presumptuous person. But Chaucer's Reeve gets it wrong. In his story, though Aleyn and the wife enter the wrong beds, neither appears presumptuous and neither, except for Aleyn's bloodied nose, is beaten. Indeed, they seem rewarded. Aleyn enjoys the daughter and, in the process, wins her love (becoming her 'deere lemman' and her 'goode lemman'), and he retrieves the stolen grain (I.4240–48). The wife, though duped, is nevertheless pleased ('so myrie a fit ne hadde she nat ful yoore' — I.4230). In the Reeve's version, the presumptuous monk's character and punishment are transferred to the miller Symkyn, the pilgrim Miller's representative in the tale. Symkyn takes too much pride in his wife's lineage and his own cleverness, and he receives the horrible beating both from the clerks and, worse, from his own wife, who unwittingly strikes the first blow.

The stories are similar also in that real or, in the Reeve's Tale, figurative demons punish the guilty party in the bedroom. In St Oswald's life, devils beat the presumptuous monk. So, if there were a closer modelling of the Reeve's Tale on the saint's life, the clerks who beat Symkyn should play the devils' roles — and, to some extent, they do, but they do so only briefly and metaphorically. Aleyn is said to go 'a twenty devel way, | Unto the bed ther as the millere lay' (I.4257–58). And when the fighting begins and the wife feels attacked, she cries 'awak, Symond! The feend is on me fall' (I.4288). But, while she believes that the clerks are fighting with each other and that one of those clerkly fiends has fallen on her, readers know that the specific 'feend' who has fallen upon her is none other than her own miller husband Symkyn — not those doing the beating, but the recipient of the beating.

So, in his own version of this episode from Oswald's life, the Reeve has been able to characterize his stand-in for the Miller as both the presumptuous guilty party and as the devil! At the same time, those Reeve's Tale characters who actually correspond to the presumptuous monk are rewarded and get to administer the punishment to Symkyn. It would seem then that someone who knew Oswald's life, or maybe a real priest, would find these ironies amusing.

A final disparity between the stories cements our impression of the Reeve as a very poor would-be priest and the loser in the comparison. He ends his tale not with penance and forgiveness of the presumptuous, as the saint's life does, but with 'the proude millere wel ybete' (I.4313). Chaucer, by juxtaposing the narratives in our minds, characterizes Osewold as clearly inferior to his namesake and his priestly pretense as presumptuous. Susanna Grier Fein persuaded us of the 'inverted applicability' of one of St Oswald's characteristics to the Reeve, but Chaucer may well have intended more.

* * *

These interpretive possibilities, no matter how far we take them, depend on Chaucer's knowledge of St Oswald the Bishop's life as it appears in the *South English Legendary* or a version similar to it. Theoretically, such knowledge might have come from his own church-going experience and be evidenced in liturgical sources. However, despite St Oswald's youth in Canterbury and Ramsey Abbey, his having been a monk in Fleury and Winchester, having founded seven monasteries, and being both Bishop of Worcester and later simultaneously

Archbishop of York, his cult was more local than national. There seem not to have been any churches dedicated to him.[15] The various St Oswald churches seem all to have been dedicated to St Oswald the King and Martyr. Moreover, although his name is included in calendars and litanies in a number of places, he seems to have had major feasts only at Ramsey in Cambridgeshire, Worcester, and perhaps Evesham (within Worcester's influence).[16]

Unfortunately, there is no record of Chaucer's having visited these three places. But the truth is that there are great gaps in our knowledge of where Chaucer may have travelled within the island from his residences in London and Kent. An exception, however, might be instructive as to the range of his travel. Derek Pearsall notes that, as a page with the Countess of Ulster's household, Chaucer went within a few years' time to Woodstock (near Oxford, about half way from London to Worcester), to Bristol (as far away as Worcester, though further to the south), and to Anglesey, Liverpool and Doncaster (all twice as far north from London as either Worcester or Cambridgeshire and spanning the breadth of the island), in addition to other locations closer to home.[17] Perhaps, then, we should not be surprised if Chaucer did at some time find his way to Worcestershire or Cambridgeshire. His wife Phillippa may have lived estranged from Geoffrey in Lincolnshire, which is due north of Cambridgeshire.[18] If so, Chaucer may have visited her. And, of course, with respect to Chaucer's setting the Reeve's Tale in Cambridgeshire, Bennett allows that Chaucer somehow 'knew what he was talking about' with respect to his handling of several matters of local color and importance.[19] Nevertheless, speculation that Chaucer could have heard the details of St Oswald's life from the pulpit remains, at best, inconclusive.

It is much more probable that he read a life of St Oswald. Chaucer (or someone thoroughly familiar with his works, speaking for him) in the famous 'retraction' does not retract, and indeed thanks, Jesus, Mary, and 'alle the seintes of heven' for allowing him to write or translate 'bookes of legendes of seintes' (X.1087–88) that are now lost to us. From one of these books, presumably, St Cecilia's life was reappropriated to become the Second Nun's Tale. It is unthinkable that Chaucer would have composed these books without hagiographic source material at hand. Indeed, he credits 'Frater Jacobus Januensis in Legenda' for his etymologies of Cecelia's name (VIII.84–85); he must, therefore, have seen the *Legenda Aurea*. Unfortunately, Oswald's life is not in that large collection. But Chaucer clearly had access to additional materials as well. Sherry Reames, in her summary of Chaucer's sources for the Second Nun's Prologue and Tale, mentions several, including two Latin abridgements of the *Passio S. Caeciliae*, one from the *Legenda Aurea* which Chaucer acknowledged and a second whose use she had previously discovered.[20] And Robert Boenig has argued that Chaucer used the *SEL* life of St Kenelm in composing the Nun's Priest's and Prioress's Tales.[21]

---

[15]   Frances Arnold-Forster, *Studies in Church Dedications; or, England's Patron Saints*, 3 vols (London: Skeffington, 1899), I, 413–15 (p. 415) and III, 21.

[16]   Alan Thacker, 'Saint-Making and Relic Collecting by Oswald and His Communities', in *St Oswald of Worcester: Life and Influence*, ed. by Nicholas Brooks and Catherine Cubitt, The Makers of England, 2 (London: Leister University Press, 1996), pp. 244–68 (esp. pp. 264–65).

[17]   Derek Pearsall, *The Life of Geoffrey Chaucer: A Critical Biography* (Oxford: Blackwell, 1992), pp. 38–39.

[18]   Ibid., 141–42.

[19]   Bennett, *Chaucer at Oxford and at Cambridge*, 116.

[20]   Sherry L. Reames, 'The Second Nun's Prologue and Tale', in *Sources and Analogues of The Canterbury Tales*, ed. by Robert M. Correale and Mary Hamel, 2 vols (Cambridge: Brewer, 2002–5), I 491–527.

[21]   Robert Boenig, 'Chaucer and St. Kenelm', *Neophilologus*, 84 (2000), 157–64. Furthermore, other scholars, notably Ann S. Haskell, have argued for the importance of allusions to saints' names in the *Canterbury Tales* and other works by Chaucer: *Essays on Chaucer's Saints* (The Hague: Mouton, 1976).

Moreover, Boenig argued for a relationship of the Kenelm vita to the other sources of the Nun's Priest's Tale, similar to the one I see here:

> I am not arguing that the *Life of St. Kenelm* suggested the bird-in-tree motif to Chaucer, for the close analogues to the Nun's Priest's Tale [...] all include the treed rooster. Doubtless Chaucer simply appropriated the detail from his direct source. But I do suggest that the influence perhaps worked the other way around: given Chaunticleer and his tree, the reference to the murdered boy king who dreamed himself as a bird in a tree was perhaps inevitable.[22]

And he argued that important parallels between the stories of Kenelm in the *SEL* and the martyred boy of the Prioress's Tale were suggested to Chaucer by the 'imaginative connection' he saw 'between him and Kenelm'.[23]

Indeed, the chances are good that Chaucer, and much of his audience, could have known a version of the *South English Legendary*. The collection's popularity can be deduced from the large number of manuscripts extant today. While undoubtedly many more copies were available in Chaucer's day, remnants of 63 *SEL* manuscripts of all sorts including either *sanctorale* or *temporale* texts survive. These include 25 complete or substantially complete manuscripts of the *sanctorale* collection and fragments of 15 additional manuscripts that may once have been similar in scope.[24] Oswald the Bishop's life is contained in 18 of these manuscripts, and thus was probably widely distributed among the manuscripts now lost. Dialectal studies indicate that the surviving manuscripts originated in areas away from London, but Oxford, Bodleian Library, MS Laud Miscellaneous 108, among the earliest of *SEL* manuscripts (though not containing St Oswald the Bishop's life), is now known to have been owned in the fifteenth century by Henry Perveys, a London draper and the son of John Perveys, a former mayor of London.[25] So other *SEL* manuscripts could easily have made their way to London and been available to its notables as well.

Chaucer may also, or alternatively, have known Oswald's life from some other source. Earlier Latin versions of the life of St Oswald, and notably the *Vita Sancti Oswaldi Eboracensis Archiepiscopi et Confessoris* of Eadmer, which became the standard life, lay the foundation for the *SEL* story. It contains the episode of a monk who falls asleep in a place special to Oswald where he is tormented by demons. However, Eadmer's version differs in some important particulars. When the monk, named Ægelricus, returns from his bath, he goes not necessarily to Oswald's bed, but either to a place where Oswald frequently sits ('Osuualdus sedere

---

[22] Boenig, 'Chaucer and St. Kenelm', pp. 159–60.

[23] Ibid., p. 163.

[24] For the total of 63, see my accounting in Virginia Blanton, 'Counting Noses and Assessing the Numbers: Native Saints in the *South English Legendaries*', in *Rethinking the 'South English Legendaries'*, ed. by Heather Blurton and Jocelyn Wogan-Browne (Manchester: Manchester University Press, 2011), pp. 233–50 (p. 247 n. 5), which offers a correction to my previous accounting in 'The Dragon in the *South English Legendary*: Judas, Pilate, and the "A(1)" Redaction', *Modern Philology*, 100 (2002), 50-59 (pp. 50–51 n. 2). The accounting is based especially on Görlach, *Textual Tradition*, viii-x, 70–130, whose sigla I employ. For the total of 25 here, I include MS Z (New Haven CT, Yale University Library (Beinecke Library), MS Takamiya 54, a manuscript that was not known at the time of Görlach's publication), and I exclude MS I from his 'major manuscripts'. For the total of 15, I include his MSS Ar, Be, Bp, Br, Cd, Gr, Lm, Pr/Wm, Rm, Qb, Ua/Wa, Ub, Wh, Ax, and Uz.

[25] See *Havelok*, ed. by G. V. Smithers (Oxford: Clarendon Press, 1987), pp. xiii–xiv, crediting A. I. Doyle. See also Christina M. Fitzgerald, 'Miscellaneous Masculinities and a Possible Fifteenth-Century Owner of Oxford, Bodleian Library, MS Laud Misc. 108', in *The Texts and Contexts of Oxford Bodleian Library, MS Laud Misc. 108: The Shaping of English Vernacular Narrative*, ed. by Kimberly K. Bell and Julie Nelson Couch, Medieval and Renaissance Authors and Texts, 6 (Leiden: Brill, 2011), pp. 87–113.

frequentius morem habebat') or — because the verb *sedere* may be taken more generally — to an unspecified place that Oswald frequently occupies, and it is there that Ægelricus sleeps. Moreover, the monk sleeps there not by mistake, except in the larger sense of the word, but because he did not revere the sanctity of the place ('non ergo ueritus sanctitatem loci'). In other respects, Eadmer's version is generally consistent with the *SEL* version:

> Frater quidam erat, professione et habitu monachus, nomine Ægelricus. Hic, laxatis balneo membris, cum fessus quiescere opus haberet, locus quietis, uae misero, is primus occurrit quem uenerandus praesul Osuualdus sedere frequentius morem habebat. Non ergo ueritus sanctitatem loci quam fuerat ex assiduitate pontificis nactus, in eo sese deiecit, somno inibi ac dulci quiete uelut sibi pollicebatur fruiturus. Et iam quiescentem lenis sopor inuoluit, sed absque mora eum ab ipsa quiete irruens demonum multitudo atrociter euoluit. Astant quippe illi plures teterrimi spiritus, et ab eo districta examinatione perquirunt quaenam illius mentem dementia ceperit quae sibi, ut se in loco tanti pontificis collocaret, surripere potuit. Ad quod rationem quam pro sui excusatione proferret nullam habentem, inuadunt, torquent, laniant, hac et illac trahunt, ab imo sursum rapientes, de sursum ad ima deicientes. Quid miser ageret? Sciebat ubi erat, nec se tanta angustia inuolutum uel loco auellere, uel ad subueniendum quenquam poterat interpellare. Tandem tamen uiolento conatu erupit in uocem, et horrido clamore infremuit. Qui circa erant ex abrupto dormientis sono perterriti, accurrunt, uociferantem pulsant, pulsantes excitant, excitatum quid dormiens passus sit diligenter interrogant. At ipse pauens ac pallens quo ausu, quid fecerit, quid aut a quibus audierit, quid pertulerit ex ordine pandit. Ad quorumcunque ergo noticiam istud perlatum est, non soli uiro, sed et iis quae sua intererant deinceps honorem ac reuerentiam per omnia deferebant.

> (There was a certain brother named [Ægelricus] who was a monk both by his vows and in his dress. When this man had relaxed his limbs in the bath, he was weary and felt a need to sleep; alas for the wretch, the first place of rest which suggested itself to him was that which quite frequently the venerable bishop Oswald was accustomed to occupy. And so, not intimidated by the sanctity of the place which it had obtained from its frequent use by the bishop, he laid himself down upon it intending to enjoy sleep and sweet rest there, just as he had promised himself. And when gentle slumber had just enfolded him in rest, without delay a multitude of hideous demons rushed upon him, and rudely snatched him from that peacefulness. For many extremely ugly spirits stood around him and asked him with insistent cross-examination what sort of madness had overrun his mind, which might seduce him in this way to set himself down in the place of such a great bishop. He had no justification which he could offer in response to this as an excuse for himself and so they attacked him, tortured him, mangled him, dragged him back and forth, snatching him up on high from the depths and then casting him down again to the depths from on high. What was the miserable wretch to do? He knew where he was and yet was unable either to tear himself away from the place in which he was so tightly constrained or to cry out for someone to come to his aid. Nevertheless, with violent effort he finally recovered his voice and roared loudly with a hideous scream. Those who were nearby were thoroughly

---

[26] The edition and translation are from Eadmer of Canterbury, *Lives and Miracles of Saints Oda, Dunstan, and Oswald*, ed. by Andrew J. Turner and Bernard J. Muir (Oxford: Clarendon Press, 2006), pp. 215–89 (pp. 276–77). However, I made two modifications to their translation to make it closer to the Latin text, marked with square brackets. Turner and Muir substitute 'Æthelric', the name of an actual monk of Worcester in Oswald's day, for 'Ægelricus' (see p. 276 n. 103). And where the Latin has the unspecific 'uiro', they substitute the man intended, i.e., 'Oswald'. For an earlier edition of the vita, see Eadmer, *Vita Sancti Oswaldi Eboracensis Archiepiscopi et Confesorsis* [sic], in *The Historians of the Church of York and Its Archbishops*, ed. by James Raine, Rerum Britannicarum medii aevi scriptores, 71, 3 vols (London: longman, 1879–94), II, 1–59 (episode on pp. 33–34).

terrified by the unexpected cry of the sleeping man; they ran to him, struck him as he cried, by striking they awoke him and when he had awakened they persistently questioned him about what he had experienced in his sleep. And, terrified and pale, he revealed step by step how bold he had been and what he had done, what things he had heard and from whom, and what he had suffered. Whenever this event was later brought to the attention of anyone, they paid honour and reverence in all matters not only to [the man] himself, but after that to those things which were important to him.)[26]

Eadmer's vita survives in three manuscripts. One was Eadmer's autograph, which would have been kept at his monastery in Christ Church, Canterbury. Another was a copy kept at the monastery of Pershore in Worcestershire, which Oswald founded. The third is of uncertain provenance, but is a collection of saints' lives, primarily English, and associated texts that may have been at Ramsey Abbey in Cambridgeshire.[27]

Some versions of Oswald's life lack the episode in question. The earliest life of Oswald, composed soon after his death in 992 by the monk Byrhtferth, also at Ramsey Abbey, does not contain it.[28] Of the lives or other works derivative of Eadmer's vita, three lack it: William of Malmsbury's *Historia Novella*, the Worcester Lectionary, and an anonymous life in a collection from Romsey Abbey in Hampshire.[29] But two others — a vita by Senatus of Worcester[30] and another from John of Tynemouth's *Sanctilogium* (sometimes ascribed incorrectly to John Capgrave)[31] — do narrate the episode of the presumptuous monk who sleeps in a place that Oswald frequently occupies. In these, as in Eadmer's account, the place is similarly identified indirectly by verb forms related to *sedere*, and so may or may not be a bed.

Two English versions are indebted to Eadmer: the *SEL* vita and also a revision of the *SEL* text into English prose undertaken after 1438 for addition to the *Gilte Legende*. Though written after Chaucer's death, it may preserve evidence of other, no longer extant versions of the story that he might have encountered. The Oswald life in the *Gilte Legende* has the episode of the monk, sleeping specifically in a bed belonging to Oswald, as in the *SEL*, but it contains an emphasis on the importance of keeping matins not found in other versions:

> but in a nyght, as this holye man and alle his monkys were at Matyns, except one monke that wente to bath hym and lefte the Matyns, and when he had do he wente and layde hym downe to slepe in Seynt Oswoldis bedde. And anone the devylle came theder and tormentyd hym fulle sore, that he cryed and made a grete noyse that alle the monkis herd it and came theder anone and fownde hym in Oswoldis bedde. And thaye askyd hym whye

[27] *Lives and Miracles of Saints Oda, Dunstan, and Oswald*, ed. by Turner and Muir, cvi–cxxiv.

[28] Available as *Vita Oswaldi Archiepiscopi Eboracensis* in *Historians of the Church of York and Its Archbishops*, ed. bu Raine, I, 399–475; see also 'Preface', I, lxv–lxvii. For the identification of the author as Byrthferth by Michael Lapidge, see Donald Bullough, 'St Oswald: Monk, Bishop and Archbishop', in *St Oswald of Worcester: Life and Influence*, ed. by Nicholas Brooks and Catherine Cubitt, The Makers of England, 2 (London: Leister University Press, 1996), pp. 1–22 (p. 2).

[29] For identification of these Latin works and of the English works mentioned in the next paragraph, see *Lives and Miracles of Saints Oda, Dunstan, and Oswald*, ed. by Turner and Muir, cxxi–cxxvii. The life from Romsey Abbey is available as *Vita S. Oswaldi*, in *Historians of the Church of York and Its Archbishops*, ed. by Raine, II, 489–501.

[30] Available as *Vita Sancti Oswaldi Archiepiscopi*, in *Historians of the Church of York and Its Archbishops*, ed. by Raine, II, 60–97 (episode on pp. 85–86).

[31] Available as *Vita Sancti Oswaldi, A Joanne Capgrave Conscripta*, in *Historians of the Church of York and Its Archbishops*, ed. by Raine, II, 502–12 (episode on p. 508). Turner and Muir state incorrectly that in this version the monk slept in Oswald's bed (*Lives and Miracles of Saints Oda, Dunstan, and Oswald*, cxxvii). The life is also available as *De Sancto Oswaldo Archiepiscopo et Confessore*, in *Nova Legenda Anglie: As Collected by John of Tynemouth, John Capgrave, and Others, and First Printed, with New Lives, by Wynkyn de Worde a.d. m d xiii*, ed.

he made suche a noyse, and he tolde theym that the devylle vexyd hym so sore because he kepte not Matyns and because that he laye in Oswoldis bedde. And then he repentyd hym, and the holye man forgaue hym that trespas and chargid his monkys to be euer after at Matyns and other seruyce in the churche.[32]

Hamer and Russell characterize the main part of the *Gilte Legende*, not including Oswald's vita, as 'a close translation, with slight modifications of the contents, of Jean de Vignay's *Légende Dorée* of about 1333–40, which in turn is a close translation of Jacobus de Voragine's *Legenda Aurea*, completed about 1267'. The Oswald vita is one of twenty-one supplementary or 'additional lives', added to the main collection in three manuscripts. These additional lives are primarily English saints' lives and, except for one, drawn from the *South English Legendary*.[33]

Among these additional lives, Manfred Görlach characterizes the *Gilte Legende* rendering of the St Oswald life as similarly 'very close' to its source, the *SEL* version. However, Görlach notes that no source for the emphasis on keeping matins has been found. Because the content did not come from the *SEL*, which was otherwise closely followed, he concludes that the detail suggests the existence of other now lost works or even oral traditions available to the *Gilte Legende* reviser and, I would add, to Chaucer as well.[34]

* * *

So, while there seems to be a variety of ways that Chaucer could have known the details of St Oswald the Bishop's story, his encountering a *South English Legendary* version seems to me the most likely. And those readers of Osewold's story in the *Canterbury Tales* who recognized the parallels to St Oswald's story and, more importantly, Chaucer's departures from it could not have failed to appreciate additional levels to the Reeve's attack upon the Miller and additional richness and irony in Chaucer's characterization of his pilgrim Osewold as a man who fancies himself a priest but who is a very poor match for his priestly and saintly namesake.

Appendix: Substantive Variant Readings among the *SEL* Manuscripts for the Lines Quoted.

The sigla are from Görlach, *Textual Tradition*, pp. viii–x.

61–70, 153–66] *lines lost, missing leaf* X.

61–70] *lines lost, missing leaf* Qa.

61 His] þe N; were wel glad] glad were G; wel] ful wel W, *omitted* PYTDER; glad] *omitted* W; of him] ynow R, *omitted* E; of] with T; þo] when GY; hi] him J, hy hym B; vnderȝite] thider ȝete W.

by Carl Horstmann, 2 vols (Oxford: Clarendon Press, 1901), II, 252–60 (episode on p. 257).

[32] Available as *St Oswald*, item 13 in *Supplementary Lives in Some Manuscripts of the 'Gilte Legende'*, ed. by Richard Hamer and Vida Russell, Early English Text Society, o. s. 315 (Oxford: Oxford University Press, 2000), pp. 173–78 (episode on p. 177, lines 95–106).

[33] *Supplementary Lives in Some Manuscripts of the 'Gilte Legende'*, ed. by Hamer and Russell, xiii–xv (quoting p. xiii). They note that among the three manuscripts of the *Gilte Legende* that preserve the additional lives, one is unfortunately now missing the quire that contained the Oswald vita. The vita is also one of six of these additional lives that were incorporated in a manuscript of Mirk's *Festial*.

[34] Manfred Görlach, 'The South English Legendary, Gilte Legende and Golden Legend', in *Studies in Middle English Saints' Legends*, Anglistische Forschungen, 257 (Heidelberg: Winter, 1998), pp. 71–145 (pp. 106, 124–25).

62 Þat(1)] þe VWGYTDER; he was] was hym RB; he] him VMAJ, saynt Oswald G; was]
   ladde WGDE; on] *omitted* WGDE, of Y, ine T; hy] *omitted* WR, he T; nolde] wolde
   W; him] he W, *omitted* MT.

63 In orisons he was] he was in orisoun G; orisons] his orisones V, his praiers W, bedes E;
   was] lay W; niȝt & day & in] day & nyȝt for be G; oþer gode] alle oþer G, alle goode
   oþer P, al oþir goed Y, holi E.

64 Þer of þe deuel hadde envie] the deuel had envye ther to W, þe deuel hedde þer to
   onde E; Þer of þe deuel] þe fende þerto G; Þer(1)] & þer B; deuel] feende Y; envie]
   comye R; and] *omitted* A; him þerof] þerof him PEB, þer fro him Y; þerof(2)] þer
   out of V, out to W, þerof to GTR, þerof owt J, out to D.

65 Ofte] fful ofte G, wel ofte B; deorne stude] derke stede WB, priue stedes PY; biniȝte
   him] hym by nyȝt G.

66 Wanne] as G; was al one inis bede] in his beodes was V, alone in his bed was W, allone
   in bed lay G; bede] bedys QPYB; &] a M; reufol] ful rewful W, rulich PYRB, reuþfol
   E; bere] chere WGY.

67 Ac] but GYT, *omitted* W, & AD; wanne] þo G; þis holyman] he E; hurde him] him
   herde ER; deoluoliche] rewfully WGR, dreduolliche AJQDEB, doelfully YT.

68 Þe signe he made] he made þe signe G; he made of þe crois] of þe crois he made on
   him VW; þe(2)] *omitted* T; &] and þenne VMAJPYDB, *omitted* W, þo E; ne hurde]
   he ne herde B; ne] *omitted* QYTDE; hurde] herde he VMAPDE, he herde WQYT,
   herde of G; him] *omitted* MD, it AJ.

69–70] *reversed* M.

69 Þo] but G, when Y, *omitted* TD; deuel] feende Y; ysey] ne sei A; þis] *omitted*
   VGMAJPYDERB, wel W; þat he] *omitted* G; nemiȝte] ne mihte wiþ drede V, myȝt
   nat WY, þerwiþ he may not G, ne miȝt þer wiþ MANQTDRB, miȝte þer wit J; him
   come] come him WGMPYDE, him ouercome T; wiþinne] ynne G.

70 mid] wiþ VWGAJQPYTDB; oþer] anoþur W; felonye] folye WR; þis] þat M; wynne]
   to winne VWGMPYTDRB.

153 As] *omitted* ER, as he B; in] *omitted* M; is] *omitted* VQaGA; orisons] preyȝeres PY;
    seint] *omitted* B; a] on a W, in G; was] at his bok was V.

154 &] as Qa; in hore bede lay] leiȝe in here bed T; in hore bede] *omitted* W, abedde
    M; hore] *omitted* G; bede] beddes QaPY; lay aslepe] aslepe were WQa; lay] weore V,
    omitted GMAJDER; aslepe] *omitted* PYDB, & slepe TR; it] as hit VWYTB, *omitted*
    GED, at hit P, as R; biuel] fyl VWQaAPYTERB; bifel þere G, þer fel D; bicas] in a
    cas Qa, siche a cas G, þat cas M, a cas J, a wonder cas D.

155 Þat] þat þe J, þe CNQ, ak PE, but Y, *omitted* T, þer R; him let baþie] þer was þat
    him bathed Y; him let] let him VWG; him] he J; let] *omitted* P; and] ac Qa; þo]
    when YE; ydo] so do GPY.

156 lay] leide him VWQaE, ȝede G, eode ligge A, ȝede ligge J, ȝode lygge P, ȝeode to ly
    Y; in] into G; ac] *omitted* WG, & MERB, but YTD; raþe] sone Y; he(2)] *omitted* EB.

157 Vour] *omitted* W; deuelen] fendes GY; come] come þere T, þer com D; & esste anon]
    anon & and axid T, anon & axid D; esste] askeden him VWQaGMPY; anon] *omitted*
    VGME.

158 In þe bed þat is maister was &] lyand in his mayster bed G; þe bed þat is maister was]
    his maystres bed þo D; þe] *omitted* VWMAJER; hou] whi D, *omitted* E; he so hardy]
    so hardi he T; so] *omitted* M.

159 Þo] and þo G, when Y, *omitted* T; ne] *omitted* WGYT; non] *omitted* VQaMAJPDE,
no W; encheson] cause W; hi him] him hi P; toke] bounde and toke E.

160 And] *omitted* VQaM; bete him so sore] so sore heo him beote VW, so sore þey beten
hym Qa; bete] hii bete M; so sore þoru þe cri] þat he cryed so þat G; so] *omitted* T;
sore] þer E; þoru þe cri] þat M; þoru] and þorw V, þat þurgh WQaAJPYDERB; þe]
his VWQaAJDER; al þe monkes] he his felawes G; al] þat alle N.

161 And(1)] thei WER; &(2)] to GYTE; holpe] *omitted* GYE, vpe R; hasteliche] *omitted*
W; esste] askd hym WE; him(2)] he.

162 And(1)] *omitted* D; in þulke bedde dude] dude in þat bed Qa; þulke] þat WGQPYTER;
wy he] *omitted* Qa; he made] madist þou T; bere] a bere W, chere Y.

163 yknewe] beknow W, wele knowen G; of] *omitted* E; al(1)] *omitted* WQaGMPYER;
and among hom al] to alle and E; and] *omitted* DR; yssriue] hii stryue R.

164 And] þei D; sede] *omitted* E; is penance was] he hedde penaunce VWG, þat hadde
penance Qa; þei] þe N; is gult were] hit were hym R; is(2)] þe VQa, þat G; gult] synne
W.

165-66] *omitted* M.

165 forȝef it him] hit forȝaf E; it him] hym þere G; þe monkes] þese oþere G; þe] his
WE.

166 By þulke cas ywar hy were] to ben bi þulke cas iwar V, & be a war of þat cas Qa, þat
þai shuld by hym be war G, þat þei bi þat cas were war D; þulke] þat WQPYTE; ywar
hy were] to be ware W, þat hi were ywar PY, þei were war TER; efsone to] & eft no
more þat þou Qa, & no more G; to misdo] amys to do T, mis to do E.

Worthy, Wycht, and Wys: Romance, Chivalry, and Chivalric Language in John Barbour's *Bruce*

James W. Titterton[1]

Introduction

In the 1370s John Barbour, archdeacon of Aberdeen, composed a narrative poem about the life of Robert I of Scotland (*r*. 1306–29) and his victory over the English in the First War of Independence. The poem, known simply as *The Bruce*, appears to have been commissioned by Robert II (*r*. 1371–90), as Barbour received a royal pension from 1378 until his death in 1395. This is said to have been granted 'for the compilation of the book of the deeds of the late King Robert the Bruce'.[2]

It is a long work, written in Old Scots, the vernacular of fourteenth-century Scotland, full of battles and ambushes, daring escapes and base betrayals. It is a story about warriors and the hard business of warfare. Its principal characters are knights, courageous and skilled in battle, stalwart in the face of hardship, and loyal to their king. They also possess finer graces and are lauded by the poet for their courtesy and generosity to both friend and foe. They are heroic figures and Barbour calls their story a *romanys* (1.446), worthy of comparison with the tales of Charlemagne or Alexander.

It seems strange, then, that so many scholars have argued that *The Bruce* is neither a romance nor chivalrous. Kliman and Cameron have even gone so far as to argue that it should be read as an anti-romance that subverted contemporary chivalric norms. Through a close study of Barbour's text and his use of chivalric language, this article will argue that *The Bruce* has been misunderstood and that it is indeed a chivalric text. Keen defined chivalry as 'an ethos in which martial, aristocratic and Christian elements were fused together. [Chivalry] is a way of life in which we can discern these three essential facets, the military, the noble, and the religious'.[3] Using this definition as a starting point, this article will outline what Barbour meant

---

[1] My thanks to Dr Alan V. Murray for his advice in the writing of this piece and his encouragement to publish my research. My thanks also to Dr Trevor Russell Smith for his comments and editorial guidance.
[2] John Barbour, *The Bruce*, ed. by Archibald A. M. Duncan (Edinburgh: Canongate, 1997), pp. 2–3. All references to book and line numbers in the text are taken from this edition and all translations are my own.
[3] Maurice Keen, *Chivalry* (New Haven: Yale University Press, 1984), pp. 16–17. For an examination of how this definition remains relevant to later medieval Scotland, see Katie Stevenson, *Chivalry and Knighthood in Scotland, 1424–1513* (Woodbridge: Boydell, 2006), pp. 1–12.

101

by the term 'chivalry' and who or what he considered 'chivalrous' by studying the vocabulary that he used to describe his knightly characters and their deeds.

The Historiography of *The Bruce*

Scholars have studied *The Bruce* for its themes of freedom and nationalism, and its significance as the first major work of vernacular Scots literature. A number have also addressed Barbour's treatment of chivalry, while the question of the poem's genre has often been bound up with the study of its content. The most prolific Barbour scholar of the last century, and the key proponent of the anti-romance/anti-chivalry theory, was Kliman.[4] She contrasted the so-called 'courtly code' with Barbour's more practical concept of chivalry: the 'objects of the standard chivalry — personal fame, defeat of unbelievers, achievement of personal salvation, a lady's love — are not appropriate to the nature of the work'.[5] Kliman regarded the minor role played by women in *The Bruce* and the characters' failure to perform any love service as evidence of Barbour's rejection of conventional chivalry.[6] Kliman also argued that Robert Bruce's use of guerrilla warfare should be seen as a rejection of the conventional tactics of 'courtly' chivalry.[7] Edward Bruce (*c*. 1280–1318), Robert's brother, more remarkable for his 'willingness to die' than his 'prowess or wisdom', is the poem's example of a 'hero in the old tradition', while Robert adopts Barbour's more practical, if unconventional, idea of chivalry.[8]

Key to Kliman's understanding of chivalry in *The Bruce* is the theme of loyalty and the role of the common people in the war for Scottish freedom. Robert Bruce is encouraged, and occasionally rescued, by his subordinates: not typical behaviour for a hero of courtly romance.[9] This extends even to commoners, who are encompassed in a 'new transcendent chivalry' motivated by love of Scotland and 'the desire for freedom'.[10] Kliman listed all the named commoners who appear in *The Bruce* and their valiant deeds, the kind 'usually associated with the chivalrous warriors of the upper class'.[11] Again, Kliman repeated her argument that *The Bruce* contains the 'theme of chivalry in conflict with strategy' and that Robert Bruce's use of cunning and deception in the poem was 'antithetical to chivalry in the usual sense'.[12]

Kliman's work is useful for providing a broad framework for studying chivalry in *The Bruce* but her assumptions about chivalry and medieval warfare are dated. In an article examining Barbour's use of rhetoric, Kliman argued that the poet used the fourth-century work of military theory Vegetius's *De re militari* to shape the content of his pre-battle speeches, although she failed to provide any evidence of a direct link between the texts.[13] Her conclusion, based on that purely hypothetical link, was as follows: '[Charles] Oman

---

[4]   Kliman's arguments about Barbour's attitude towards chivalry draw extensively on the work of Wittig. See for example Kurt Wittig, *The Scottish Tradition in Literature* (Edinburgh: Oliver and Boyd, 1958).

[5]   Bernice W. Kliman, 'The Idea of Chivalry in John Barbour's *Bruce*', *Medieval Studies*, 35 (1973), 477–508 (p. 478).

[6]   Kliman, 'Idea of Chivalry', pp. 479–81.

[7]   Kliman, 'Idea of Chivalry', pp. 490–92.

[8]   Kliman, 'Idea of Chivalry', p. 493.

[9]   Kliman, 'Idea of Chivalry', p. 497.

[10] Kliman, 'Idea of Chivalry', p. 505.

[11] Bernice W. Kliman, 'The Significance of Barbour's Naming of Commoners', *Studies in Scottish Literature*, 11 (1973), 108–13 (p. 109).

[12] Kliman, 'Significance of Barbour's Commoners', pp. 110–11.

[13] Bernice W. Kliman, 'Speech as a Mirror of *Sapientia* and *Fortitudo* in Barbour's *Bruce*', *Medium Ævum*, 44 (1975), 151–61.

refs to most battles in the Middle Ages as between chivalrous maniacs, seeking glory rather than victory. So for Barbour to use Vegetius as a model of behaviour for his ideal hero is a significant departure from romance and even historical norms'.[14] Oman's 'chivalrous maniac' model of medieval warfare had been superseded even when Kliman wrote the above statement. As far back as 1954, Verbruggen dismissed Oman's arguments as 'facile', lacking 'both synthesis and critical insight'.[15] Fifty years of military history has demonstrated that there was a science to medieval warfare, in which effective leadership and strategic acumen were more important than brute force.[16]

Despite this glaring flaw, Kliman's interpretation has influenced many later scholars.[17] For instance, Purdon and Wasserman took Kliman's conclusions and suggested that *The Bruce* was intended to call Scottish knights away from the glamour of conventional chivalry and towards more practical service under the Stewart kings.[18] Cameron (formerly Väthjunker) repeated the idea that, in criticising the conduct of Edward Bruce, Barbour 'rather than redefining the code of chivalry [...] rejects it'.[19] On the subject of James Douglas (*d.* 1330), whom Barbour portrays as Robert Bruce's chief lieutenant, she wrote that he 'does not conform to the courtly concepts of chivalry any more than his swarthy physique does', and 'it is impossible to call Douglas an "ideal knight" without redefining the concept of chivalry beyond recognition'.[20] She would go on to elaborate on this theme, claiming that Barbour was redrawing the boundaries of chivalric virtue to emphasise *mesure* or cunning, as employed by Robert Bruce and Douglas, over thoughtless courage, as exemplified by characters such as Edward Bruce and Thomas Randolph, earl of Moray (*d.* 1332).[21]

Stevenson largely agreed with Kliman on Barbour's portrayal of chivalry, arguing that he 'modified the practice of chivalry to fit in his stories'.[22] Scenes like the infamous 'Douglas Larder', in which James Douglas had the blood of an English garrison which he had executed mixed with the contents of a wine-cellar, are instances in which Barbour's attempt to portray

[14] Kliman, 'Speech as a Mirror', pp. 151–52.

[15] Jean F. Verbruggen, *The Art of Warfare in Western Europe During the Middle Ages, from the Eighth Century to 1340*, trans. by Sumner Willard and Sheila C. M. Southern, 2nd rev. edn (Woodbridge: Boydell, 1997), p. 2.

[16] The literature on medieval military history is vast. Key texts include Philippe Contamine, *War in the Middle Ages*, trans. by Michael Jones (Oxford: Blackwell, 1984); John France, *Western Warfare in the Age of the Crusades, 1000–1300* (London: UCL Press, 1999); John Gillingham, 'Richard I and the Science of War in the Middle Ages', in *War and Government in the Middle Ages in Honour of J. O. Prestwich*, ed. by John Gillingham and James C. Holt (Woodbridge: Boydell, 1984), pp. 78–91; Helen Nicholson, *Medieval Warfare: Theory and Practice of War in Europe, 300–1500* (Basingstoke: Palgrave Macmillan, 2004); Raymond C. Smail, *Crusading Warfare, 1097–1193* (Cambridge: Cambridge University Press, 1956); Matthew Strickland, *War and Chivalry: The Conduct and Perception of War in England and Normandy, 1066–1217* (Cambridge: Cambridge University Press, 1996); Verbruggen, *Art of Warfare*.

[17] See Anne M. McKim, 'James Douglas and Barbour's Ideal of Knighthood', *Forum for Modern Language Studies*, 17 (1981), 167–80; Phoebe A. Mainster, 'How to Make a Hero: Barbour's Recipe', *Michigan Academician*, 20 (1988), 225–38.

[18] Liam O. Purdon and Julian N. Wasserman, 'Chivalry and Feudal Obligation in Barbour's *Bruce*', in *The Rusted Hauberk: Feudal Ideals of Order and their Decline*, ed. by Liam O. Purdon and Cindy L. Vitto (Gainesville: University Press of Florida, 1994), pp. 77–95.

[19] Sonja Väthjunker, 'A Study in the Career of Sir James Douglas' (unpublished doctoral thesis, University of Aberdeen, 1992), p. 178.

[20] Väthjunker, 'Study in the Career of Douglas', p. 258.

[21] Sonja Cameron, 'Chivalry in Barbour's *Bruce*', in *Armies, Chivalry and Warfare in Medieval Britain and France: Proceedings of the 1995 Harlaxton Symposium*, ed. by Matthew Strickland (Stamford: Watkins, 1998), pp. 13–29 (pp. 18–21).

[22] K. Stevenson, *Chivalry and Knighthood*, p. 154.

a chivalric ideal was forced to defer to the evidence of history. This is a key point that will be expanded on below. Stevenson differed from Kliman's interpretation on one significant subject: according to Stevenson, Edward Bruce's reckless courage was not chivalric at all but was 'an abandonment of a key part of chivalric knighthood' because he placed personal glory before victory.[23]

The idea that Barbour presents a marginal or radical interpretation of chivalry was repeated again in a recent collection of essays on *The Bruce*. Purdie interpreted Barbour's emphasis on prudence and cunning as a rejection of medieval romance's fixation on displays of reckless bravery.[24] Likewise, she interpreted two incidents from the poem in which noblemen do gallant service to a woman, namely John Webiton's death in fulfilment of his vow to defend Douglas Castle and Robert Bruce's decision to halt his army in order to allow a laundress to give birth, as sly jokes on Barbour's part, intended to highlight to his audience 'the limitations of romance as a lens though which to read Bruce's history'. Given-Wilson also stated that Barbour's depiction of Bruce 'did not always measure up to the chivalric ideal' because he employed ruses.[25] According to Given-Wilson, this anticipated the content of later 'chivalric biographies', such as Jean Cuvelier's life of Bertrand du Guesclin (*d.* 1380) and the biography of Marshal Boucicaut (1366–1421).

Romance, *Chanson* or Biography?

Closely associated with the question of chivalry and *The Bruce* is the debate concerning its genre. Barbour calls it a *romanys* (1.446) but a number of scholars have questioned whether it is truly a 'romance', often citing what they believe to be its unconventional attitude towards chivalry as evidence that it should be seen as a broadly 'historical' text.[26] This is symptomatic of a larger issue in medieval studies: there is no satisfactory definition of 'medieval romance' that encompasses all the disparate texts that have been categorised under that name. In the twelfth century, the term 'romance' simply referred to texts translated from Latin into the vernacular, the 'romance languages'. In time, it came to encompass any narrative in the vernacular.[27] According to Sergi Mainer, 'the most general, inclusive and completely acceptable definition

---

[23] K. Stevenson, *Chivalry and Knighthood*, p. 157.

[24] Rhiannon Purdie, 'Medieval Romance and the Generic Frictions of Barbour's *Bruce*', in *Barbour's Bruce and its Cultural Contexts: Politics, Chivalry and Literature in Late Medieval Scotland*, ed. by Steve Boardman and Susan Foran (Woodbridge: Brewer, 2015), pp. 51–74 (pp. 70–71).

[25] Chris Given-Wilson, 'Chivalric Biography and Medieval Life-Writing', in *Barbour's Bruce and its Cultural Contexts: Politics, Chivalry and Literature in Late Medieval Scotland*, ed. by Steve Boardman and Susan Foran (Woodbridge: Brewer, 2015), pp. 101–18 (here 116).

[26] See *Barbour's Bruce: A Fredome Is a Noble Thing!*, ed. by Matthew P. McDiarmid and James A. C. Stevenson, 3 vols (Edinburgh: Scotish Text Society, 1985), I, 45; R. James Goldstein, *The Matter of Scotland: Historical Narrative in Medieval Scotland* (Lincoln: University of Nebraska Press, 1993), pp. 133–36; Phoebe A. Mainster, 'Folkloric Elements in Barbour's *Bruce*', *Michigan Academician*, 19 (1987), 49–59 (pp. 50–58); Joachim Schwend, 'Religion and Religiosity in *The Bruce*', in *Scottish Language and Literature, Medieval and Renaissance: Fourth International Conference (1984) Proceedings*, ed. Dietrich Strauss and Horst W. Drescher (Frankfurt am Main: Lang, 1986), pp. 207–15 (pp. 207, 213). For an excellent overview of different attempts to classify *The Bruce*, see Purdie, 'Medieval Romance', pp. 53–55.

[27] Sergi Mainer, *The Scottish Romance Tradition, c. 1375–c. 1550: Nation, Chivalry and Knighthood* (Amsterdam: Rodopi, 2010), p. 12.

which can be given is that romance is a narrative of a certain length'.[28] This definition, however, is too broad to be very useful for a modern critical study.

Cameron argued that *The Bruce* strays too far from the 'courtly romance' model to be considered part of the same genre: the characters 'fail to engage in the popular chivalric pursuits of winning ladies, fighting in tournaments and sleeping with their lord's wife'.[29] John Finlayson, in his attempt to define the medieval romance, distinguished between the 'heroic' narratives of the *chanson de geste* and the 'romantic' by the emphasis they place on martial qualities, 'on the ends which they are made to serve, and on the contexts within which they operate'.[30] In a heroic narrative, 'the hero tends to fight in defence of his lord or society, or in furtherance of political ends', whereas in romance 'the hero is conceived of basically as an individual, not as essentially a representative of his society' who engages in solitary adventures for his own glory.[31] Finlayson further differentiates between the simple 'romance of adventure', an episodic series of knightly deeds, and the more sophisticated 'courtly romances', such as the works of Chrétien de Troyes or the poem *Sir Gawain and the Green Knight*, in both of which the knightly deeds serve to highlight the inner struggle of the characters.[32] If one accepts Cameron and Finlayson's definitions of romance then *The Bruce* should be considered a heroic narrative, a latter-day *chanson de geste*.

Mainer has argued that the above definition of romance is too restrictive and that it gives undue preference to the 'sub-genre' of courtly romance, as exemplified by Chrétien and his imitators:

> this creates difficulties for a broad analysis of the genre insofar as both the intellectual and socio-political contexts as well as the aesthetic values of a romance composed in Champagne in the late twelfth century cannot be judged in the same way as one written, for example, in fifteenth-century Scotland.[33]

Mainer has argued for the 'cultural distinctiveness and singularity of Scottish romance'.[34] Discussing *The Bruce* as the first (surviving) Scottish 'historical romance', he described it as an 'eclectic romance'. It is written in octosyllabic couplets, a typical feature of French 'courtly romance', has a 'martial, masculine and male-centred narrative' typical of epic literature, and marginalises the courtly world of love affairs and tournaments in a manner similar to contemporary Anglo-Norman and Middle English romances.[35] Barbour's adaptation of older, foreign romance traditions created a form of distinctively Scottish romance that promoted the ideal that the good of the 'commonwealth' should be placed above individual glory: 'the traditional quest for identity and a place within feudal society is transformed into a search for the consolidation of shared values'.[36]

Kaeuper used *The Bruce* as an example of a 'historical account' that was seen by contemporaries as akin to 'accounts in imaginative literature' such as the Arthurian romances.[37]

---

[28] Mainer, *Scottish Romance*, p. 14.
[29] Cameron, 'Chivalry in Barbour's *Bruce*', p. 14.
[30] John Finlayson, 'Definitions of Middle English Romance', *Chaucer Review*, 15 (1980), 44–62, 168–81 (p. 52).
[31] Finlayson, 'Definitions of Romance', p. 53.
[32] Finlayson, 'Definitions of Romance', pp. 56–57.
[33] Mainer, *Scottish Romance*, pp. 12, 14 (quote).
[34] Mainer, *Scottish Romance*, p. 16.
[35] Mainer, *Scottish Romance*, p. 29.
[36] Mainer, *Scottish Romance*, p. 257.
[37] Richard Kaeuper, 'The Societal Role of Chivalry in Romance: North-Western Europe', in *The Cambridge*

Yet this distinction between history and romance is modern, not medieval, as can be seen in Barbour's own use of the term. He describes his *romanys* as a story of 'sympill folk and worthy' (1.463), who were in 'gret distress' but eventually came to 'gret hycht and till honour' through the grace of God and their own 'full gret hardynes' (1.447–52). He emphasises the disparity in numbers between his heroes and their enemies, and in one instance states that the odds were at least a thousand to one (1.453–55). In the same section, Barbour compares his heroes to the biblical Maccabees:

> Thai wrocht sua throu thar vasselage
> That with few folk thai had victory
> Off mychty kingis as sayis the story,
> And delyveryt thar land all fre,
> Quharfor thar name suld lovyt be (1.472–76)

The same comparison was made by Robert Bruce's supporters in the Declaration of Arbroath (1320).[38] Barbour's use of it here in conjunction with the term *romanys* alerts us to the fluidity of contemporary genre boundaries. We would not normally connect the Hebrew Scriptures with medieval romance but, in the fourteenth century, such a comparison was both logical and appropriate. Judas Maccabeus was one of the Nine Worthies, 'the tally of nine supreme heroes' who were key figures in what Keen called 'the historical mythology of chivalry'.[39] The Worthies included such solidly historical figures as Alexander the Great and Godfrey of Bouillon alongside (from a modern perspective) the mythical Hector of Troy and King Arthur. The boundaries between Scripture and myth, history and romance were not clearly defined to the medieval mind.[40]

It is this very fluidity of genre that informs Barbour's use of romantic *exempla* in *The Bruce*. He explicitly compares the deeds of his heroes, men of the recent past, with Greek and Roman heroes known to the medieval audience through the *romans antiques*, a sub-genre of romance concerning heroes that predated Chrétien's Arthurian tales and remained popular into the fourteenth century.[41] Describing John Comyn's betrayal of Robert Bruce, Barbour equates Bruce with Alexander, Julius Caesar, and Arthur, all famous heroes brought low by treachery (1.510–60). In Book 6, Barbour invites his audience to choose who 'that mar suld prysit be': Robert Bruce, who held a ford alone against two hundred men, or Tydeus of Thebes, a hero of the *Roman de Thèbes*, who defeated fifty men singlehanded (6.271–86). These comparisons are not just reserved for Robert Bruce. James Douglas is compared to Hector in both looks and deeds (1.395–405). Thomas Randolph's capture of Edinburgh Castle is compared to Alexander's capture of Tyre in the *Roman d'Alexandre* (10.706–40).[42]

Barbour uses the term *romanys* three more times in *The Bruce*. Describing the hardships that befell Robert Bruce, Barbour declares that he 'herd never in romanys tell | off man sa hard frayit as wes he | that efterwart com to sic bounté' (2.46–48). Barbour again makes the explicit connection between *romanys* and a triumph over great odds. In the midst of his

---

Companion to Medieval Romance, ed. by Roberta L. Kruger (Cambridge: Cambridge University Press, 2000), 97–114 (here 98).

38 *The Declaration of Arbroath*, ed. by James Fergusson (Edinburgh: Edinburgh University Press, 1970), p. 8.

39 Keen, *Chivalry*, pp. 121–24.

40 Susan Foran, 'Biography, Romance and Chivalry: Barbour's *The Bruce* and Chandos Herald's *La Vie du Prince Noir*' (unpublished doctoral thesis, Trinity College Dublin, 2006), pp. 19–20.

41 Purdie, 'Medieval Romance', p. 61

42 For other examples of romantic *exempla* see Barbour, *The Bruce*, 1.339–41, 2.531–50, 3.187–266, 3.267–98,

hardships, while crossing Loch Lomond in a tiny boat, Bruce reads to his men the 'romanys of worthi Ferambrace', encouraging them with the tale of how a few men successfully held the castle Aigremore against a great host of pagans (3.435–66). The connection between *romanys* and the few defeating the many is repeated a third time in Barbour's description of Edward Bruce's campaigns in Galloway. Edward Bruce, we are told, 'discumfyt commounly | mony with quhone' (9.492–93) and that if men were to rehearse all the deeds 'off his hey worschip and manheid | men mycht a mekill romanys mak' (9.496–97).

Purdie attempted to argue for a 'friction' between the romantic and historical elements in *The Bruce*, arguing that the former, which was understood to be fabulous, conflicted with Barbour's desire to present a truthful account of real events and people: 'most [medieval] authors will make their generic intentions clear one way or another, but Barbour does not, choosing instead to evoke both categories with confusing determination'.[43] Purdie never satisfactorily demonstrates that Barbour or his audience would have considered a *romanys* to be inherently fiction or to contain fabulous elements such as magic spells or giants. Based on the evidence above, Barbour appears to have understood *romanys* to mean a narrative in which heroic individuals, such as the Maccabees or Charlemagne's paladins, overcome great odds through their acts of valour.[44] The struggle of Robert Bruce and his followers against the English provided such a narrative from recent history, after he had edited out certain inconvenient facts.[45]

If *The Bruce* is not strictly a 'romance', would it be better to call it an 'epic', a fourteenth-century *chanson de geste*? This is also problematic, as *The Bruce* differs in several key respects from the typical *chanson*.[46] *The Bruce* is written in octosyllabic couplets, while *chansons* were composed in assonated or mono-rhyme stanzas with lines of ten or twelve syllables.[47] The heroes of the *chansons* are typically preoccupied with fighting pagans or exacting vengeance for personal wrongs, neither of which strictly applies to *The Bruce*.[48] Neither Bruce nor his followers possess special swords or horses, nor do they quarrel much among themselves.[49] The only major similarity is the appearance of a treacherous villain, a role fulfilled by John Comyn (1.477–568).[50] To confuse the matter further, modern scholarship regards the aforementioned 'romanys of worthi Ferambrace' as an 'established *chanson de geste*'.[51] Some later *chansons* self-identify as romances, in the manner of *The Bruce*.[52] Whatever distinctions

---

5.238–306, 14.312–16, 20.531–78.

[43] Purdie, 'Medieval Romance', p. 53.

[44] Foran, 'A Great Romance', pp. 3, 9–13.

[45] Mainster, 'How to Make a Hero', pp. 230–31.

[46] Like romance, *chanson de geste* is a broad genre that is difficult to define satisfactorily. Kay has likened the *chansons* to a family who share common characteristics that are not necessarily present in every member of that family: Sarah Kay, *The 'chansons de geste' in the Age of Romance: Political Fictions* (Oxford: Clarendon Press, 1995), pp. 8–9.

[47] *Handbook of Medieval Studies: Terms, Methods, Trends*, ed. by Albrecht Classen, 3 vols (Berlin: De Gruyter, 2010), II, 1684.

[48] Marianne Ailes, 'What's in a Name? Anglo-Norman Romances or *chansons de geste*?', in *Medieval Romance, Medieval Contexts*, ed. by Rhiannon Purdie and Michael Cichon (Cambridge: Brewer, 2011), pp. 61–75 (pp. 69–74).

[49] Jessie Crosland, *The Old French Epic* (Oxford: Blackwell, 1951), pp. 278–88.

[50] Crosland, *Old French Epic*, pp. 276–78.

[51] Ailes, 'What's in a Name?', p. 66.

[52] Kay, *'Chansons de geste'*, p. 7.

modern scholars might draw, medieval audiences evidently did not see the two genres as wholly distinct.

A third possibility is to categorise *The Bruce* as a vernacular 'chivalric biography'.[53] This genre first gained popularity in the late fourteenth century, around the same time that Barbour was writing. These texts, almost all written in Middle French or Anglo-Norman, chronicled the careers of noted historical knights.[54] Some, like the lives of Boucicaut and Bertrand du Guesclin mentioned above, concerned knights of middling or noble birth, while others had royal subjects, such as Guillaume de Machaut's life of Pierre I of Cyprus (*r.* 1358–69), *La Prise d'Alexandrie*, and Chandos Herald's life of Edward of Woodstock (1330–76), *La Vie du Prince Noir*. In Ferris' perceptive statement, chivalric biography 'focusses on the person as knight, not on the knight as person'.[55] The subject is usually portrayed in a highly generic, idealised fashion, beginning with his precocious youth, his desire to do great deeds leads him into an exemplary martial career through which he acquires love and loyal followers, before finally making a worthy end.[56] Given-Wilson described the line between 'truth and fiction' in these texts as 'hazy', as they were largely based on oral testimony and recollection of specific deeds and incidents.[57] It was up to the author to collate these recollections, arrange, edit and enhance them to create a portrait of his subject.

A useful comparison can be made between *The Bruce* and the two chivalric biographies referred to above: the *Prise d'Alexandrie* and *Vie du Prince Noir*. Neither author describes his text as a romance but their works possess significant similarities to *The Bruce*.[58] All three are written in octosyllabic couplets, the traditional form for courtly romance. They are all concerned with a royal protagonist who was renowned as a warrior and a ruler in their own lifetime: Robert Bruce, Pierre I of Cyprus, and Edward of Woodstock (later known as the Black Prince). Each protagonist has a supporting character, a knight notable for both their prowess and loyalty to the protagonist.[59] In *The Bruce* this role is fulfilled by James Douglas (2.149–74). Pierre is supported by Perceval of Coulonges.[60] In the *Vie du Prince Noir*, Woodstock is aided by the author's patron, John Chandos.[61]

---

[53] As did Duncan, for example: Barbour, *The Bruce*, p. 6.

[54] Antonia Gransden, *Historical Writing in England*, 2 vols (London: Routledge and Kegan Paul, 1974–82), ii, 80–82; Sumner Ferris, 'Chronicle, Chivalric Biography and Family Tradition in Fourteenth-Century England', in *Chivalric Literature: Essays on Relations between Literature and Life in the Later Middle Ages*, ed. by Larry. D. Benson and John Leyerle (Kalamazoo: Medieval Institute Publications, 1980), pp. 25–38 (p. 29); Elisabeth Gaucher, 'Entre l'histoire et le roman: La Biographie chevaleresque', *Revue des langues romanes*, 97 (1993), 15–30; Richard Barber, *The Knight and Chivalry*, rev. edn (Woodbridge: Boydell, 1995), pp. 140–46.

[55] Ferris, 'Chronicle, Chivalric Biography and Family', p. 35.

[56] William T. Cotton, 'Teaching the Motifs of Chivalric Biography', in *The Study of Chivalry: Resources and Approaches*, ed. by Howell Chickering and Thomas H. Seller (Kalamazoo: Medieval Institute Publications, 1988), pp. 583–610 (p. 591); Elisabeth Gaucher, 'La Chevalerie dans les biographies chevaleresques (xiiie — xve siècles)', *Revue des langues romances*, 110 (2006), 145–64.

[57] Given-Wilson, 'Chivalric Biography', p. 114; Ferris, 'Chronicle, Chivalric Biography and Family', p. 35.

[58] Foran, 'Biography, Romance and Chivalry', p. 63; Guillaume de Machaut, 'Edition critique de la *Prise d'Alexandrie*', ed. by Sophie Hardy (unpublished doctoral thesis, Université d'Orléans, 2011), lines 259–62.

[59] Given-Wilson identified the depiction of the hero 'in the context of his war-band' as a key feature of chivalric biography: Given-Wilson, 'Chivalric Biography', p. 107.

[60] Guillaum de Machaut, 'Edition critique de la *Prise*', lines 1961–86.

[61] Chandos Herald, *La Vie du Prince Noir*, ed. by Diana B. Tyson (Tübingen: Niemeyer, 1975), lines 573–75: 's'i furent Chaundos et Audeléle; l cils deuz eurent grand renomée, l et furent ordeignez au frayne l du Prince, sachez de certaine'.

All three poems are primarily interested in warfare and knightly deeds. Machaut's text differs in that his subject's antagonists are Saracens, not fellow Christians.[62] While Barbour and Chandos Herald are focused on the heroic actions of their protagonists, they also make a point of recognising the virtues of their enemies as valiant Christian knights in their own right.[63]

Like Barbour, Machaut and Chandos Herald make a point of comparing their heroes to the Worthies of romance. Chandos Herald describes Edward of Woodstock as 'the most valiant prince in the world, if one was to search the whole earth, one would not find his like since the days of Charles [the Great], Julius Caesar, or Arthur'.[64] Machaut is more poetic, depicting a scene in which the god Mars laments that his 'good and dear friends', Alexander, Caesar, Joshua, and the other Worthies, are all dead. He proposes that he and his fellow gods 'work to set up a good Godfrey [of Bouillon] and to find a man ready and able to defend his land'.[65] The gods consent and so the Christian God creates Pierre, who is showered with gifts by the Olympians.[66]

All three authors emphasise the virtues and accomplishments of their heroes but none of them had complete creative freedom: they were all bound to well-known history and had to accommodate some of the less praiseworthy aspects of their subjects' lives into the heroic narrative. Barbour could not completely gloss over Bruce's murder of Comyn (2.25–49) or the failure of Edward Bruce's Irish campaign (18.175–84). Although Machaut is able to portray Pierre's murder as a martyr's death, with the king exhorting the Virgin to receive his soul with his dying breath, he was unable to omit the lurid tales of injustice and torture that marred Pierre's reign.[67] Edward of Woodstock's life lacks a heroic sequel to the Spanish campaign due to the wasting illness that consumed him in the final years of his life. All Chandos Herald can say is that he made a 'very noble end', complete with a pious confession and a farewell to his household.[68]

The Bruce is a *romanys* in the sense that Barbour uses the term: it is a narrative of heroic and chivalric deeds, in which men triumph in the face of great odds. Modern critics may find that too narrow a definition but, if it is not a *romance*, it is undeniably *romantic* in form and intent. It is written in verse and was intended to both entertain, being a story both *suthfast* and *said in gud maner* (1.3–5), and to commemorate the knightly deeds of its heroes (1.17–36) who were comparable to the heroes of romance. In this it shares many key features with the emerging genre of 'chivalric biography'. This returns us to the question of whether Barbour's depiction of chivalry in his poem was in keeping with contemporary understandings of 'chivalry'.

---

62 For example Guillaum de Machaut, 'Edition critique de la *Prise*', lines 2257–497.

63 For example Chandos Herald, *Vie du Prince*, lines 309–17, 1015–60. For *The Bruce* see below.

64 Chandos Herald, *Vie du Prince*, lines 43–54: 'de plus vaillant prince du mounde | si come il est tourny a le rounde | ne qui fuist puis les temps Claruz, | Jule Cesaire ne Artuz'.

65 Guillaum de Machaut, 'Edition critique de la *Prise*', lines 45: 'mi bon et chier amy', 63–67: 'si deveriens tuit labourer | au bon Godefory restorer, | et querir homme qui sceüst | maintenir sa terre et deüst'.

66 Guillaum de Machaut, 'Edition critique de la *Prise*', lines 69–258.

67 For example Guillaum de Machaut, 'Edition critique de la *Prise*', lines 8243–378.

68 Chandos Herald, *Vie du Prince*, line 4109: *tres noble fin*.

Word	Uses	Word	Uses
Averty	4	Manhed(e), -heid | Manly, -lie	37
Avisé, avysy	10	Nobil(l), Noble	40
Bald, bauld	10	Prowes, Prowes(s)	3
Bounté, bownté	56	Prys, price	10
Chevalry, Chevelry	40	Renoun(e), -non(e)	23
Courage	6	Skill	3
Curtas, -ais	16	Slicht	19
Deboner, -eir	4	Stalwart	28
Douchty	40	Stout	53
Empris(e), Emprys(e)	5	Sturdy	41
Forsy, Forsie	1	Subtilté, Sutelté	14
Hardy	126	Val(o)ur, -or	14
Hardi-, Hardyment	19	Worschip	46
Honest	2	Worthy, -ie	113
Honour, Honor	25	Wicht, Wycht	73
Juparty, Jupardy	1	Wis(e), Wys(e)	33
Large, Larges	3	Wit, Wyt	25
Lufand	1		

Table 1. Chivalric words in *The Bruce*

Chivalric Language in *The Bruce*

This section will examine how Barbour uses the language of chivalry to highlight his heroes' many virtues that made them worthy to be compared to figures of romance.[69] Although Barbour's use of such adjectives is 'often formulaic, repetitive and alliterative', their very repetition emphasises those qualities that Barbour and his audience found admirable.[70]

The term 'chivalry' and its derivations, referring to knightly deeds or qualities, appear forty times in *The Bruce*, as shown in the table above.[71] Barbour uses it in a variety of ways. One can possess chivalry (3.155). Men are described as being full of it (2.214, 2.248, 2.338, 14.518). The English garrison at Inverkip, we are told, 'lovyt fast' their comrade Philip Mowbray's 'chevalry' after he escaped an ambush (8.74–106). Having a leader who possesses chivalry comforts soldiers (14.83–84). It is the stuff of romance: Arthur conquered the twelve kingdoms of Britain 'throu chevalry' (1.549–51) and the unnamed king in the romance of Fierabras recovers holy relics from the pagans 'throu his chevalry' (3.454–62). One can also achieve chivalry (3.180, 20.15). The vanguard of the English army at the battle

---

[69] Tyson has undertaken a similar study of the *Vie du Prince Noir*, including a very cursory comparison with *The Bruce*. She notes that Barbour places more insistence on the virtues of prudence and cunning than Chandos Herald but does not offer any substantive conclusions about Barbour's approach to chivalry: Diana B. Tyson, 'The Vocabulary of Chivalric Description in Late Fourteenth-Century Biography', in *Barbour's Bruce and its Cultural Contexts: Politics, Chivalry and Literature in Late Medieval Scotland*, ed. by Steve Boardman and Susan Foran (Woodbridge: Brewer, 2015), pp. 119–36.

[70] K. Stevenson, *Chivalry and Knighthood*, p. 152.

[71] I have distinguished this use of the word from its use as a collective noun for a body of heavy cavalry, which occurs a further 19 times in Barbour, *The Bruce*, 2.210, 2.224, 2.289, 2.406, 3.244, 4.187, 6.460, 7.511, 8.157, 8.208, 9.558, 10.716, 11.85, 11.89, 11.97, 14.150, 14.508, 15.572, 16.79.

of Bannockburn (1314) is described as full of 'young men and joly [who] | Yarnand to do chevalry' (11.531–32). Other characters also do chivalry (2.348, 6.12, 12.496) and win 'gret price off' it (1.25, 3.175).

All of the above examples have a military or warlike context. Barbour never uses 'chivalry' to refer to scenes of love or courteous speech. Crucially, he tells his audience on two occasions that he will not go into detail about an event because 'gret chevalry done wes nane' (10.816–17, 13.750–51). This indicates Barbour's purpose in writing: to commemorate the 'gret chevalry' done by his heroes and to entertain his audience in the telling. That does not mean that his heroes are entirely warlike or that they are valued only for their military prowess. The subject of the poem is war and the deeds of warriors but Barbour also emphasises the other virtues they possess: courteousness, generosity, and intelligence.

'Worthy, wycht and wys' (2.173) is a formula that Barbour uses to describe his heroes on several occasions.[72] *Worthy* and *wycht* are the second and third most common virtues referred to in *The Bruce* (see Fig. 1). In this context, *worthy* means 'of high value as a soldier, brave [...] honourable; of noble rank' or 'of high moral worth or value, attracting honour and respect'.[73] *Wycht* is a more explicitly martial word. Derived from the Old Norse *vígt*, it means 'physically strong, powerful robust; mentally strong, brave, bold especially in battle'.[74] The third virtue, *wys*, is quite different: 'possessing sound judgement, sensible, prudent, clever, skilled, competent, sharp-witted'.[75] Together these three represent the three areas in which Barbour's heroes excel: they both win and retain honour by their deeds, they are strong in battle but are also prudent and sharp-witted. These are the three categories that will be used below to examine the other words Barbour uses to describe his characters' virtues.

The majority of the chivalric words in *The Bruce* are *wycht* words that describe a character's prowess and courage in battle. The word *prowess* itself is used only three times in the whole poem (9.508, 12.292, 20.240) but Barbour uses other synonyms that convey the same idea.[76] By and large the most common word he uses to describe characters is *hardy*, 126 times. It is commonly used in early Scottish verse as a term of commendation, describing someone who is 'bold, brave, daring; stout, valiant'.[77] Related words used by Barbour include *hardiment*, *manheid*, *stalwart*, and *vasselage*. There is also an indication that these words carried honourable and noble associations. Robert Bruce laments that the three assassins sent to kill him had turned traitor: 'for rycht wycht men all thre war thai' (7.494).

The word *bounté* is both a *wycht* and *worthy* word. It can mean 'excellence of character', 'courage' or 'deeds of valour', 'a good estate or condition', or 'goodness in giving; liberality'.[78] It is often difficult to tell in what sense Barbour is using it. Characters possess it (10.279, 11.425, 13.113, 14.19, 16.191). It is a key quality of good knighthood and governance. Edward Bruce kills an Englishman called Mandeville, 'a knycht that of all Irland | was callit best and of maist

---

[72] See also Barbour, *The Bruce*, 4.534, 10.278. Two of the three (usually *worthy* and *wycht*) are paired at 1.22, 1.401, 2.201, 2.263, 2.337, 6.484, 7.424, 8.266, 9.51, 10.536, 11.133, 12.495, 12.525, 12.585, 13.285, 16.163, 16.377, 17.237, 17.310, 19.78, 19.162, 19.794, 20.193, 20.374.

[73] *A Dictionary of the Older Scottish Tongue from the Twelfth Century to the End of the Seventeenth*, ed. by William A. Craigie and others, 12 vols (Chicago: University of Chicago Press, 1937–2002), xii, 309–11.

[74] *Dictionary of the Older Scottish Tongue*, xii, 171–72.

[75] *Dictionary of the Older Scottish Tongue*, xii, 229.

[76] I have not included the word *mycht* or its derivations. Barbour uses it so freely that it retains no relevance for the study of chivalry in *The Bruce*.

[77] *Dictionary of the Older Scottish Tongue*, iii, 52.

[78] *Dictionary of the Older Scottish Tongue*, i, 318.

bounté' (15.206–07). At the very end of the poem, Barbour expresses the hope that Robert Bruce's descendents will 'leid weill the land, and ententyve | be to folow in all thar lyve | thar nobill eldrys gret bounte' (20.625–27). *Bounté* is also useful: James Douglas achieved his goals while fighting in the Forest of Ettrick 'throu wyt and throu bounté' (9.683). It is something that can be achieved. Robert Bruce comes to *bounté* after great hardship (2.46–48), presumably in the sense of a 'good condition'.

Like chivalry, *bounté* is occasionally used as a verb, something that a person does. Robert Bruce does 'honour and bounté' to two French knights captured from the English army at Byland in 1322, eventually freeing them without a ransom (18.537–44). Earlier in the poem, when he is ambushed by the Mac na Dorsair brothers, Robert Bruce did 'ane outrageous bounte': he threw one of his assailants from his horse, split his skull with a sword blow, and then killed another who had seized his stirrup (3.129–46). Barbour uses the same word to describe the generosity of a magnanimous victor and the feat of killing two enemies in a tight place, a clear example of the dual nature of medieval chivalry.

Turning now to *worthy* words, those concerned with reputation and honour, it should be remembered that Barbour's stated aim in writing *The Bruce* was to preserve the glorious memory of his heroes (16.534–39). Characters in the text are particularly concerned with honour. One can win honour through valour in battle (2.357, 2.400, 8.318, 14.237, 14.277). Fighting courageously can also preserve one's honour (2.341, 8.252, 11.270). Before Bannockburn, Robert Bruce tells his men: 'bott all wate ye quhat honour is, | contene you than on sic a wis | that your honour ay savyt be' (12.315–17). Fighting is not the only thing that can be done honourably. After Bannockburn, Robert Bruce ensures that all the 'gret lordis slain there are buried in haly place honorabilly' (13.672–74). One can also 'do' honour to another person. When James Douglas travelled to Seville in 1330 to carry the Bruce's heart into battle against the Saracens, he was honoured above all others by the English contingent (20.366–72).

Barbour himself discusses the nature and value of *worschip* in *The Bruce*. *Worschip* means 'honour', 'renown', or 'worthiness, prowess or valour (chiefly in battle)'.[79] Barbour places this discussion after Robert Bruce's defence of a ford against two hundred men (described above), declaring that 'worschip is a prisit thing' (6.327) because it causes men to be loved if it is consistently pursued. It has two extremes, 'fule-hardyment and cowartys' (6.339–40). True *worschip* is the 'mene betuix tha twa' (6.349), when a man is neither too rash nor too cautious in his deeds. 'For hardyment with foly is vice | bot hardyment that mellyt is | with wyt is worschip' (6.357–59). Robert Bruce's action at the ford exemplifies this. His 'wyt' recognised that the ford was narrow enough for a single man to hold, his 'hardyment' gave him the strength to face so many alone (6.361–70). It is this emphasis on the need for both physical prowess and prudent insight that has led some scholars to claim that *The Bruce* is an anomaly in medieval chivalric literature.[80]

Barbour regularly uses certain words to emphasise his heroes' cleverness and cunning in warfare. The word *avisé*, meaning 'prudent' or 'careful', is a trait ascribed to both James Douglas (1.302) and Robert Bruce (8.385).[81] Barbour uses it to describe Robert Bruce's decision to dig earthworks before Bannockburn (11.355–80) and a commander's ability to deploy his forces effectively (2.274, 2.347).

---

[79] *Dictionary of the Older Scottish Tongue*, XII, 299–301.
[80] Cameron, 'Chivalry in Barbour's *Bruce*', pp. 18–21; Kliman, 'Significance of Barbour's Commoners', pp. 110–11.
[81] *Dictionary of the Older Scottish Tongue*, I, 152.

'Wit' and its derivations have a similarly broad usage. At Bannockburn, Thomas Randolph's division defends itself *wittily* against the English vanguard (11.601). Robert Bruce is *wytty* at the end of the battle because he holds his army together against an English counterattack (13.437–39). *Wit* can also mean insight. In a later engagement, seeing the Scots feigning flight to draw his men into an ambush, the English commander John Hainault comments: 'yone folk ar governyt wittily' (19.471). Robert Bruce is described as *witty* when he recognises a group of assassins sent to kill him (7.134).

The use of the word *sutelté* in *The Bruce* is particularly interesting. It has a range of meanings: 'craftiness', 'ingenuity', 'a trick, stratagem', or 'cunning or ingenious workmanship'.[82] In *The Bruce* it is used to refer to the specialist skills of a military engineer (17.240, 17.662–71) and a silversmith (20.315) but also to stealth and deception in warfare. James Douglas seeks to take Roxburgh Castle in 1314 by *sutelté*, not open assault (10.361). Thomas Randolph's stealthy seizure of Edinburgh castle that same year, compared to Alexander's capture of Tyre (see above), is also described as a *sutelte* (10.540). Describing his plan to attack a group of sleeping enemies, Robert Bruce tells his men:

> For werrayour na fors suld ma
> Quhether he mycht ourcum his fa
> Throu strenth or throu sutelté
> Bot that gud faith ay haldyn be (5.85–88)

The use of deception and stealth in *The Bruce* and whether they should be considered chivalrous will be discussed below. For now it is enough to say that Barbour made a point of describing the prudence, cunning and strategic acumen of his heroes, not just their courage and raw strength.

There is a final category of chivalric words not covered by the formula *worthy, wycht and wys*. They can be grouped under the heading of 'courtly' words. Although the poem has very few courtly or ritual scenes of the kind common to chivalric literature, and no significant female characters, Barbour does stress his heroes' courtliness and generosity on several occasions. *Curtais* and its derivations appear on sixteen occasions.[83] James Douglas is described as greeting Robert Bruce by bowing 'ffull curtasly' (2.154). Robert Bruce's decision to halt his army to allow a laundress to give birth is described as 'a full gret curtasy' (16.293). *Curtais* also has overtones of magnanimity and generosity. At the parliament of August 1320, when Robert Bruce permitted Ingram de Umfraville to dispose of his Scottish lands and go into England as a protest against the execution of David Brechin, it is described as 'curtassy' (19.125). The related word *larges* appears three times, in connection with James Douglas (1.363), Thomas Randolph (10.293), and Robert Bruce (20.234).[84]

Barbour uses the language of chivalry to highlight his characters' strengths and virtues. In keeping with the poem's subject, he most frequently uses words to emphasise their prowess and strength in battle but he does not neglect their other achievements. He shows a concern with their honour and reputation, both as warriors and as men of worth. He describes their prudence and cunning in warfare and their generosity, both to their followers and to their defeated foes.

---

[82] *Dictionary of the Older Scottish Tongue*, x, 118–19.

[83] *Dictionary of the Older Scottish Tongue*, i, 790: 'courteous, of good manners or breeding'.

[84] *Dictionary of the Older Scottish Tongue*, iii, 560: 'liberal in giving or in expenditure; generous, open-handed, munificent'.

Chivalry and Chivalric Deeds in *The Bruce*

The Bruce is a poem about war and warriors. Its heroes are knights and much of the action is violent. Describing the Scottish sieges of Norham and Alnwick in 1327, Barbour says: 'apert eschewys oft maid thar war | and mony fayr chevalry | eschevyt war full douchtely' (20.14–16). The poem is a catalogue of this sort of *fayr chevalry*, especially stories of a few men overcoming many. Barbour declares that three *poyntis* of war will be prized for evermore: James Douglas defeating ten thousand men with fifty, Edward Bruce defeating fifteen hundred with fifty, and the French knight John de Soulis defeating three hundred with fifty (16.493–522). The story of Robert Bruce overcoming a gang of assassins singlehanded is repeated four times, with only minor alterations (3.93–146, 5.523–658, 6.571–674, 7.79–232). In this, at least, Barbour adhered to a conventional understanding of chivalry. Physical prowess was the key virtue in medieval chivalry, the quality that knights prized above all others, so to focus on deeds of prowess in his narrative is unquestionably chivalrous.[85]

It is somewhat surprising to find that, in a poem about a national struggle against a foreign invader, Barbour does not ignore the valorous deeds performed by the enemy. *Fayr chevalry* is *fayr*, regardless of who does it. Giles d'Argentan, Edward II's bodyguard at Bannockburn, is called 'the thrid best knycht perfay | that men wyst lyvand in his day' (13.321–22).[86] Two English knights, Thomas Ughtred and Ralph Cobham, attack the Scots alone at Byland. Cobham, Barbour says, was known as 'the best knycht of all that land' but, when he fled where Ughtred was taken prisoner, Ughtred was 'prisit our him' (18.390–436). Two French knights are also captured in the same encounter. Robert Bruce receives them 'as frendis' because they fought for the English, not because of 'wreyth na ivill will', but because their 'gret worschip and bounté' would not allow them to avoid battle (18.527–36). In *The Bruce*, the values of chivalry, and the respect for those who embody them, are international.

Emphasising the strength and virtue of their enemies only enhances the reputation of Barbour's heroes but there is more at work here than simple poetic exaggeration. By emphasising the international nature of chivalry in his poem, Barbour elevates his subjects to the status of international heroes. Robert Bruce and his followers are not just Scottish heroes: they are to be admired alongside Arthur, Charlemagne, or Godfrey of Bouillon, as paragons of the international code that was chivalry.

As mentioned above, the lack of female characters in *The Bruce* has led some critics to declare it to be neither romantic nor chivalrous. Yet love and service to ladies do feature in *The Bruce* and in unquestionably chivalric form. John Webiton, an English knight slain defending Douglas Castle in 1307, is found with a letter from his mistress, promising that he could ask for her love and service if he could defend the castle for a year (8.488–99).[87] Purdie claimed that Barbour was 'cheerfully indifferent' to Webiton's fate and that the incident serves as an example of how Barbour sought to distance his text from pure romance, where such love service was common.[88] This is an anachronistic interpretation, based more on modern distaste for such seemingly-irrational behaviour than textual evidence. Barbour does not criticise

---

[85] Richard W. Kaeuper, *Chivalry and Violence in Medieval Europe* (Oxford: Oxford University Press, 1999), pp. 129–49.

[86] According to Walter Bower, D'Argentan was acclaimed as the 'third best knight' of his day by Edward II of England's chief herald, surpassed only by Emperor Henry VII and Robert Bruce. Duncan theorises that Bower may have taken this acclamation from Barbour, however: Barbour, *The Bruce*, p. 496.

[87] For historical examples of this kind of love-service, see Keen, *Chivalry*, pp. 212–13.

[88] Purdie, 'Medieval Romance', p. 70.

Webiton for recklessness, as he does Edward Bruce, or for any other failing. It is far more likely that Barbour thought that this story was an example of *fayr chevalry* that his audience would appreciate.

The Scots also perform love service in *The Bruce*. Shortly after Robert Bruce's defeat at Methven (1306), his queen 'and other ladyis fayr and farand' (2.517) join him at Aberdeen and accompany the army into hiding. Barbour compares them to the women who helped undermine the walls of Thebes in the *Roman de Thèbes* (2.531–50). He praises love because it allows men to make light of suffering (2.523–30).[89] While hiding in the hills, Barbour highlights the role James Douglas played in hunting for the ladies, bringing them venison or fish (2.573–81).

> Bot off all that ever thai war
> Thar wes nocht ane amang thaim thar
> That to the ladyis profyt was
> Mar then James of Douglas (2.585–88)

We see here an example of Barbour turning a difficult fact, Robert Bruce's exile and privations in the wild, into something chivalrous: a chance for James Douglas to display his worth by serving the ladies. In *The Bruce*, what could have been a shameful episode is elevated to the status of a *romanys*.

Religion and religious language are of peripheral concern in *The Bruce*.[90] Consequently the religious dimensions of chivalry are not dwelt upon, except at the very end of the poem. As he lies dying, Robert Bruce repents of the innocent blood he has spilled (20.177–81). He laments that he will be unable to go on crusade to make atonement, so instead one of his followers is chosen to carry his heart into battle against the Saracens (20.182–99). It is clear that Barbour did not consider the Wars of Independence an adequate substitute for a crusade but as a factor that prevented Bruce from taking the cross.

A critical question in *Bruce* scholarship is whether Barbour's portrayal of chivalry is in keeping with contemporary values. Particularly controversial is the Scots' repeated use of deception and ambush.[91] In this Barbour was being faithful to history. Following his defeat at Methven Robert Bruce was forced to flee into the wild with the remnant of his following.[92] According to the *Vita Edwardi Secundi*, Robert Bruce, 'knowing that he was unequal to the king of England in strength as much as fortune, declared to his men that it would be better to move in arms against out king secretly than to contend for his right in open battle'.[93]

Barbour's treatment of this 'secret' warfare is largely positive. In keeping with his celebration of men who possess *wyt* and *sutelte*, he delights in tales of deception and cunning.

---

[89] For a similar sentiment in a contemporary chivalric work, see Geoffroi de Charny, *The Book of Chivalry: Text, Context, and Translation*, ed. by Richard W. Kaeuper and Elspeth Kennedy (Philadelphia: University of Pennsylvania Press, 1996), pp. 118–22.

[90] Schwend, 'Religion and Religiosity', p. 208.

[91] Cameron, 'Chivalry in Barbour's *Bruce*', pp. 14–22; Kliman, 'Idea of Chivalry', pp. 490–92; Purdie, 'Medieval Romance', p. 73; Given-Wilson, 'Chivalric Biography', p. 116.

[92] Thomas Gray, *Scalacronica, 1272–1363*, ed. by Andy King, Surtees Society, 209 (Woodbridge: Boydell, 2005), p. 56: *qi enboterent le dit Robert de Bruys a tiel meschef qil ala a pee par lez mountez et de ile en ile, et a la foitz a tiel meschief, qe auscun foitz ne auoit nuly od ly, qar com tesmoignent lez croniclis de sez gestis.*

[93] *Vita Edwardi Secundi*, ed. by Wendy R. Childs (Oxford: Clarendon Press, 2005), p. 24: 'Robertus enim de Brutz, sciens se tam ex uiribus quam ex fortuna sua regis Anglie imparem, decreuit sibi magis expedire contra regem nostrum arma latenter mouere quam in bello campestri de iure suo contendere'. See also Geoffrey W. S. Barrow, *Robert Bruce and the Community of the Realm of Scotland*, 4th edn (Edinburgh: Edinburgh University Press,

When Bruce perceives that Perth cannot be taken by 'strenth or mycht [...] he thocht to wyrk with slycht' (9.351–52). The Scots openly withdraw from the siege, then return under cover of night to scale the walls with ladders (9.353–454). James Douglas also launches many ambushes against his enemies. In 1308, when he returned to Douglasdale to claim his heritage, Barbour notes that:

> [...] he wes wys
> And saw he mycht on nakyn wys
> Werray his fa with evyn mycht
> Tharfor he thocht to wyrk with slycht (5.267–70)

Douglas secretly gathers those men still loyal to him, then surprises the English garrison in church on Palm Sunday, massacres them, and seizes the castle (5.271–428). Campaigning in England, James Douglas declares to Thomas Randolph, who proposes attacking a much larger English force, that 'it war na outrage I to fewar folk aganys ma I avantage quhen thai ma to ta' (19.306–08).

The use of trickery also has negative connotations in *The Bruce*. At Methven, Aymer de Valence's decision to attack Robert Bruce despite giving his word not to fight that day is described as 'slycht', opposed to 'mycht' (2.326–29). On two occasions Robert Bruce is challenged by other characters about his use of deception. First Aymer de Valence challenges him to a pitched battle at Loudon Hill (1307), saying:

> [Bruce's] worschip suld be mar,
> And mar be turnyt in nobillay,
> To wyn him in the playne away
> With hard dintis in evyn fechtyng
> Then to do fer mar with skulking (8.136–40)

Bruce reacts angrily to this message because 'Schyr Aymer spak sa heyly' (8.143) but nonetheless accepts the challenge. On the second occasion, he is confronted by his nephew Thomas Randolph. Admonished by his uncle for refusing his allegiance, Randolph responds:

> Ye chasty me, bot ye
> Aucht bettre chastyt for to be,
> For sene ye werrayit the king
> Off Ingland, in playne fechtyng
> Ye suld pres to derenyhe rycht
> And nocht with cowardy na with slycht (9.747–52)

On this occasion Bruce responds that it may come to 'playne fechtyng' before long but he still rebukes Randolph for his 'proud wordis' and has him imprisoned until he knows 'the rycht and bow it' (9.753–58).

It is possible to interpret Valence and Randolph's challenges as the voices of conventional wisdom, challenging the Bruce's underhand behaviour and setting him on the road to Bannockburn, where he finally achieves his right in *playne fechtyng*. Yet it is Thomas Randolph who captures Edinburgh Castle for Bruce by scaling the walls at night, an act described by Barbour as requiring 'slycht' (10.520). *The Bruce* is not neatly divided into two halves, pre-Bannockburn *skulking* and post-Bannockburn *playne fechtyng*. The Scots continue to employ ambushes and other deceptions (for example 15.11–64, 16.335–401). Robert Bruce himself

2005), p. 221.

defends the use of such deceptions: it does not matter whether a warrior overcomes his enemy through force or trickery, so long as 'gud faith ay haldyn be' (5.88). Read in this light, it becomes clear why Valence's deception at Methven is condemned but Bruce's ambushes are not: Valence broke his word not to attack until the morning.

Even a cursory reading of medieval chronicles will reveal that medieval combatants were willing to employ all manner of tricks and stratagems to defeat their enemies.[94] This does not mean that idealistic chivalric literature acknowledged such ruthless pragmatism, however. Scholars from Kliman onwards have assumed that Barbour was unusual for recognising the reality of warfare in a way that ran contrary to the glamourous 'chivalric ideal'. Yet this assumption is undermined by evidence from other texts. Contemporary military and chivalric writers described stratagems as legitimate in times of war. Honoré Bouvet (*d.* 1410), in his *Arbre de batailles,* declared that: 'according to God and according to the Scripture I may defeat my enemy by ingenuity or by deception without doing sin, once the war has been judged and declared and ordered between him and me, and I have given him defiance'.[95] This parallels Bruce's statement about keeping *gud faith* with one's enemies. Stratagem was also sanctified by ancient and authoritative texts such as Vegetius' *De rei militari* and Frontinus' *Strategemata.* Although it is uncertain whether these texts were used as sources of practical advice in the Middle Ages, they were widely copied, translated and adapted into other works on warfare and chivalry.[96]

Admiration for cunning was not just restricted to theory. In the early thirteenth century, the Anglo-Norman poet who composed the verse biography of William Marshal (*d.* 1219) had Henry II of England praise the Marshal as *corteis* (courtly; a worthy man) for suggesting a stratagem to deceive Philippe II of France: Henry was to pretend to disband his army then secretly reassemble it and attack when Philippe did not expect it.[97] If this had been considered dishonourable, the poet would have changed or omitted it altogether, as he did with other inconvenient events in the Marshal's career.[98]

An admiration for cunning can also be found in other, more overtly literary texts. In Wace's *Roman de Brut*, composed for the court of Henry II of England, the Trojan leader Brutus (and supposed ancestor of Wace's royal patron) is depicted luring his enemy into a trap in order to save his own men. Wace declared: 'one must use trickery and cunning to destroy one's enemy, and to rescue one's friends one must enter great danger'.[99] The *Roman de Thèbes,*

---

[94] For a detailed study of this neglected subject, see James W. Titterton, 'Trickery and Deceit in Medieval Warfare, *c.* 1050–1320' (unpublished doctoral thesis, University of Leeds, 2019).

[95] Honoré Bouvet, *L'Arbre des batailles*, ed. by Ernest Nys (Brussels: Muquardt, 1883), p. 143: 'selon Dieu et selon l'escripture je puis vaincre par engien ou par barat mon ennemy sans faire pechié depuis que la guerre est jugiée et notifiée et ordonnée entre lui et moy et que je l'ay defié'.

[96] For the use and reception of Vegetius and Frontinus in the Middle Ages, see Richard Abels and Stephen Morillo, 'A Lying Legacy? A Preliminary Discussion of Images of Antiquity and Altered Reality in Medieval Military History', *Journal of Medieval Military History*, 3 (2005), 1–13; Christopher Allmand, 'A Roman Text on War: The *Strategemata* of Frontinus in the Middle Ages', in *Soldiers, Nobles and Gentlemen: Essays in Honour of Maurice Keen*, ed. by Peter Coss and Christopher Tyerman (Woodbridge: Boydell, 2009), pp. 153–68; Allmand, *The 'De re militari' of Vegetius: The Reception, Transmission and Legacy of a Roman Text in the Middle Ages* (Cambridge: Cambridge University Press, 2011); Sydney Anglo, 'Vegetius's *De re militari:* The Triumph of Mediocrity', *Antiquaries Journal*, 82 (2002), 247–67.

[97] *History of William Marshal*, ed. by Anthony J. Holden, Anglo-Norman Text Society, Occasional Publications Series, 4–6, 3 vols (London: Anglo-Norman Text Society, 2002–6), line 7800.

[98] See David B. Crouch, 'Biography as Propaganda in the *History of William Marshal*', in *Convaincre et persuader: Communication et propagande aux xiie et xiiie siècles*, ed. by Martin Aurell (Poitiers: CESCM, 2007), pp. 503–12.

[99] Wace, *Roman de Brut: A History of the British*, ed. by Judith Weiss, rev. edn (Exeter: Exeter University Press,

which Barbour refers to in his own text, features an incident in which the besiegers lure the garrison out from the castle of Montflor by feigning flight.[100] Even the pioneer of Arthurian romance himself, Chrétien de Troyes, depicted his heroes employing guile to achieve their goals. In *Cligés*, the hero Alexander has his troops disguise themselves with their enemies' shields in order to infiltrate Windsor Castle.[101] Far from being an exception, tales of cunning ruses were an established, if marginal, element of chivalric literature.

Chivalry, in *The Bruce*, consists largely of brave deeds done by knights in battle. They are to be remembered and praised, regardless of who did them. They may be deeds of strength, done in pitched battle, or deeds of skill and cunning, such as an ambush or stealthy assault on an enemy stronghold. This appreciaton of *slycht* does not mean that Barbour's text is not chivalric or that his understanding of chivalry was a radical departure from established values. Chivalric literature before and after *The Bruce* could and did celebrate cunning alongside boldness.

Conclusion

The Bruce is both chivalrous and romantic, although it does not fit neatly into modern conceptual categories. Barbour possessed limited creative freedom in writing his poem. Certain inconvenient facts, such as the murder of Comyn and the failed Irish campaign, were too well-known to be wholly redacted from his narrative. Barbour's task as a poet was to take the complex, morally-ambiguous history of Robert Bruce and recast it in a romantic style, presenting his subject in the most heroic, chivalrous manner possible.

When Barbour writes of *chevalry*, he means primarily the hard business of fighting. This is how men win, retain, and demonstrate their honour, the public estimation of their personal worth, summed up in words like *bounté* and *worschip*. Yet Barbour's heroes are not brutes, valued only for their ability to crack skulls. He takes care to emphasise their mastery of the other virtues that make up a *worthy* knight. They are generous, magnanimous to the defeated enemy, and open-handed to their followers. They also possess a gentler side. Robert Bruce condescends to halt his whole army out of concern for a washerwoman. The fearsome James Douglas devotes himself to fishing and hunting to serve the ladies in the wild.

Some of the details may stretch credulity but there is a healthy streak of practicality in Barbour's narrative: not every problem is resolved with a pitched battle. When a superior English force besieges Berwick, Robert Bruce orders Douglas and Randolph to harry northern England to draw the English forces away (16.500–21). Characters who neglect to use strategy to gain an advantage are criticised (12.454–76, 12.546–60, 16.119–42, 16.246–58, 18.28–58). Barbour laments that Edward Bruce did not possess his brother's *mesur* (9.665) but let pride and stubbornness bring about his untimely death in battle (18.175–84).

It is in this context that we must read the Scots' use of guile and deception in *The Bruce* and Barbour's approval of their 'secret warfare'. This kind of fighting may not seem honourable by modern standards, but if one defines chivalry according to Barbour's own standards, as the great and valorous deeds done by knights, then ambush and deception can be interpreted as

---

2002), lines 363–66: 'boisdie e engine deit l'en faire | pur destrure son adversaire, | e pur ses amis delivrer | deit l'en en grant peril entrer'.

[100] Purdie, 'Medieval Romance', p. 72.

[101] Chrétien de Troyes, *Cligés*, ed. by Stewart Gregory and Claude Luttrell (Cambridge: Brewer, 1993), lines 1827–37.

chivalrous. The business of knights, the 'chivalry', was warfare. To master the skills of war, one needed more than a strong right arm, one needed intelligence and cunning too.

Barbour attempts to cast his protagonists, particularly Robert Bruce and James Douglas, as chivalric heroes comparable with the Nine Worthies. Occasionally the mask slips. Bruce commits sacrilege by murdering Comyn before the high altar. He and his followers must flee into the wild hills like outlaws, without horses or even shoes (2.513). This is the tension between history 'as it was' and history as Barbour wishes to portray it. Some facts he ignores, such as Robert Bruce doing homage to Edward I of England. Others he interprets as romantic episodes. James Douglas provides venison, a noble dish, for the ladies in the wilderness. Bruce compares his plight to that of romantic heroes. The murder of Comyn is incorporated into the grand narrative arc, and with the benefit of hindsight Barbour could interpret it (and Bruce's subsequent hardships) as the downturn of fortune's wheel, preparing for the upturn that would culminate in Bannockburn and the establishment of the Stewart dynasty (13.635–83).

It is important that we take chivalry seriously as a vital and dynamic force in medieval culture, not simply dismiss it, like Antonia Gransden, as 'a veneer on a basically violent and often barbaric society'.[102] Barbour's understanding of the terms *romanys* and *chevalry* may differ from modern scholarly definitions but that does not invalidate them or make him 'anti-chivalry'. In studying *The Bruce* we learn not only 'what happened' but what contemporaries thought about it, namely the qualities they admired in men and the deeds they thought worth remembering. We gain a valuable insight into the dreams and aspirations of the medieval warrior class: not just how they thought the world was, but how they thought it should be.

---

[102] Gransden, *Historical Writing*, ii, 60.

Middle Yiddish and Chaucer's English Considered as Fusion Languages

Jennifer G. Wollock

The classification of languages is not a preoccupation for many readers of Middle English. Every language is a world of its own, an 'old-growth forest of the mind'.[1] The existing tools serve them well; the simple but visually powerful 'language tree' model shows how languages derive from one another as if along biological lines, each branching off from a parental trunk into a separate leafy branch, well exemplified by an attractive recent version by Minna Sundberg.[2] For most students of Middle English, this orientation provides sufficient background. Their concern is with the wonders of English, distinctive features of a language still too little explored.

Others, however, consider that many languages, notably Middle English, still require more specific tools for their understanding. The 'language tree' depicts English among West Germanic languages branching off from one another — but what happens when languages fuse together? Here this simple, elegant, visually clear model fails us; it glosses over what is in fact a complex, dynamic problem of linguistic contact and interplay, as multiple languages recombine to form the English of the Middle Ages. Middle English demands to be understood in a way that promotes our better appreciation of its sources and nature. In this paper I would like to discuss the usefulness of conceptual tools (notably Max Weinreich's term 'Fusion Language') originally developed for a different member of the West Germanic linguistic family, Yiddish, to clarify the situation of Middle English — and which apply, in analogous ways, to both languages.

The 'language tree' offers a clear, linear, static image of a fully developed, mature organism. It puts the stress on a single line of parentage, without complications. The challenge to students of language development is to arrive at a better way of visualizing and describing the situation, one that reflects the full history of each language without minimizing the importance of their respective Germanic origins, but also without erasing the other contributing linguistic forces that make them distinctive. The symbiosis that shapes a language — more complex with some than with others — demands much more recognition than it has

---

[1]   Wade Davis, *The Light at the Edge of the World* (Vancouver: Douglas & MacIntyre, 2009), p. 9. My thanks to Isabelle Barrière for pointing out this quotation, and for much expert linguistic advice.
[2]   'A Comprehensive Overlook of the Nordic Languages in the Old World Language Families', in *Stand Still, Stay Silent, Volume 1* (Portland, OR: Hiveworks, 2018), p. 196, accessed from <http://www.sssscomic.com/comic.php?page=196> [accessed 20 April 2020].

been afforded so far. It requires not merely a visual representation, but an articulation that sorts languages according to their full historical trajectories.

Approaching the problem of classifying Chaucer's Middle English from history and comparative literature rather than linguistics, which means dealing with language as it is used over time, in literary texts written in multiple languages, has offered me a different perspective on the subject than that of a full-time linguist, if not the status of an outside observer. My students in Texas used to say to me, in another connection, 'you're not from around here, are you?', and that is my situation here as well. As a stranger in town, let me attempt to bring a contrasting viewpoint to the recurrent conversation on Chaucer's Middle English as a possible pidgin or creole of Old French.[3]

Finding an adequate descriptive framework for Chaucer's language is not a new problem. The literature divides itself into two camps. The first focuses on how to describe this particular language, the Middle English of the later fourteenth century, as a kind of hybrid; the second insists that no amount of stress on its hybrid character must be allowed to distance it from the family of Germanic languages or impugn its essential Englishness. This is not a simple territorial struggle over which 'stock language' is more important to Chaucer's English, German or French (i.e., a longstanding European nationalist rivalry still smouldering on the linguistic front), but speaks to the larger problem of how to describe and understand languages of the type that Jespersen in 1905 described as 'mixed languages'.[4]

The hypothesis that Middle English can be best explained as a pidgin or creole of Old French has resurfaced from time to time among scholars of historical linguistics since Charles James Nice Bailey and Karl Maroldt first proposed it in 1977.[5] Fabienne Toupin further extended this line of discussion in an article published in 2008.[6] The title of the collection in which her article appears — *Une Espace colonial et ses avatars* — bears witness that the appeal of this approach would seem to stem at least in part from postcolonial studies, a sweeping influence that has reshaped scholarly understanding on a broad historical front since the later years of the twentieth century.

A major problem with the idea of Chaucer's English as a creole of Old French, however, is that this approach narrows the historical-linguistic focus to the historical relationship between these two languages.[7] In the process it necessarily leaves out the inconvenient and complicated previous history of the Indo-European languages concerned. Earlier contacts between West Germanic dialects — which after the Germanic-speakers migrated to Britain

---

[3] The earliest version of this paper was delivered on 29 July 2006 at the New Chaucer Society biennial congress at Fordham University in New York, as part of a panel organized by Dr Fabienne Toupin of the University of Tours, 'Is Middle English a Creole of Old French?' I am most grateful to Dr Toupin, a specialist in the linguistic development of medieval English, for drawing my attention to this subject, and for her cogent analysis of the problem.

[4] Otto Jespersen, *Growth and Structure of the English Language*, 9th edn (Garden City, NY: Anchor Books/Doubleday, 1960) [first publ. 1905], pp. 39–41. For discussion of the resistance to the concept of 'mixed languages' in neogrammarian historical linguistics see Edwin Ardener, 'Social Anthropology and the Historicity of Historical Linguistics', *Social Anthropology and Language*, 67 (1971), 209–41 (esp. pp. 220–22).

[5] Charles James Nice Bailey and Karl Maroldt, 'The French Lineage of English', in *Langues en contact: Pidgins, Creoles*, ed. by Jürgen M. Meisel (Tübingen: Narr, 1977), pp. 21–53.

[6] Fabienne Toupin, 'Des Phénomènes de pidginisation et de créolisation en moyen anglais', in *Une Espace colonial et ses avatars: Naissance d'identités nationales*, ed. by Florence Bourgne, Leo M. Carruthers and Arlette Sancery (Paris: Presses universitaires Sorbonne, 2008), pp. 179–201.

[7] Brandy Ryan, 'Middle English as Creole: "Still trying not to refer to you lot as 'bloody colonials'"' (2005) <http://www.chass.utoronto.ca/~cpercy/courses/6361ryan.htm> [accessed 11 October 2019]. See also Toupin, 'Des Phénomènes'.

promoted regional variants of Old English — the Celtic languages of Britain, the Latin of the Church, and the North Germanic of the Vikings had all left their mark on Old English well before the advent of the Normans. The evidence supporting the concept of Middle English as a 'creole' focuses instead on features that scholars argue reflect 'pidginization', particularly the loss of grammatical inflections and gender.[8]

It does seem to me, as an interested spectator following the contest from a distance, that the existing tools are inadequate. The term 'creole' can be redefined and broadened to serve many purposes, but in linguistics it still best describes an asymmetric binary relationship between two languages, one a prestige language, the other a language socially and culturally subordinated to it. The result is the product of the unequal union of these two partners. This characterization of Middle English is only made possible by ignoring the past and future of the language — its trajectory or directionality — as well as much of Chaucer, let alone other Middle English writers. Problems of this kind have indeed led many current linguistic thinkers to debate the usefulness of the 'creole' designation for languages long identified in this way.[9]

To cope with this problem, various other descriptive terms have been suggested, for instance, 'hybrid language' (preferred by Nicole Z. Domingue) or Ellen Prince's 'contact language'.[10] These are too broad, and not really descriptive except in the most general terms. Where 'creole' is specific and restrictive, even allowing for definite confusion over the meaning of that term, these substitutes are too abstract. Another persistent term, 'mixed language' (*vermischte Sprache*), originated as a pejorative label (as applied to Yiddish in 1733 by the missionary and linguist Johann Heinrich Callenberg, and to English by German students of the history of language as early as the seventeenth century).[11] These terms contrast the 'mixed' language, by implication if not directly, with other languages that are understood to be 'pure' — a doubtful possibility in the extreme. Again, we find ourselves straying across the border into the realm of the politics of language, although this realm may be impossible to avoid when attempting to cope with such a subject. Having reached this impasse, it may be useful to look at another medieval language of a comparable type, one in much the same boat when it comes to linguistic terminology and the socio-politics, philosophy, mythology, or psychology of language. That language is Yiddish.

Although their linguistic timelines are not synchronized with one another, the points of correspondence between these two major Germanic languages have long been numerous and familiar, to Yiddishists, at least.[12] As Joachim Neugroschel writes, '[The Haskala (the Jewish

8   See David DeCamp's 'Introduction to the Study of Pidgin and Creole Languages', in *Pidginization and Creolization of Languages*, ed. by Dell Hymes (London: Oxford University Press, 1971), pp. 13–42. De Camp updated his work in 'The Development of Pidgin and Creole Studies', *Pidgin and Creole Linguistics*, ed. by Albert Valdman (Bloomington: Indiana University Press, 1977), pp. 13–20.

9   See the ongoing discussions of Michel DeGraff and Derek Bickerton, continuing the exchange from DeGraff, 'Against Creole Exceptionalism', *Language*, 80 (2004), 828–33, and their successors, e.g., Michel DeGraff, 'Against Creole Exceptionalism (Redux)', *Language*, 80 (2004), 834–39, and 'Linguists' Most Dangerous Myths: The Fallacy of Creole Exceptionalism', *Language in Society*, 34 (2005), 533–91. See also Isabelle Barrière, 'L'Haïtianophonie aux États-Unis' [The Haitianophone World in the United States], *Haïti Liberté*, 4.3 (2010), 18–19.

10 See a full discussion of the history of the problem in Richard J. Watts, 'The Construction of a Modern Myth: Middle English as a Creole', in his *Language Myths and the History of English* (New York: Oxford University Press, 2011), pp. 83–113. For Domingue, see p. 90.

11 Jean Baumgarten, *Introduction to Old Yiddish Literature*, trans. by Jerold C. Frakes (Oxford: Oxford University Press, 2005), pp. 14–15. See also Jerold Frakes, *The Politics of Interpretation: Alterity and Ideology in Old Yiddish Studies* (Albany: State University of New York Press, 1989).

12 Max Weinreich, 'History of the Yiddish Language: The Problems and Their Implications', *Proceedings of the*

Enlightenment)] castigated [Yiddish] as a mishmash jargon — though any educated person knew that a major tongue like English (on which the sun never set) was far more of a fusion language than Yiddish could ever strive to be'.[13]

Like Old English, Yiddish is West Germanic in origin (though from a different branch), and seems to have first appeared as a result of Jewish settlement in the Rhineland in the ninth and tenth centuries, four or five centuries after the earliest surviving Old English phrase was engraved in runic letters on the Undley Bracteate, a gold medallion found in Suffolk in 1882. In each case there are not two but multiple contributing component languages. English stems from at least four West Germanic Old English dialects, as well as Danish, Latin, Norman French, and 'French of Paris'. Yiddish combines two kinds of Judeo-French (northern and southern Laaz), Hebrew, Aramaic, German, and, later, various Slavic languages, beginning with Old Czech around the fourteenth century. In both cases the dominant language is Germanic, but contributing component languages introduce distinctive complications and make it possible for the speaker or writer to communicate with a variety of multilingual or monolingual acquaintances in a variety of contrasting registers depending on choice of vocabulary. My discussion in this paper will not focus on the entire trajectory of either language, or on the vexed question of which dialect represents the original parent from which either one of them sprang, but on the formation of Middle English, leading to the fourteenth-century language of Chaucer (*c.* 1342–1400), as compared with the emergence of Middle Yiddish in the works of a comparable poet who was also a pioneering scholar of Hebrew and Yiddish, Eliahu Levita (also known as Elye Bokher) (1469–1549). It is important to emphasize from the outset that the two languages are at different stages of development as they appear in the work of these two key witnesses, with Middle English much more advanced in its process of fusion.

In his 2013 article for the first issue of the new *Journal of Jewish Languages*, Alexander Beider analyzes 'Language Tree' (i.e. 'Germanistic') and 'Judeo-centric' approaches to the study of the history of Yiddish, and finds for the 'Germanistic' 'Language Tree' model, while admitting that a combination of both methods would provide a better framework for understanding its trajectory.[14] A full response to his proposal from the standpoint of the English specialist demands a different paper — one that could discuss the benefits of the knowledge of Middle English for the better understanding of the development of Yiddish. Here, grappling with Middle English, the historical linguist rejoices in a well-established 'Germanistic Language Tree' from which its English branch springs without dispute. What the student of Middle English (and, incidentally, Old French) lacks, and what the present

---

American Philosophical Society, 103 (1959), 563–70.

[13] Neugroschel, p. 142. See also Lytton Strachey, 'Racine', in *Books and Characters, French and English* (New York: Harcourt, Brace and Co., 1922), p. 13. 'Owing mainly, no doubt, to the double origin of our language, with its strange and violent contrasts between the highly-coloured crudity of the Saxon words and the ambiguous splendour of the Latin vocabulary, owing partly, perhaps, to a national taste for the intensively imaginative, and partly, too, to the vast and penetrating influence of those grand masters of bizarrerie — the Hebrew Prophets — our poetry, our prose, and our whole conception of the art of writing have fallen under the dominion of the emphatic, the extraordinary, and the bold. No one in his senses would regret this, for it has given our literature all its most characteristic glories[…].' See also his essay on Sir Thomas Browne for its discussion of Browne's manipulation of Latinate and Saxon words, pp. 38–43.

[14] Alexander Beider, 'Reapplying the Language Tree Model to the History of Yiddish', *Journal of Jewish Languages*, 1 (2013), 77–121. See also Beider's important new study, *Origins of Yiddish Dialects* (Oxford: Oxford University Press, 2015). For an astute response and critique, see Alec Burko, 'The New Yiddish Dialectology: A Review of Alexander Beider's *The Origins of Yiddish Dialects*', *In geveb*: *A Journal of Yiddish Studies* (2016), 1–15.

paper attempts to supply, are the key tools supplied for Yiddish by what Beider identifies as a 'Judeo-centric', or what might be termed, in the case of English, an 'Anglo-centric' slant. Both viewpoints have merits, and both are necessary for the better analysis of these two cognate languages at different stages of their histories.

'Fusion languages', to return to the term Max Weinreich proposed for Yiddish, are built from the daily experience of including or excluding conversational partners, flashing instant linguistic signals to those in the know while confounding the uninitiated. This feature proves of special importance for both Middle English and Yiddish literature. These languages, with their built-in contrasts, hybrid words and expressions, and multi-level synonyms, make code-switching and sophisticated compounding techniques almost irresistible to the writer as literary tools within his or her native tongue. It is worth adding that code-switching was of great interest to Chaucer. He darts between French, Latin, or Northumbrian dialect, puncturing flights of aureate learned rhetoric with down-to-earth native English translations: 'For th'orisonte hath reft the sonne his lyght — I This is as muche to seye as it was nyght';

> the gentile, in estaat above
> She shal be cleped his lady, as in love;
> And for that oother is a povre womman,
> She shal be cleped his wenche or his lemman.[15]

Both English and Yiddish spring from the differential multilingualism of the communities that produced them, each with substantial bilingualism in the center, trilingual or quadrilingual learned populations, and important monolingual groups in different social layers. The work of the late Joshua Fishman, a language sociologist, suggests that this high degree of variable multilingualism within the community would seem to be the key factor in generating 'fusion languages' (or language-fusion effects).[16]

Indeed, it was to cope with this complex linguistic situation that the preeminent Yiddish linguist Max Weinreich proposed the term 'fusion language' (in Yiddish, *shmeltsshprakh*) in 1940.[17] This term has been criticized as 'pre-theoretical' and without an established technical definition.[18] Yet it is the one that most Yiddishists still find most satisfactory, and Weinreich did define it in a 1956 article in *Romance Philology*:

> I use 'fusion language' as the label for 'a type of language in which the fusion principle is dominant;' this presupposes another language type in which a different principle — which we may call 'lineal' — dominates. The two principles are construed as opposite poles of an axis; each, to a varying degree, is perceptible in any language, and any language may be thought of as occupying the continuum between the two extremes. Consequently, 'lineal language' and 'fusion language' are ideal types which never occur in reality; but few will hesitate to place, let us say, Icelandic, Gaelic, or Lithuanian nearer one pole and English, Rumanian [*sic*], or Yiddish closer to the opposite pole, while French or Russian may be

---

[15] All references to Chaucer are from *The Riverside Chaucer*, gen. ed. Larry D. Benson (Boston: Houghton Mifflin, 1987): *The Franklin's Tale*, p. 182, ll. 1016–17; *The Manciple's Tale*, p. 285, ll. 217–20, the latter a trenchant comment on class influence in word choice.

[16] Joshua A. Fishman, 'Post-Exilic Jewish Languages and Pidgins/Creoles: Two Mutually Clarifying Perspectives', *Multilingua*, 6 (1987), 7–24.

[17] Dovid Braun, 'A reply to Vulf Plotkin [re: Yiddish is not a 'mixed' language]', *Mendele*, 6.2 (February 2002) <http://yiddish.haifa.ac.il/tmr/tmr06/tmr06002.txt> [accessed 11 October 2019].

[18] Laszlo Cseresnyesi, 'On the Term "Fusion Language"', in *Sum: Creolistics*, ed. by Ann Dizdar, *Linguist List*, 7.1721 (6 December 1996), <https://linguistlist.org/issues/7/7-1721.html> [accessed 11 October 2019].

assigned intermediate places. Obviously, many languages that we choose to label 'lineal' may give us that impression simply because their early history is insufficiently known.[19]

Even today, mainstream linguistics tends to regard 'lineal' or 'genetic' development of languages as its gold standard, and anything else (including fusion or contact effects) as aberrant. Whether this simplistic, pseudo-Darwinian bias is still appropriate to the study of languages is a question worth asking, particularly as biology itself moves toward recognizing more complex forms of hybridization and symbiosis in all forms of life. The simple tree model is no longer adequate.[20]

Languages created by fusion are often accused of not being languages at all, but degenerate forms of the language they grow out of. Yiddish, which has never 'had an army and a navy', has attracted such opinions for a long time, but this is even true of English at a time when the English did not enjoy much prestige on the Continent. Until the later nineteenth century, very few Germans knew English. In the sixteenth century many German authors — not least Martin Luther — looked down on English, characterizing it much as did Justus Georgius Schottelius (who in 1641 called it *spuma linguarum*, 'the scum of language'), and (in an interesting psycholinguistic reaction to the different rhythmic nature of English with its strong stresses on initial syllables and fondness for alliteration, 'rum, ram, ruf by letter' as Chaucer phrased it) described it as sounding like the barking of dogs. In a fascinating study, William Jervis Jones provides many examples of German writers from the sixteenth century on through the eighteenth century expressing this general impression of English as a motley language.[21]

Among linguists the term 'fusion language' is largely restricted to Yiddish, or by extension on rare occasions, to Modern Hebrew, Romanian, Greek, and sometimes Afrikaans. (Maltese would seem to be another excellent candidate for inclusion in this category.) There are linguists who object to it in the case of Yiddish, notably the late Ellen Prince, or more often ignore it, but to my knowledge nothing better has been proposed, and arguments against it are scarce.[22] The advantage of the term is first of all that it describes the language not just as a 'hybrid', but a hybrid of a specific type, which is, as it happens, the same specific type as Middle English.

The idea of Yiddish as simply a curious if not corrupt sub-dialect of German with a few loan words and insignificant grammatical variations seems to be whistling past the graveyard; it really does not do justice to the language's distinctive character or its striking non-Germanic elements — for Neil Jacobs, features unlike those of any other Germanic language.[23] This is

---

[19]   Max Weinreich, 'The Jewish Languages of Romance Stock and their Relation to Earliest Yiddish', *Romance Philology*, 9 (1956), 403–28; see also Max Weinreich, 'Yiddish, Knaanic, Slavic: The Basic Relationships', in *For Roman Jakobson: Essays on the Occasion of his Sixtieth Birthday*, ed. by Hugh McLean, Horace G. Lunt and Cornelis H. Van Schooneveld, compiled by Morris Halle (The Hague: Mouton, 1956), pp. 622–32.

[20]   See, for example, Jordana Cepelewicz, 'Interspecies Hybrids Play a Vital Role in Evolution', *Quanta Magazine*, 5 (August 24, 2017) <https://www. quantamagazine.org/interspecies-hybrids-play-a-vital-role-in-evolution-20170824> [accessed 11 October 2019]; Lucía Morales and Bernard Dujon, 'Evolutionary Role of Interspecies Hybridization and Genetic Exchanges in Yeasts', *Microbiology and Molecular Biology Review*, 76 (2012), 721–39; David Quammen, *The Tangled Tree: A Radical New History of Life* (New York: Simon and Schuster, 2018); Loren H. Rieseberg, 'The Role of Hybridization in Evolution: Old Wine in New Skins', *American Journal of Botany*, 82 (1995), 944–53.

[21]   Justus Georgius Schottelius, *Teutsche Sprachkunst* (Braunschweig: Gruber, 1641), p. 141; William Jervis Jones, *Images of Language: Six Essays on German Attitudes to European Languages from 1500 to 1800* (Amsterdam and Philadelphia: John Benjamins, 1999).

[22]   Ellen Prince, 'Yiddish as a Contact Language', in *Creolization and Contact*, ed. by Norval Smith and Tonjes Veenstra, Creole Language Library, 23 (Amsterdam: Benjamins, 2001), pp. 263–90.

[23]   Neil Jacobs, *Yiddish: A Linguistic Introduction* (Cambridge: Cambridge University Press, 2005), p. 17.

also the problem with defining Chaucer's Middle English as a pidgin, creole, or sub-dialect of Old French. The genesis of both languages is markedly different from that of either a pidgin or a Creole, an issue well discussed for Yiddish by Joshua Fishman, and for Middle English by Richard J. Watts in 2011. As Fishman points out, Yiddish shares with pidgins and Creoles 'the disparateness of their etymological components' and a 'frequent "non-standard" (that is, "dialectal") image'. Yet no post-exilic Jewish language originates in the way that classic pidgins and creoles do, as a simplified medium of communication for 'dislocated members of a newly constituted aggregate' with no common language, who 'must communicate with one another on a make-shift basis as much as they are forced to do so with their masters'. This was no more the case for Yiddish than it was for English. The ninth-century Jews, like the eleventh-century English, already had their own languages. One should note that Old Yiddish developed among a population that had been not just bilingual but multilingual for centuries. Dovid Katz traces this multilingualism as far back as the encounter of Hebrew and Aramaic in the ancient Near East.[24] Fishman concludes: 'thus, the genesis of a post-exilic Jewish language [PEJL] is an instance of language spread from, initially, intergroup to, primarily, intragroup purposes'. As the language is adapted by its new community of speakers for their own purposes, different speech networks may be at different stages in the chain of linguistic developments, and, indeed, these groups may be 'differentially instrumental in bringing about the ultimate distancing between PEJLs and their coterritorial correlates'.[25]

The term 'fusion language' brings with it an alternative way of thinking about language. It stresses the integrity and interrelationship of the multiple components of the language, as opposed to the binary asymmetry of the classic creole, with one language seen as superior, the speech of the ruling class, and the other as inferior, or the 'mixed' language as opposed to other 'pure and unmixed' languages. As the Yiddish poet Matisyahu Mieses pointed out in 1908, and Weinreich reiterated in 1956, all European languages are hybrids of one sort or another; Dovid Katz would go further and see all languages as fusion languages in origin.[26]

Another linguist interested in language mixing was the Soviet academician Nikolai Yakovlevich Marr (1865–1934). Although Marr's controversial linguistic theories were not accepted outside the USSR and were discredited by Stalin himself in 1950, emphasis on hybridization as a key factor in the evolution of languages is one element of his theory that cannot be so easily rejected. Another is his insistence on the importance of sociolinguistic factors (albeit from a Marxist-Leninist perspective) in linguistic evolution. Marr was 'one of the first to insist that languages coalesce, as much as they "derive", that constructing family trees is to over-simplify a process by which one language absorbs another'.[27] During the short time that Max Weinreich studied at the University of St Petersburg (1912), Marr was Dean of the Faculty of Oriental Languages there. More significantly, Weinreich, as a linguistic theorist in Poland in the 1920s and 30s, would certainly have been aware of Marr's ideas. But, having studied linguistics at Marburg (1919–23), Weinreich would by that time have

---

[24] Dovid Katz, *Words on Fire: The Unfinished Story of Yiddish* (New York: Basic Books, 2004), pp. 13–15.

[25] Fishman, 'Post-Exilic Jewish Languages', pp. 13, 8.

[26] Getzel Kressel, 'Matisyahu Mizes un di polemik vegn yidish', *Di Goldene Keyt*, 28 (1957), 143–63; Katz, *Words on Fire*, p. 14. Weinreich, 'The Jewish Languages', pp. 12–13.

[27] Donald Rayfield, 'Nikolai Marr' (16 March 2015), <http://britishgeorgiansociety.org/events/11-past/206-nokolai-marr-a-talk-by-donald-rayfield-17-february> [accessed 11 October 2019]. See also Patrick Sériot, *Structure and the Whole: East, West, and non-Darwinian Biology in the Origins of Structural Linguistics* (Berlin: De Gruyter, 2014), pp. 117–118 and 136–37. Sériot provides much additional information on the interest in hybridization theory in European and particularly Eastern European linguistics of the 1920s and 30s.

been thoroughly imbued in the German linguistic tradition. He would certainly have known the work of Jespersen.

Without going to extremes, the advantages of seeing Chaucer's Middle English as a fusion language (as against seeing it as a 'creole' or simply Germanic or French), and of bringing in Yiddish as a parallel case, are numerous. It interested me to see the term 'fusion' recur several times without explanation in Otto Jespersen's classic account of Middle English from 1905, and again in Baugh and Cable's description of the development of Middle English. An examination of the parallel and complementary trajectories of English and Yiddish makes it clear that the Middle English of 1350 was well ahead of Yiddish in its process of fusion. The two languages develop along parallel lines at different rates: Old English forms in the context of fifth-century migrations to Britain, encountering Old Norse and Norman French around the ninth to eleventh centuries and entering its 'middle' period around the twelfth century; Yiddish begins with Jewish migrations to the Middle Rhine region in the ninth to tenth centuries, encountering Slavic (Old Czech) around the mid-thirteenth century, and entering its 'middle' period around the fifteenth century.[28]

Both Katz and Max Weinreich call attention to the combination of elements from different source languages in the same word as a sign of a fusion language. The *-nik* suffix (*shlimazlnik, olrightnik,* or, worse yet, *nogoodnik* in today's Yinglish) combines German, English, or Hebrew roots with a Slavic ending; the feminine personal name *Blumke* unites the German *blum,* 'flower', with the Old Czech diminutive *-ka.* Jespersen notes the same feature in Middle English, and remarks that this practice of combining native words with foreign affixes is an uncommon feature of the language as compared with other languages more resistant to external elements. Jespersen regarded this type of 'hybridism', commonplace in Middle English, as much rarer in other languages, though it is more frequently found in Germanic than in Romance languages.[29] Familiar English composite words that bring together French and English elements in this way (as in 'shepherdess') reveal code-switching so pervasive that it appears even within the word itself, not to mention within a phrase or sentence.

Katz and Weinreich both adapt (with some reservations) Ber Borekhov's (1881–1917) hypothesis that Yiddish uses different components for different purposes, due in part to the differential multilingualism of the population: German or Slavic (or, in the Middle Yiddish poet Eliahu Levita's case, Italian) for everyday domestic or marketplace use, Hebrew or Aramaic terms for tasks related to the Jewish community and communal experience.[30] The English tendency to use French for the culinary and courtly spheres, Latin for learning and religion, and English for agricultural and domestic life, as in the familiar examples *cow/beef, sheep/mutton, veal/calf,* with the animal changing its name and nationality as it is slaughtered and enters the kitchen, ties in with this observation. This stratification of layers within the fusion language connects with the cultivation of rhetorical 'registers' that combine to give the fusion languages a special literary character.

The term 'fusion language' takes into account directionality — what might be called the dynamics of the language as it develops. Middle English is not in the process of becoming

---

[28] See Albert C. Baugh and Thomas Cable, *A History of the English Language,* 3rd edn (Englewood Cliffs, NJ: Prentice-Hall, 1978), pp. 50, 177; Baumgarten, *Introduction to Old Yiddish Literature;* Weinreich, 'History of the Yiddish Language'.

[29] Jespersen, *Growth and Structure of the English Language,* pp. 109–11.

[30] For a pertinent overview, see Barry Trachtenberg, 'Ber Borochov's 'The Tasks of Yiddish Philology', *Science in Context,* 20 (2007), 341–52.

French, though without question it becomes more frenchified than before. It becomes Modern English. Yiddish is not becoming Russian or Modern Hebrew. In fact, the fusion language idea helps explain the directionality of English — why it was not replaced altogether by French in the aftermath of 1066, in the way that conquerors' languages so often supplant those of the conquered — just as it helps explain why Yiddish does not become altogether Slavic as the Jewish population of Europe was pushed further and further into Eastern Europe, though it is significantly slavicized. Ongoing fusions of Yiddish, English, and Modern Hebrew in present-day British, American, and Israeli speech are fascinating subjects of current linguistic research.[31]

The term 'fusion language' emphasizes the nature of the resulting language, rather than over-stressing the role of one or another component. In fact, the components become inextricable parts of a new language that has its own identity, integrity, and dignity. As the late Yiddish philologist Mordkhe Schaechter (1927–2007) liked to insist, a Hebrew word or a Slavic word adopted into Yiddish is a Yiddish word in good standing, a fully functional and fully integrated element of a new system, just as a French word has the potential to become a perfectly respectable Middle English word, and indeed, to be productive, when combined with non-French elements to produce new English words.[32] Baugh and Cable list early combinations of French loan-words with English endings: 'for example, the adjective "gentle" is recorded in 1225 and within five years we have it compounded with an English noun to make "gentlewoman" (1230) [...] It is clear that the new French words were quickly assimilated, and [that they] entered into an easy and natural fusion with the native element in English'.[33] As Jespersen noted, the compounding of the native word with non-native affixes, uncommon in more isolated linguistic situations, seems to be a defining marker of fusion languages. In Eliahu Levita's Middle Yiddish *Bove Bukh* of 1507–8 words of Hebrew origin are inflected according to German grammatical usage on a regular basis.[34] We see this same productive fusion of French and English continuing into Chaucer's phase of Middle English as well, and beyond him into the fifteenth century. It might be argued that they are woven out of code-switching.

For Chaucer studies, and indeed for medieval English studies across the board, one benefit of the concept of the 'fusion language' may be a more sophisticated appreciation of the resources such a language offers to the attentive writer (and, consequently, reader). Chaucer is well aware of this, as he plays with contrasts between courtly (or, for that matter, legal) French terms and *burel* (simple, rude) English, and flights of aureate or legal Latinity or Latin tags, like the Pardoner's *Radix malorum est Cupiditas*, the Summoner's *questio quid juris*, or the Nun's Priest's *mulier est hominis confusio*, 'woman is man's ruin', mistranslated with a wink as 'woman is mannes joye and al his blis' for a differentially multilingual audience of male and female pilgrims.[35]

---

[31] For an example, see Isabelle Barrière's study 'The Vitality of Yiddish among Hasidic Infants and Toddlers in a Low SES Preschool in Brooklyn', *Yiddish — a Jewish National Language at 100: Proceedings of the Czernowitz Yiddish Language 2008 International Centenary Conference*, Jews and Slavs, 22 (Jerusalem-Kyiv: Hebrew University of Jerusalem, 2010), pp. 170–96.

[32] Mordke Schaechter, personal communication. August 18, 1997.

[33] Baugh and Cable, *A History of the English Language*, p. 166.

[34] Jerry C. Smith, 'Elia Levita's *Bovo-Buch*: A Yiddish Romance of the Early Sixteenth Century' (unpublished Ph.D. dissertation, Cornell University, 1968), p. 544.

[35] *Radix malorum est Cupiditas* (1 Timothy 6. 10), *Pardoner's Prologue*, p. 194, l. 334; *Questio quid iuris*, *General Prologue* to the *Canterbury Tales*, p. 33, l. 646; *The Nun's Priest's Tale*, p. 257, ll. 3163–64.

The comedy of Chaucer's love-lyric 'To Rosemounde' as an expression of frustrated love is rooted in the joys and perils of code-switching in the Middle English of the later fourteenth century.[36] The elusive lady Rosamounde takes form within a frame of courtly French, between the elegant, formal opening address *Madame* (first occurring in English *c.* 1300) and the refrain's closing note of the 'daliaunce' again and again denied to the speaker as he snatches at sonorous but incongruous French words (*oynement, galantine*) from medicine and the kitchen (along with the geographical Latin of *mappemounde*) and mashes up the French and English forms of the name *Tristan* (from the original perhaps Pictish *Drust*, Welsh and Cornish *Drystan*, later to appear in French as *Tristan* and English as *Tristram*) to get 'Tristam'. A sprint through the online *Middle English Dictionary* brings out the novelty of many of the French and Latin polysyllabic words.[37] *Cercled, mapemounde, jocounde, galantine, daliaunce* all appear first in English in this poem: *oynement* turned up in 1290, *crystal* in 1300. Chaucer shares the honor of the earliest *MED* instances of *revell* and *daunce* with the early alliterative romance *William of Palerne* (*c.* 1350–61). The polysyllables tend to stand out, while earlier French *beauté* (*c.* 1275), *curtaysly* (*Ancrene Riwle*, 'kurtesye', *c.* 1225), *divine* (F. *deviner*, twelfth century), and Latin borrowings like *shrine*, from *scrinium* (a chest or box), *walwed* (from *volvere*, 'to roll'), are much more deeply embedded among the short words of Germanic origin so beloved of George Orwell — *chekes, teres, wo, herte, founde, bounde, mery, blis, trewe, brenne, lyst*.[38] In true fusion language style, *walwed* is domesticated as a weak verb with its non-Latinate dental preterite (*-ed*), *curtays* becomes an English adverb with its equally English suffix *-ly*, and *was* combines with the ancient Indo-European negative particle *ne* that French and Old English shared to form the ubiquitous negative contraction *nas*. When the poet concludes the final stanza, 'Do what you lyst, I wyl your thral be founde, | Thogh ye to me ne do no daliaunce', he strikes a powerful note by diving not just deep into the Old English register (over the entire penultimate line) to identify himself as his lady's 'thral', her abject slave (originally, a 'gofer', a servant running with a message), but by choosing an Old Norse loan-word over the more pejorative French possibility, *vileyn*, or, for that matter, the Anglo-Saxon alternative *cherl*. The Northern *thral* is, for Chaucer, a strong word to be used at key moments: in *The Man of Law's Tale* its embattled heroine Constance sighs that 'Women are born to thralldom and penance | And to be under mannes governaunce'.[39] In *The Franklin's Tale*, the narrator retorts that 'Wommen desiren to han sovereignte | And nat to be constrained as a thral, | And so doon men, if I sooth seyen shal'.[40] In *The Physician's Tale*, the doomed Roman maiden Virginia is ruled a slave by the predatory judge Appius Claudius, with "The cherl shal have his thral, this I awarde".[41] On all occasions, the word *thrall* strikes a dire note, suggesting the depths of servitude. At the same time, the teasing key word *daliaunce* — covering any form of social interaction from a friendly greeting to a romp in the shrubbery — that ends each stanza, remains courtly and French. The contrast between courtly, learned, elegant polysyllables and the stark monosyllables of the 'pyk' (already in Old English, with Latin or Celtic roots) surrounded by his French sauce, or of the 'thral' enslaved to his lady,

---

[36] *Riverside Chaucer*, p. 649.
[37] *Middle English Dictionary* (Ann Arbor: University of Michigan Press, 1952–2001), <https://quod.lib. umich.edu/m/med/> [accessed August 8 2018].
[38] George Orwell, 'Politics and the English Language', *Horizon*, vol. 13, issue 76 (1946), 252–65.
[39] *The Man of Law's Tale*, p. 91, ll. 286–87.
[40] *The Franklin's Tale*, p. 179, ll. 769–770.
[41] *The Physician's Tale*, p. 192, l. 202.

is what makes the poem funny and poignant, even for readers so accustomed to the fusion character of English that these linguistic effects are barely noticed.

As the Ukrainian linguist Alexander A. Potebnja noted in 1904, our sensitivity to these linguistic roots may well become blunted over time, though they persist in the form and sound of the word and the internal images it has the potential to generate.[42] 'To Rosemounde' stands out as a *tour de force* demonstrating the art of the fusion language in action. The series of jarring, comic discords called up by the sounds and varied linguistic origins of the words contribute to conjure up a series of incongruous mental images that illuminate the speaker's struggle to find the words to court his unresponsive lady.

A century and a half later, Eliahu Levita would deploy the resources of a Yiddish enriched both by learned Hebrew and the Italian of his adoptive country in a variety of poetic ventures, in particular his delightful version of *Bevis of Hampton*, the *Bove-Bukh*. From the title page on into his preface he describes himself as *Elia Bokher* (Heb. *Bakhu*), *Elia ha-mechaber*, and *Elia Levi*, introducing himself as (according to his nickname) still a bachelor (*bakhur*), but also *The Author* (*ha-mechaber*), and using three familiar Hebrew terms to define himself as youthful, the writer in command of his book, and a man whose pedigree connects him to the Levites, the tribe entrusted by Moses with the musical component of the service in the temple in Jerusalem. These three words paint his portrait for the Yiddish-speaking reader as he or she opens the book, investing the poet in progressive layers of dignity. (This is, for the Jewish reader, his *yikhes*, i.e., his pedigree as a poet and, indeed, a sort of musician.) The opening is spiced with a little *gematria* for his learned readers who appreciate the numerical values of the letters of the Hebrew alphabet: '*Elye Ha-mekhaber* equals the year'. (To decode the message the knowledgeable reader adds up the Hebrew letters in the author's name to make the number 302 — 5302 in the Jewish reckoning, 1541 CE.) Its flash from the allusion to his ancestors' divine service to Elye Bokher's own service to 'all pious women' that has led him to publish this romance builds its humor on the simultaneous parallelisms and contrasts of the situation, packed into the language itself. It is left to the male or female readers, to learned colleagues or *frume vayber* (pious women), to decide what comedy lurks in the shift from the temple to the contemporary Jewish household, from the choral music of the Levite of old to the chivalric romance translated from the Italian that entertains the Sabbath-observant Jewish wife, or from religious service to the courtly service offered to ladies. There is much more to come, but the opening lines already suggest the range of possibilities. The fusion language changes its flavor as the speaker crosses linguistic borders. For the Yiddish-speaking reader not resident in Italy the poet (who was also a distinguished lexicographer) supplies a glossary of the Italian words that pepper his Yiddish, from *ancora* to *stora*.[43] Here, too, the prestige language embedded within the everyday vernaculars encourages harmonic or dissonant effects at the touch of a key. The instrument — the fusion language — is as sophisticated as a pipe organ, and as responsive as a pennywhistle.

To say that Chaucer's Middle English is x% French by computer analysis is to flatten out completely where and when and how Chaucer uses his different French registers (Frenches of England or of Paris, of the court or of the law), as well as his regional and socially

---

[42] John Fizer, *Alexander A. Potebnja's Psycholinguistic Theory of Literature: A Metacritical Inquiry* (Cambridge, Mass.: Harvard University Press, 1986), pp. 31–33.

[43] Jerry C. Smith, *Elia Levita Bachur's Bovo-Buch: A Translation of the Old Yiddish Edition of 1541* (Tucson: Fenestra, 2003), pp. 105–106. Levita himself published the first Yiddish-Hebrew dictionary, *Shemot Devari*, in collaboration with Paul Fagius, his publisher (Isny, 1542).

marked English and Latin registers, against one another — the versatility, sophistication, and opportunities of a fusion language. As in Yiddish, the component languages form a flexible entity with its own distinct identity as a language, capable of being very French or very Germanic or very Latinate or very English or all four at once. Such a language is slippery and difficult to pin down, a medium eminently suitable to Chaucer himself.

The parallels between Middle English and other fusion languages, notably Yiddish, offer plenty of opportunities for technical comparative linguistic studies, things unattempted yet in prose or rhyme. They also offer innumerable opportunities for the literary scholar to see how a skillful poet — Chaucer or Elia Bokher Levita — can take advantage of the full range of resources of such a complex fusion of disparate elements. Other effects drawing on the character of English as fusion language can be seen throughout Middle English literature, including the stark contrasts of aureate and vulgar as they recur throughout *Piers Plowman* (whose running Latin allusions help to make it more of a 'fusion poem' than perhaps any other that we have) or for dramatic characterization in, say, *Mankind*, where the rudest of the little vices tells the dignified Mercy that his 'body is full of Englisch Laten', as indeed it is.[44] They carry on through the Early Modern period with Shakespeare's Monsieur Le Beau of *As you Like It*, to mention one obvious instance, up into the aureate academic registers of our own day. These languages are nobody's pidgin.

What the situation really demands is the reintegration of literature and language studies (philology or linguistics, as you please) envisioned in J. R. R. Tolkien's 'Valedictory Address to the University of Oxford' of 1959.[45] Tolkien's own experience as a philologist at Leeds over the five years he taught there (1920–25), and upon his return to Oxford, underlines the difficulty of bringing these conflicting visions of English studies into some kind of alignment. Today, almost a century later, we still need to reconnect the shards, if we are to understand either language or literature, English or Yiddish.

In conclusion, it seems important to return to the fundamental questions raised by this discussion. What does the term 'fusion language' and the suggested analogy between Middle English and Yiddish contribute to our understanding of Middle English? Why do this? First, because Yiddish is an analogue to Middle English, developing from a different combination of Germanic and non-Germanic sources along a distinct but parallel timeline, from differentially multilingual populations. Both languages have been too often misunderstood, and indeed denigrated as languages. The continuing discussion, throughout history down to the present, of whether such hybrids are truly languages at all, or represent some degenerate form of the 'parent' language deserves to be recognized as belonging to the politics and psychology of language. This has to do with the 'ethical' evaluation of language, evoking standards of 'purity' that reflect the cultural biases of the writer. Yiddish and English may be better understood together than separately.

The advantage of the 'fusion language' term is clarity. It seems desirable to have an appropriate descriptive name to aid in classifying and grouping such languages. 'Mixed language', one suggested alternative term, is a large generic category covering all sorts of

---

[44] 'NEW-G[U]ISE: Ey, ey, yowr body is full of Englisch Laten! | I am aferde it will brest.' *Mankind*, in *Medieval Drama*, ed. by David Bevington (Boston: Houghton Mifflin, 1975), p. 907, ll. 124–25.

[45] Michael Drout, 'J. R. R. Tolkien's Medieval Scholarship and its Significance', *Tolkien Studies*, 4 (2007), 113–76. See also Tom Shippey, *The Road to Middle Earth: How J. R. R. Tolkien Created a New Mythology* (Boston: Houghton Mifflin, 2003), pp. 273, 332, 337–38. J. R. R. Tolkien, 'Valedictory Address to the University of Oxford', in *The Monsters and the Critics*, ed. by Christopher Tolkien (London: HarperCollins, 1997), pp. 224–40 [first publ. London: Allan and Unwin, 1983].

languages, perhaps every language on the planet. Like the 'mixed breed' dog, every breed of dog is technically a mixture of earlier varieties. Does it really mean anything, other than to point out that languages do mix, and some are more mixed than others? 'Mixed language' does not specify the nature or extent of the mixture of elements within the language. Terms like 'pidgin', 'creole', and 'fusion language' denote subgroups within this much larger 'mixed language' field. Of these, only 'fusion language' stands up to the critique of 'Creole Exceptionalism'.

'Fusion language' represents a clarification as a term for Middle English, resulting in a higher degree of specificity. It describes a particular subset of languages (among them Albanian, English, Garifuna, Maltese, Yiddish) within the broad category of 'mixed languages'. It counters the misleading mental image conjured up by the familiar 'language tree' diagram, in which languages are shown branching out from a parental stem representing its original language family (e.g. Proto-Indo-European). The trajectory is linear, growing out in one direction only. Old English is customarily represented in this way as a West Germanic language descendant of Ingvaeonic (North Sea German) dialects and migrating to Britain in the fifth century. The 'language tree' model does not begin to express the idea of languages from different branches of the tree merging to form new independent languages. This is the phenomenon described by the term 'fusion language'.

The concept of 'fusion language' directs attention toward necessary new directions in the study of language formation and affiliation. Such studies should bring linguistics into productive dialogue with recent work on the modeling of biological descent. This approach has deep roots in the history of linguistic thought. Antecedents of Weinreich's ideas of linguistic blending can be seen in the work of Jespersen and Marr, and others discussed by Sériot.[46] From this perspective Middle English and Yiddish are eminently comparable, and equally relevant to literary scholarship: future comparative studies will offer students of both languages a chance to arrive at deeper insights into the origins and nature of Chaucer's and Elye Bokher's languages and of language in general.

Where the 'language tree' model emphasizes lineal descent in one direction, the term 'fusion language' stresses the strength and endurance of bonds that unite disparate linguistic strands, melting or fusing them together in a new language with its own unique character. Of the two taxonomic terms, 'fusion language' is the stronger and more accurately descriptive, focusing attention on the distinctive way in which languages form by recombining. The subset of 'mixed languages' that share the 'fusion language' features of origin and structure should be identified as a group and need an appropriate name, such as this one, which has the merit of historical priority. In this way, scholars can get a more accurate picture of the relationships between languages, and how individual languages develop. The 'fusion language' idea corrects the innate bias inherent in the 'language tree' by putting the emphasis on coming into contact, fusing into one — the linguistic equivalent of marriage, biological symbiosis and genetic recombination.

---

[46] Sériot, *Structure and the Whole.*

REVIEWS

P. S. Langeslag, *Seasons in the Literatures of the Medieval North*. Cambridge: Brewer, 2015. viii + 250 pp. ISBN 9781843844259.

It is probably a cliché by now — and certainly ought to be — that any research that helps us to understand the human relationship with climate is time well spent; this meticulous monograph on the cultural history of seasonality can, then, only be a welcome addition to our understanding of the Middle Ages. Its explorations flow mostly along the familiar channels of the medieval English canon carved out by the philologically-minded founders of English degrees in the decades around 1900: the most prominent sources include the so-called Old English elegies, not least *The Wanderer* and *The Seafarer*; *Beowulf*; the *Íslendingasögur*, particularly *Grettis saga*; and Middle English romances, pre-eminently *Sir Gawain and the Green Knight*. The study's frame of reference is far wider, eclectically bringing in other reference-points as required — a wide range of English and Icelandic literary texts; welcome nods to adjacent writing in French (such as Chétien de Troyes's *Yvain*), Latin (Alcuin of York), Irish (*Buile Suibne*) and Welsh (*Pwyll Pendefig Dyfed*); climate-history (e.g. pp. 14–16), place-names (e.g. p. 88), Old English prognostics (pp. 154–58), and more. But its main contributions lie in rereading the canon from a new vantage point.

The subject of this book, one learns, is not easy to come to grips with: this study indicates how, for all their material importance in shaping the social organisation of north-western Europe, seasons *per se* are seldom the concern of literary texts, and are to a profound degree a property of genre. Langeslag finds the ancient two-season division of the year into winter and summer more analytically useful than English's present preference for a four-season system, and even the chapter that is ostensibly devoted to summer ends up making many of its most interesting points about winter: the gorgeously snowy scene from the *Très Riches Heures du Duc de Berry* that adorns the cover is misleadingly late for a book which tends not to range far beyond the thirteenth century, but certainly indicates the season which it finds most intellectually fertile. Drawing on Mikhail Bakhtin's idea of the chronotope, a term coined to represent the way that time and space are mutually constitutive in literary writing, Langeslag provides repeated case-studies of how seasons constitute themselves in medieval experience as transformations of space, cyclically reshaping how people interact with their environment.

The book's introduction is a brisk and hard-nosed tour of the material realities of climate in medieval England and Scandinavia. Thereafter, perhaps unsurprisingly given the nebulousness of the season as a literary construct and the geographical, chronological, and generic range of the primary sources, the content of chapters tends to be rather kaleidoscopic.

The first three chapters focus on Old English and Old Icelandic material. Chapter 1, 'Myth and Ritual', happily does not work within the paradigms of the early twentieth-century Myth and Ritual School; indeed, 'rather than perpetuate the misleading nomenclature of Christian and Pagan', the chapter refreshingly positions its sources on a spectrum from orthodox (such as Augustine of Hippo), through heterodox (*Genesis B*), to 'suspected non-Christian religious elements' (*Vǫluspá*; quoting p. 29). It contemplates the intersections between reality and ideology in religious writing, bringing a firm grasp of Latin Christian writing to bear on Old English poetry and the Eddas, and on historical phenomena like month-names and winter feasts.

Chapter 2, 'Winter Mindscapes', explores the psychogeographies of winter in the Old English elegies, emphasising the role of winter not as a literal season but as a source of connotation and symbolism. It proceeds to Grendel's mere, and thence to the role of winter in the construction of the racial otherness of giants and Sámi people in Old Norse literature. Through these different analyses, it argues that 'geographical features peripheral to social space become distrusted in consequence of their unfamiliarity [...] Narrative literature responds by projecting this unease back onto the landscape in a more tangible form, whether by attention to the landscape's cold and stormy features or by the allocations to these regions of a supernatural counterpart embodying the danger associated with them' (p. 111). Chapter 3, 'Winter Institutions', retreads this journey by using the same or similar texts to contemplate what a busy time the season of winter in fact is in the literature under study. It devotes considerable space to the walking dead in Old Icelandic literature; these figures have received a great deal of attention in recent years, but reading their activities in relation both to seasonality and, through that, diurnality, gives Langeslag the opportunity to present some new perspectives on their hauntings. The chapter also takes on the seldom contemplated place of seasonality in *Beowulf*. It traces how *Beowulf* and sagas construct the seasonal constraints on social space, as well as the capacity of those constraints to foment social discord.

Chapter 4, 'Summer Adventure', turns to the warm season and to Middle English romance (which rubs shoulders here with dream-visions both English and Scandinavian, and, in a dialogue too seldom attempted, Old Norse *fornaldarsǫgur*). While several of the narrative texts addressed earlier in the book also feature plenty of aestival activity, Langeslag explores how romance especially is, as a genre, constituted by summer. Characteristically, though, the chapter's freshest insights come when it uses this observation to emphasise how unusual is the hibernal setting of *Sir Gawain and the Green Knight*, and how resonant its association of winter with the supernatural is with Old English and Old Norse literature.

The book is not unaware of the precipitous rise of ecocriticism as a field (p. 64), but, surprisingly, does not enter into dialogue with it; Gillian Rudd's influential 2007 *Greenery: Ecocritical Readings of Late Medieval English Literature* makes no appearance, for example. It would have been interesting to understand more clearly why these theoretical developments left the author cold, as they clearly did. But as research that might broadly be described as ecocritical gains ever greater prominence in medieval studies, ecocritically minded scholars will find in *Seasons in the Literatures of the Medieval North* both helpful new angles on canonical texts and a rich scattering of unexpected insights on other sources. It encourages us to look beyond weather or human-animal relations to the imaginative force and social consequences of cyclical time, and challenges us to read space as a function of time.

ALARIC HALL   UNIVERSITY OF LEEDS

David R. Carlson, *John Gower: Poetry and Propaganda in Fourteenth-Century England*. Cambridge: Brewer, 2012. viii + 245 pp. ISBN 9781843843153.

It seems common for the best late-fourteenth/early-fifteenth century English poets to question the order of things. Accordingly, those who appear to have 'collaborated' with the English monarchy, most important among them John Gower, are sometimes given a back seat. Gower wrote a number of short texts in Middle English, Anglo-Norman, and Latin, as well as the monumental poem *Confessio amantis*, which comments on various aspects of culture, society, and contemporary events. David Carlson's monograph, the subject of the present review, goes some way towards restoring Gower's reputation and position within the medieval canon.

The first five chapters provide the necessary context of the state-writer relationship in fourteenth-century England. Carlson first compares short poems on the battle of Bannockburn (1314) by William Baston and Laurence Minot. He raises the difficulties in determining whether a poet's work was patronised, given that it was in their best interest to loudly declare their (potential or actual) patrons, while it was in poor taste to be seen commissioning a poem about one's own actions (pp. 5–25). Carlson argues that 'official' newsletters and correspondence were considered as authoritative sources that were then used by other writers, especially chroniclers, such as Robert of Avesbury and Henry Knighton (pp. 26–43).[1] Carlson then shows how poems produced in early- to mid-fourteenth century England (such as those by Minot and the Calais Anonymous) had intentions that are similar to those of the previously discussed state-supporting letters, but took on a different form (pp. 44–67). He makes a very interesting case study of contemporary English sources on the battle of Nájera in Spain (1367), such as *Gloria cunctorum*, Edward of Woodstock's letter to his wife Joan of Kent, and Walter Peterborough's *Victoria belli in Hispania*, to illustrate the varied interaction between newsletters and panegyric verse (pp. 68–92). Carlson finishes this section with another case study, this time on a single text, Richard Maidstone's *Concordia* (1392), and examines how it employs both official and unofficial sources (pp. 93–109).

Only in the final four chapters of his book does Carlson directly address Gower, his ostensible main subject. He first provides background context for Gower by covering texts written during and after Richard II's deposition and how, even in the absence of any evidence of their direct commissioning, these writings legitimise Henry IV's actions (pp. 110–52). Then, in his longest chapter, Carlson argues that Gower's *Chronica tripertita* is a state sponsored text. This argument is primarily based on his analysis of the many instances in which Gower's text seems to rely on the official *Record and Process* (pp. 153–96). Carlson clearly illustrates this relationship through a large table that displays corresponding passages (pp. 158–61). He then shows how Gower's use of state texts was not thoughtless, but rather meant to promote the state and Henry IV's rule (pp. 197–226). He suggests that Gower was commissioned by the state, although he earlier acknowledges that this cannot be known

---

[1] It should be noted that, in addition to those cited by Carlson, such documents are interpolated into several other mid-fourteenth century chronicles of England. See most notably Adam Murimuth, 'Continuatio chronicarum', in *Adae Murimuth; Robertus de Avesbury*, ed. by Edward Maunde Thompson, Rolls Series, 93 (London: Eyre, 1889), pp. 3–276; the continuation of the *Bridlington Chronicle*, in *Chronicles of the Reigns of Edward I and Edward II*, ed. by William Stubbs, Rolls Series, 76, 2 vols (London: Longman, 1882–83), II, 93–151; John of Tynemouth's *Historia aurea*, unedited and surviving most fully in London, Lambeth Palace Library, MSS 10–12; and the 1327–47 continuation of the *Long Anglo-Norman Prose Brut*, unedited and surviving only in London, British Library, MS Cotton Tiberius A VI, fols 184^r–199^r.

with any certainty. This final chapter clears up some lingering issues, most importantly by showing how Gower was not the mindless scribe of the crown, as some claim, through careful consideration of the several instances in which Gower criticises the state. On the other hand, Carlson suggests that some of Gower's other writings might be considered 'official verse panegyric', 'conceived and written' to praise Henry IV (p. 209). He ends his book with a short but fascinating consideration of Gower's opportunism through an examination of how he took verse that he had first written for Richard II and adapted it so that it was instead for his usurper, Henry IV (pp. 212–13).

Interesting and compelling as they are, it is sometimes difficult to accept some of the arguments and observations made in the book. As is not uncommon with non-specialists, Carlson demonstrates only passing familiarity with the many complicated issues of medieval war, such as when he derides it for (supposedly) being conducted solely for financial gain (pp. 28–31).[2] He unfairly dismisses Edward III's claim to the throne of France, along with the many other difficult issues that are brought up in many English texts throughout the Hundred Years War, as insincere and merely propaganda (pp. 44–47).[3] He relies on existing translations whenever possible, creating a number of problems in interpretation, such as, when quoting Baston, he relies on Morgan's popular and overly stylistic translation instead of Latham's scholarly translation (p. 6 n. 1).[4]

Carlson provides a useful examination of a complicated subject in an accessible and stimulating format. His arguments are clear, concise, and follow a logical direction. It is made particularly interesting and fresh through his engagement with many lesser-known texts. It is especially helpful to see how the English state continued to rely on a variety of writers for support throughout the fourteenth century, despite the changing social and political conditions. I was very happy that Carlson examined texts written in all three languages of late medieval England, side by side, rather than just Middle English, which is too often studied in isolation. Carlson's arguments and observations are always thorough and rewarding, and they will surely encourage further study of Gower's fascinating writings, as well as the other political poems of medieval England, that are too often overlooked.

TREVOR RUSSELL SMITH   UNIVERSITY OF LEEDS

---

[2]   See recent works on chivalry, and the importance of reputation and fighting for one's lord, most recently Richard Kaeuper, *Medieval Chivalry* (Cambridge: Cambridge University Press, 2016).

[3]   Craig Taylor, 'Edward III and the Plantagenet Claim to the French Throne', in *The Age of Edward III*, ed. by James S. Bothwell (Woodbridge: York Medieval Press, 2001), pp. 155–69.

[4]   Robert Baston, *Metrum de praelio apud Bannockburn*, trans. by Edwin Morgan (Edinburgh: Scottish Poetry Library, 2004); Baston, 'De striuelinensi obsidione', trans. by Ronald E. Latham, in Walter Bower, *Scotichronicon*, ed. by Donald E. R. Watt and others, 9 vols (Aberdeen: Aberdeen University Press, 1987–98), vi, 366–75, 458–60.

Also published by *Leeds Studies in English* is the occasional series:

LEEDS TEXTS AND MONOGRAPHS

(ISSN 0075-8574)

Recent volumes include:

Approaches to the Metres of Alliterative Verse, edited by Judith Jefferson and Ad Putter (2009), iii + 311 pp.

The Heege Manuscript: a facsimile of NLS MS Advocates 19.3.1, introduced by Phillipa Hardman (2000), 60 + 432pp.

The Old English Life of St Nicholas with the Old English Life of St Giles, edited by E. M. Treharne (1997) viii + 218pp.

Concepts of National Identity in the Middle Ages, edited by Simon Forde, Lesley Johnson and Alan V. Murray (1995) viii + 213pp.

A Study and Edition of Selected Middle English Sermons, by V. M. O'Mara (1994) xi + 245pp.

Notes on 'Beowulf', by P. J. Cosijn, introduced, translated and annotated by Rolf H. Bremmer Jr, Jan van den Berg and David F. Johnson (1991) xxxvi + 120pp.

Úr Dölum til Dala: Guðbrandur Vigfússon Centenary Essays, edited by Rory McTurk and Andrew Wawn (1989) x + 327pp.

Staging the Chester Cycle, edited by David Mills (1985) vii + 123pp.

The Gawain Country: Essays on the Topography of Middle English Poetry, by R. W. V. Elliot (1984) 165pp.

For full details of this series, and to purchase volumes, or past numbers of *Leeds Studies in English*, please go to <http://www.leeds.ac.uk/lse>.

9 781845 49771